WHERE PERSIMMON WAS KING

Published in the United States by
Beckham Publications Group, Inc.
P.O. Box 4066, Silver Spring, MD 20914

ISBN 9780980238068

Library of Congress Control Number: 2008923940

10987654321

WHERE PERSIMMON WAS KING

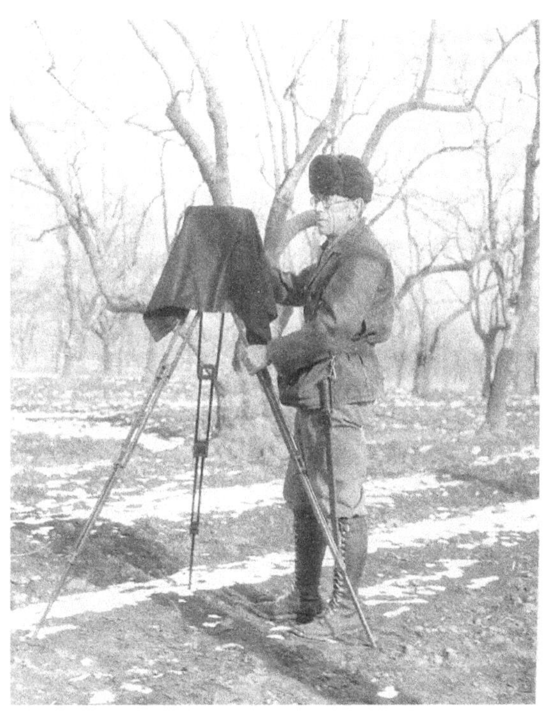

P.H. DORSETT'S PHOTOGRAPHIC TOUR
AROUND PEKING, CHINA
1924 - 1931

Edited by WILLIAM H. PRESTON

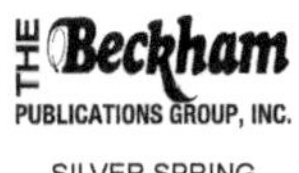

SILVER SPRING

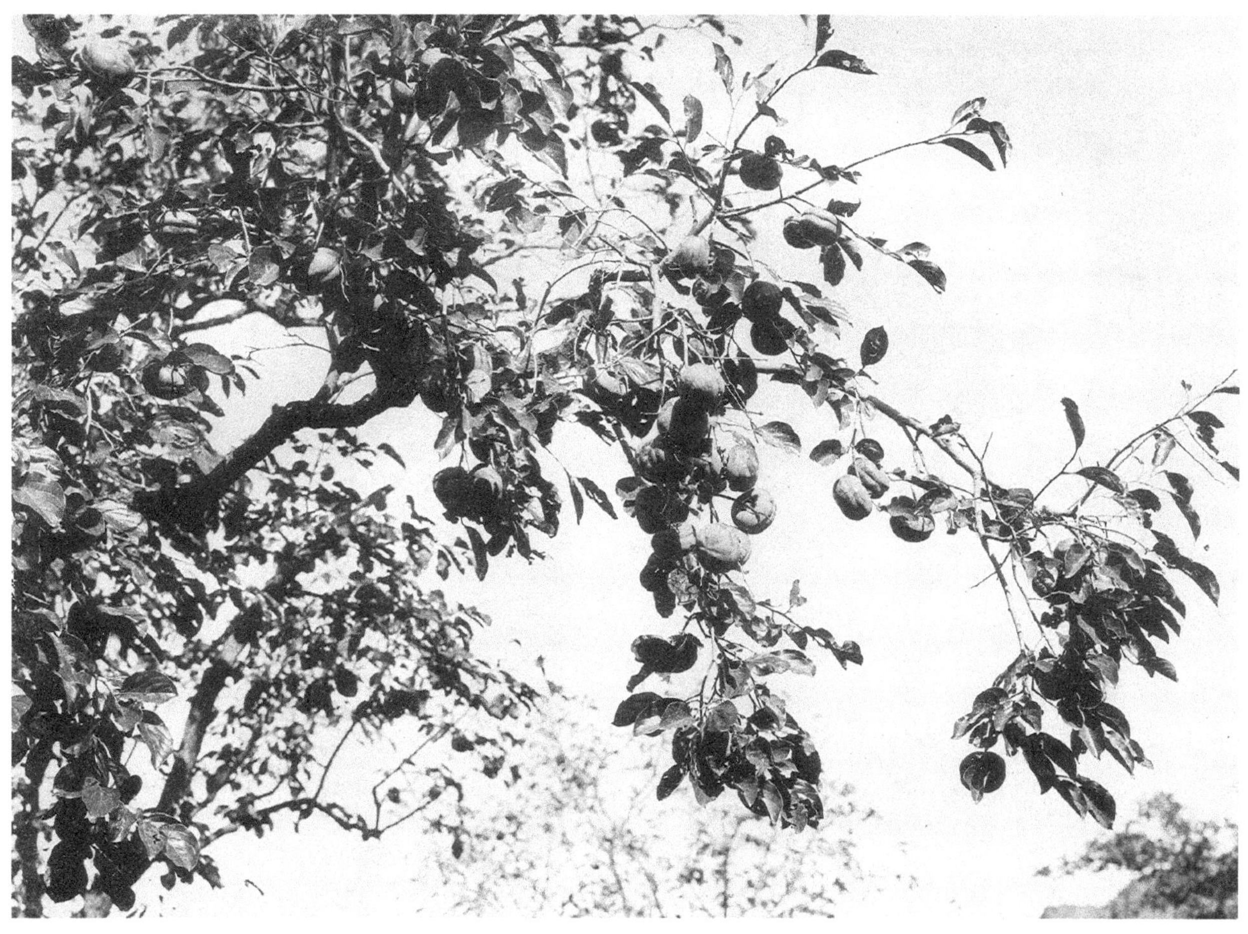

29475. *Oct. 7, l924. Tai Ling Chuang, en route to the Ming Tombs. A nearby picture of fruiting branches of large Chinese persimmons in an orchard.*

太陵園 village, Tai Ling Yuan
大柿子 TA Shih Tzu
Large persimmon

CONTENTS

PREFACE

That old brown box! I'd forgotten all about it. Sitting on a closet shelf for forty-five years, never opened, it was a mystery. It was near my persimmon records, and I guessed it contained old shipping records of persimmon scion wood.

So I opened it recently and I knew I had guessed wrong! It was a collection of about 200 photographs of persimmon fruits, trees, workers, and related views. Upon closer examination, many had handwritten legends and Chinese writing. Many were dated, ranging from 1924 to 1930.

Where did they come from? Who took the pictures? How did I get them? This took some deep recollection (not easy for an old duffer like me!). Eventually I recalled that some of the offices at the USDA New Crops Research Branch at Beltsville, MD were being cleared of old unneeded papers and records. Since Eugene Griffith and I, both working at the Glenn Dale, MD Plant Introduction Station at the time, were both interested in persimmons, the box was given to us to do with as we wished. Gene had no desire to keep them, so I took them and put them on my closet shelf after a cursory look.

Now I have studied the pictures further. A trip to the National Agricultural Library in Beltsville revealed that these photographs were taken by Palemon Howard Dorsett on several plant exploration trips to Asia during the 1920's. Dorsett was a plant explorer, paid by the USDA to locate and collect plants, seeds, and scions that might be useful as crops or in crop breeding in the U.S. He was also an avid and expert photographer, and the National Agricultural Library already had many boxes of his photographs and records organized into big booklets according to general subject matter.

These booklets were held in the "Special Collections" section of the National Agricultural Library, and one could peruse them only with special gloves. My examination of these booklets revealed that my old brown box of photos would be part of this collection, but of course it was never included for some unknown reason. Since some of my photos had no legends, this collection was probably "unfinished business".

I immediately organized my photos according to photo negative number, and I could then track Dorsett's travels to the extensive persimmon growing region north of Peiping (now Beijing). He and his son, James, explored the region in 1924-5, and he returned there in 1930-31.

Fortunately, he and his son published a USDA Circular (#49) titled *Culture and Outdoor Winter Storage of Persimmons in the Vicinity of Peking, China* in 1928. This publication was of major value in assessing the importance of the photos. I have used this paper, Dorsett's notes, his photo legends, and his excellent photographs extensively in this book.

ACKNOWLEDGMENTS

My interest in the Oriental persimmon began in 1958, when I worked at the U. S. Department of Agriculture Plant Introduction Station at Glenn Dale, Md. To my knowledge there were no persimmon trees at the Station, but there was an employee there, Eugene Griffith, who had attended the University of Maryland with me, and who knew the fruit and imparted his enthusiasm for it. He had traveled widely, including to China and Japan in the 1930's and 1940's, and he knew of the fruit's great flavor, and the tree's potential hardiness. We shared many memorable experiences, locating varieties, learning about persimmon culture and uses, and meeting other persimmon enthusiasts.

Special thanks go to (probably) Harold Winters, who rescued the box of Dorsett's persimmon photographs during the clearing of an office at Beltsville, and delivered the box to Eugene and me in (about) 1960. I don't recall the details of this transfer, and of course the photos had no names on them to indicate their original source. Anyway, I ended up with the photos.

When I looked for a source for the photos in 2007, I went to the U. S. Department of Agriculture's National Agricultural Library. The front desk staffer Mike Terbourg gave me all kinds of support for searches, files, plant explorers, etc., but when he directed me to the Dorsett files, my search for the source of the photos ended.

The next step was to examine the Dorsett files in the Special Collection section, and I got a great deal of assistance from Emelie George Rubin. She helped me locate more Dorsett files and photos on persimmons, which allowed me to expand the story about this crop in and around Peking, China, when Dorsett visited there. Thanks go to Susan Fugate, Head, Special Collections, who arranged to transfer 49 digital photos of the Dorsett collection to the publisher.

I appreciate the help supplied by Eric Lindstrom of the National Geographic Society, in locating some of the many towns and villages mentioned by Dorsett.

Special thanks go to Barry Beckham, publisher and CEO of The Beckham Publications Group, Inc., who guided me through the intricacies of producing this book.

Finally, I wish to express my heartfelt thanks to my wife, Corinne, for her guidance and many computer rescues in preparing this document for publication.

William H. Preston, Jr.

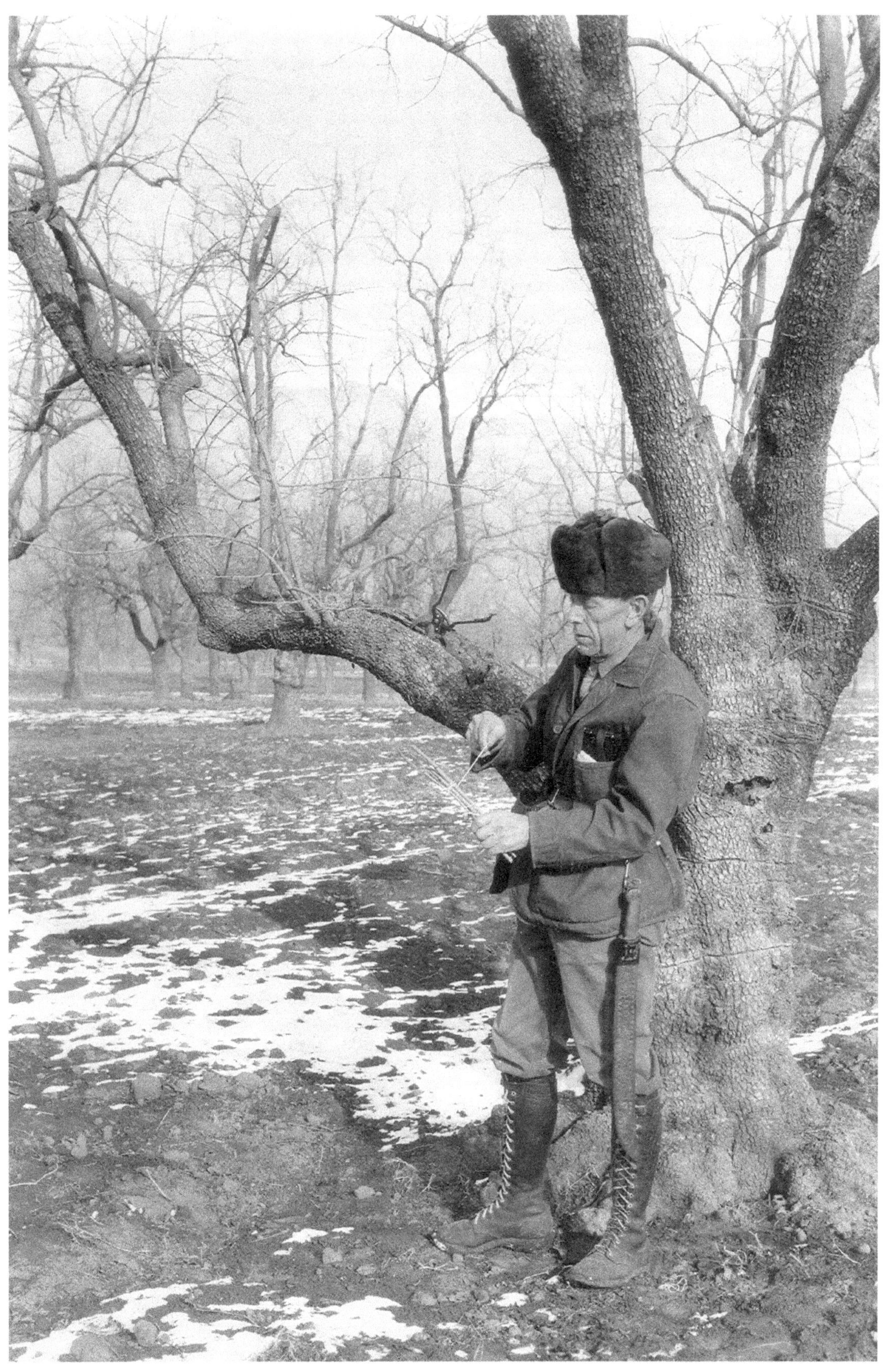

46439. *P. H. Dorsett standing next to a very old Chinese persimmon tree and collecting scions.*

SIGNIFICANCE OF PERSIMMON CULTURE IN NORTH CHINA

When P.H.Dorsett visited persimmon orchards north of Peking (Peiping), China in 1925-31, he found an amazing horticultural operation taking place there. An agricultural explorer from the U.S. Department of Agriculture, he was assigned to observe and collect plants in China and other Asian countries that might show promise as introductions for U.S. agriculture.

In North China he found many orchards of Chinese persimmons (Diospyros kaki) and a few significant varieties being grown there. An expert photographer, he captured views of persimmon culture wherever he observed it. As a result, he produced a collection of photographs that tell the story of persimmon culture in the areas he visited. This collection of pictures, along with his narration, reveals a phenomenal effort made by the Chinese to establish, grow, harvest, store, process, transport, and sell persimmons for the markets in local population centers, principally in and around Peking.

The significance of his findings have not yet been realized by most persimmon afficionados and many horticulturists in the U.S. This is the principal reason for the publication of this book. Listed below are the most important situations and practices Dorsett observed:

(1) A major horticultural industry supplying huge quantities of persimmon fruit to one of the world's largest northern cities.

(2) An outdoor cold-storage system that maintained persimmon fruits in good condition for up to 6 months from harvest.

(3) An astringency-removal technique that rendered the fruits edible within a day's time, set up to process large quantities of fruit.

(4) The extensive use of human, donkey, mule, and camel transportation to move the harvest of persimmons from the orchards and storage areas in the country, to the processing kilns and markets in the city on a carefully-arranged supply schedule.

(5) The selection and employment of persimmon varieties and grafting understock that were hardy enough to withstand the winters of North China, and appealing enough to result in a consistent widespread demand for the fruit.

(6) Living evidence that the persimmon had been cultivated and successfully grafted as an orchard fruit in this northern climate for hundreds of years.

BIOGRAPHICAL SKETCH of P.H. Dorsett

[Source: USDA National Agricultural Library's Special Collection notes]

1862	Born Palemon Howard Dorsett on April 21 in Carlinville, Macoupin County, Illinois.
1884	Received Bachelor of Arts degree from the University of Missouri.
1891	Joined United States Department of Agriculture (USDA) Section of Plant Pathology under the supervision of Beverly Thomas Galloway, and engaged in experiments on the treatment of diseased plants with Bordeaux mixture.
1892	Married Mary Virginia Payne on September 12.
1898	First work published, *The Selection of Violets.*
1899	Dorsett jointly authored *The Use of Hydrocyanic Acid Gas for Fumigating Greenhouses and Cold Frames* with Albert Fred Woods, which was revised and published again in 1903 and l908.
1900	Dorsett's *Spot Disease of the Violet* published as *USDA Bulletin No. 23.*
1904-1907	Supervised the USDA Plant Introduction Garden at Chico, California.
1907	Dorsett returned to the Washington, D.C. area following the deaths of his wife and eldest daughter. He began a commercial horticultural business in Alexandria, Va.
1909	Dorsett's youngest daughter died during the winter months, and he rejoined USDA Bureau of Plant Industry in the Office of Seed and Plant Introduction.
1913	Published USDA Bulletin No. 28: *Experiments in Bulb Growing at the United States Bulb Garden at Bellingham.*
1913-1914	Left October 4, 1913, on his first foreign plant expedition to Brazil with Archibald Dixon Shamel and Wilson Popenoe. They published *USDA Bulletin No. 445: The Navel Orange of Bahia, with Notes on Some Little Known Brazilian Fruits,* in 1917, as a report of this expedition.
1914	Worked with David Fairchild on the development of Japanese flowering cherry trees.
1915	Established Miami, Florida, Plant Introduction Garden, with David Fairchild and Wilson Popenoe.

1917	Published *The Plant Introduction Gardens of the Department of Agriculture* in the *Yearbook of Agriculture 1916*.
1921	Traveled on plant exploration expedition to Panama with David Fairchild.
1924-1925	Traveled on plant exploration expeditions in Manchuria, China, accompanied by his son James (Jim) Dorsett.
1925-1926	Traveled on plant exploration expeditions in Ceylon (Sri Lanka), Sumatra, and Java (Indonesia) with David Fairchild. The expedition was recounted in Fairchild's *Exploring for Plants.*
1926-1927	Traveled on plant exploration expeditions in Manchuria, China, from spring (left Java in mid-April) 1926 to 1927.
1927	Death of only son, Jim, on October 8, in Washington, D. C.
1928	Wrote *Culture and Outdoor Winter Storage of Persimmons in the Vicinity of Peking, China,* jointly authored with his son and published as *USDA Circular No. 49.*
1928-1932	Traveled on Dorsett-Morse Oriental Agricultural Exploration Expedition to Japan, Korea, and China.
1932	Retired from the USDA.
1932-1933	Joined the Allison Vincent Armour agricultural expedition to the British West Indies and Guianas (Carribean).
1936	Awarded the 13th Frank N. Meyer Medal by the Council of the American Genetic Association for distinguished actions related to the collection, preservation, or utilization of germ plasm resources.
1943	Died in a Washington, D.C. nursing home on April 1.

PERSIMMON TERMINOLOGY

The principal crop discussed in this book is the Oriental persimmon, presumed native to China, and officially given the Latin name *Diospyros kaki.* It is also known as the Kaki persimmon, the Japanese persimmon, and the Chinese persimmon. Dorsett studied the crop in China and generally referred to it as the Chinese persimmon.

Another persimmon native to China and used as understock for grafting by the Chinese is the black date persimmon, *Diospyros lotus.* Dorsett observed and described this crop.

In the U.S., we are familiar with our native persimmon *Diospyros virginiana*, and I have mentioned it in the text occasionally. It is often used in this country as an understock for grafting Oriental persimmon varieties.

ENGLISH AND CHINESE TERMINOLOGY

Some of Dorsett's photographs had legends that used Chinese terms, indicating that he was attempting to learn the language. If you travel to China or discuss persimmons with Chinese people, this listing may be helpful.

Persimmon	*Shih tzu*
Large persimmon	*Ta shih tzu*
Small persimmon	*Hsaio shih tzu*
Lantern persimmon	*Teng lung shih tzu*
Tree	*Shu*
Orchard	*Yuan*
Black date tree	*Hei ts'ao shu*
Large dried persimmon	*Ta Shih ping*
Small dried persimmon	*Hsaio shih ping*
Black date dried persimmon	*Hei ts'ao ping*
Persimmon picking hook	*Shih tzu k'ou tzu*
Persimmon storage	*Shih tzu ch'ang*
Ring bud grafting	*T'ao t"ung chien*
Sticking bark (shield bud) grafting	*Chan pi chien*
Donkey (small) saddle-basket(pannier)	*Lung tuo*
Camel basket (pannier)	*Tuo kuang*

BEIJING—A HISTORY OF NAMES

When P.H. Dorsett traveled to north China in 1924-5, the city now named Beijing was called Peking. When he traveled there in 1930-1, the city had the new name of Peiping. A brief review of the naming of this ancient and large city, now with a population of over seven million, may be helpful to readers.

- Ch'i (capitol of Yen)(before 1000 AD)
- Yenching (by Tartars, from 1000-1264)
- Khanbalik (by Mongols, 1264-1421)
- Peking (by Ming Dynasty, etc. 1421-1928)
- Peiping (1929-1949)
- Beijing (1949 to present)

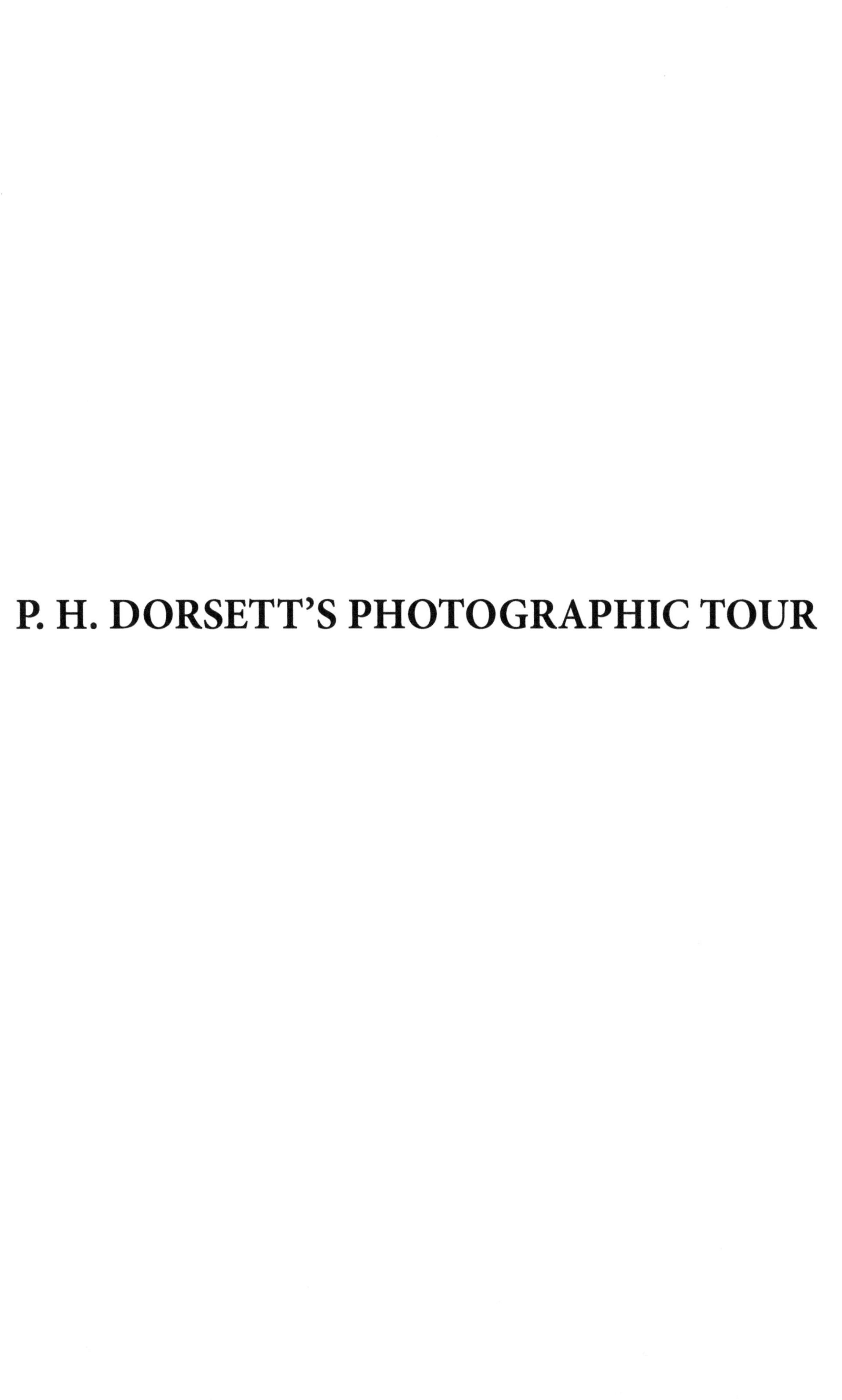

P. H. DORSETT'S PHOTOGRAPHIC TOUR

HISTORY

For centuries the Oriental persimmon has been cultivated in Japan and China, the probability being that it was originally grown in China, whence it was introduced into Japan at a very early date. The late Frank N. Meyer found top-worked trees in China that appeared to be very old, and he reported large sections of that country devoted entirely to persimmon culture. In Japan trees are grown singly or in small groves throughout the country.

It is probable that the persimmon is the most commonly used staple fruit in the Orient, its importance being comparable to that of the apple in the United States. During the long period of cultivation in China and Japan many distinct horticultural varieties have arisen and cultural practices have become greatly specialized.

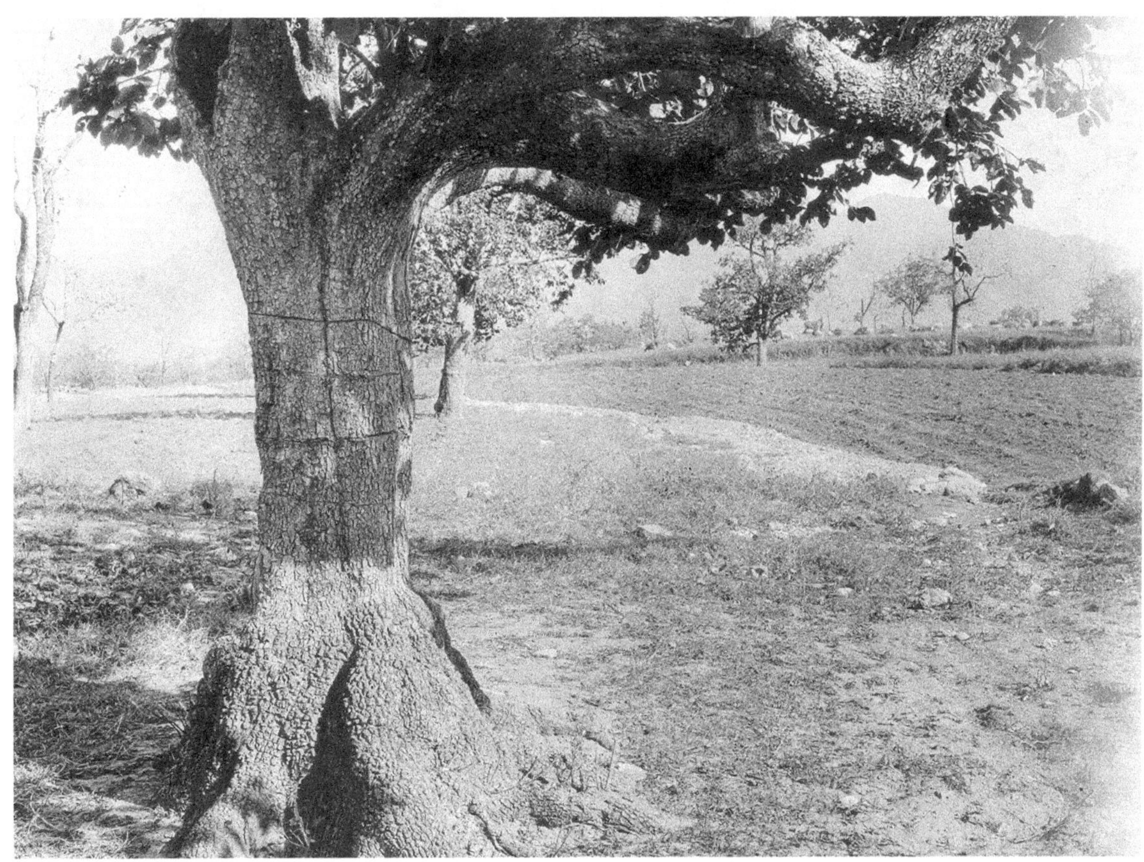

29486. *Oct. 8, 1924. Ming Tombs region. A close-up picture of the trunk and part of the limbs of the 400-year-old Lantern persimmon tree shown also in #29485.*

燈籠柿子樹 Teng Lung Shih Tzu Shu
Lantern persimmon tree

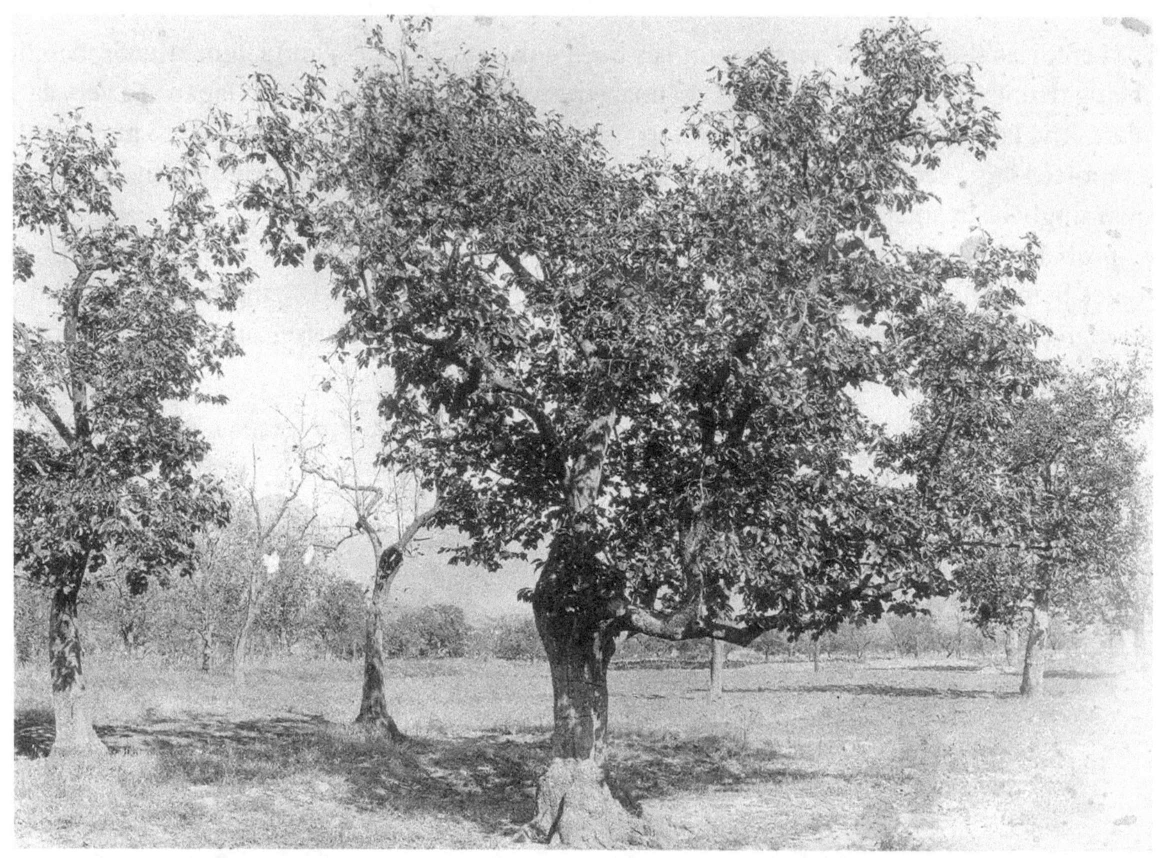

29485. *Oct. 8, 1924. Ming Tombs region. A close-up picture of the largest and also one of the oldest persimmon trees in the region. This is a Lantern variety and is reckoned to be 400 or more years old.*

明陵 Ming ling, Ming Tomb
柿子樹 Shih Tzu shu
Persimmon tree

U. S. EXPLORATION

The introduction of the oriental persimmon into the United States is recorded by Prince as early as 1828, and in 1856 Commodore Perry obtained seeds during his epoch-making visit to Japan. These seeds were planted at the Naval Observatory in Washington, D. C., and four years later one of the trees bore fruit. No distribution of seedlings was made, and after a few years the original trees died.

In 1863 another lot of seed was introduced by William Saunders of the United States Department of Agriculture, and it is reported that at least one of the trees distributed as a result of this importation produced a good crop of fruit. The first introduction of grafted trees, made by the Department in 1870, included a number of good varieties, such as Hachiya, Tanenashi, and Yemon. These trees were distributed throughout the southern states and California. From this time on extensive importations were made from Japan, not only by the Department but also by private growers, resulting in the establishment of the oriental persimmon in California and certain parts of the South.

In 1894 and again in 1895 the United States Department of Agriculture made efforts to introduce living plant material of the large oriental persimmon from the region west of Peking, where it was known to be in cultivation. The pomologist of the Department solicited the cooperation of Charles Denby, then United States Minister to China, in this important work. The minister and his son, Charles Denby, Jr., then secretary of the legation at Peking, forwarded scions of two varieties, which they reported on at the time. Unfortunately, this material did not survive the long ocean voyage, and it was not until 1905 that the Department made another specific attempt to introduce living plant material of the large persimmons from China. In that year Frank N. Meyer, agricultural explorer in the Office of Foreign Plant Introduction of the Bureau of Plant Industry, was successful in importing live scions of the large Chinese persimmon grown commercially in the Ming Tombs region northwest of Peking.

More recent introductions of the (astringent) Hachiya and nonastringent Fuyu have stimulated greatly the interest of American fruit growers in this new plant introduction from the Orient, and already their cultivation is being extended in parts of the southern United States and more notably throughout California.

[Ed.: Sponsored by the U.S. Department of Agriculture, P.H. Dorsett and his son James explored for plants, including persimmons, in northern (Manchurian) China in 1924 and 1925. Dates on photographs taken on this trip indicate that they were in persimmon growing areas from late September through late November, 1924, then returned again in early January, 1925, and again in early March, 1925.

In a later USDA-sponsored trip Dorsett was accompanied by soybean specialist William J. Morse (collecting soybean varieties was the principal purpose of the trip). In November, 1930, and later, Dorsett was again in the persimmon growing region of north China and he took more photographs of persimmon culture and fruit processing, storage, and transport.]

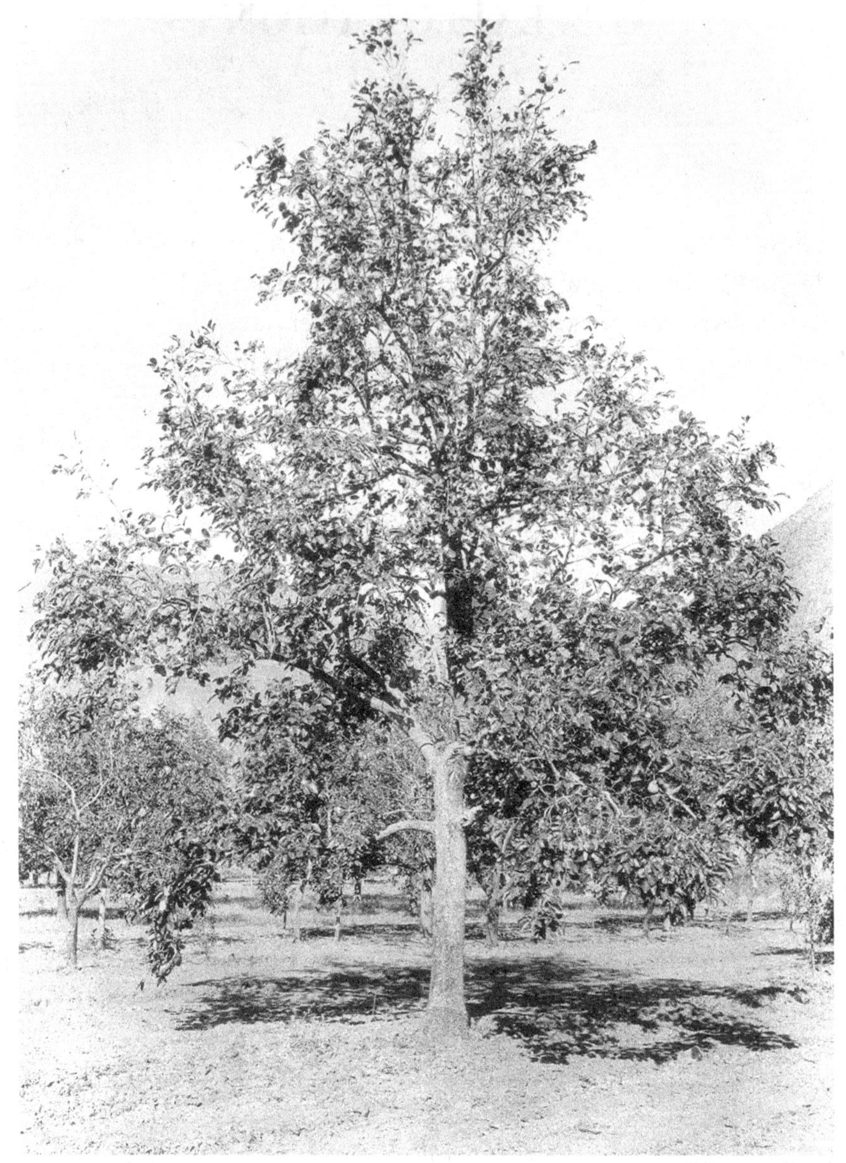

29482. *Oct. 8, 1924. Tai Lung Yuan village. A close-up picture of a good tree of the large Chinese persimmon in an orchard.*

太陵園 village, T'ai Ling yuan
柿子樹 shih Tzu shu
persimmon tree

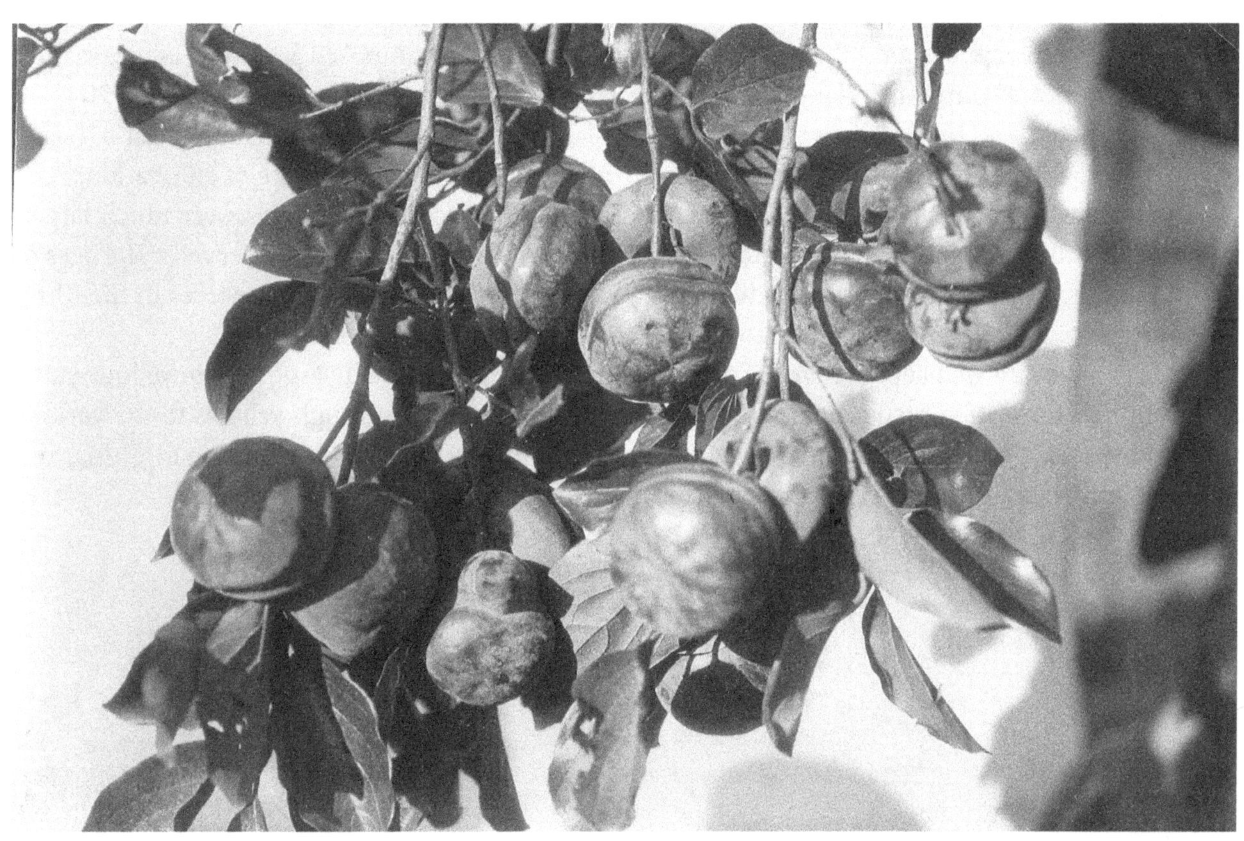

Req. 438. *Close-up picture of large Chinese persimmons on a tree branch of the variety Ta mo pan shi tzu (large persimmon) grown in great quantities in North China orchards.*

PERSIMMON ORCHARDS

Most of the persimmon orchards of northeastern China are located in the foothill areas of the larger valleys and in the more or less level areas along the smaller rivers and mountain streams, appearing at their best in deep, well-drained, decomposed granite or alluvial sandy loam. The trees are commonly planted in rows which are about 30 feet apart, the trees being 20 to 30 feet apart in the rows. The orchards are usually interplanted to smaller-growing fruit trees or to beans or other annual crops, and as a rule are kept free from weeds and in a good state of cultivation.

The trees we inspected averaged 15 inches in diameter, but occasionally trees were much larger. One tree measured 68 inches in circumference, and many of similar size were observed. The ages of the trees in the average orchard were generally stated as 75 to 100 years, and a few trees in the Ming Tombs region northwest of Peking were reported to be 400 to 500 years old.

At harvest time a well kept orchard of oriental persimmons, laden with large golden yellow fruits, and in full costume of gorgeous colored foliage, ranging from green through yellows to the various shades of pink, red, and even dark maroon, is a most glorious spectacle not uncommon in China, and grander, more beautiful, and even more spectacular than the orange groves of America.

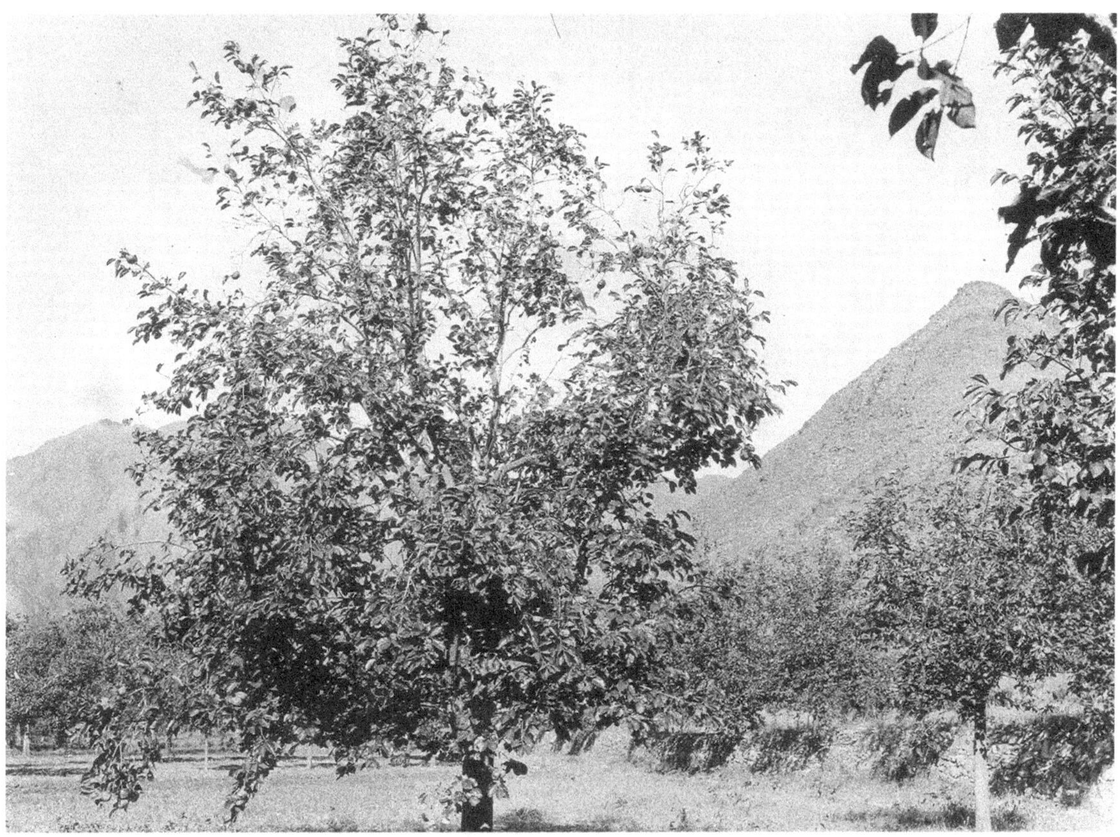

***29483.** Oct. 8, 1924. Tai Ling Yuan. A close-up picture of one area of the good average large-fruited persimmon trees in one of the orchards.*

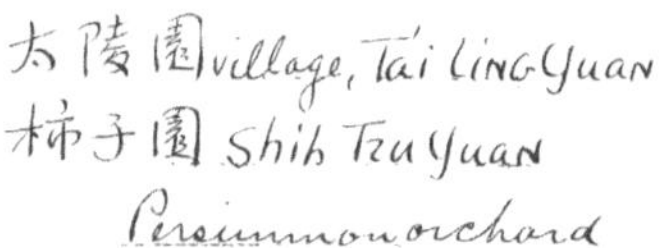

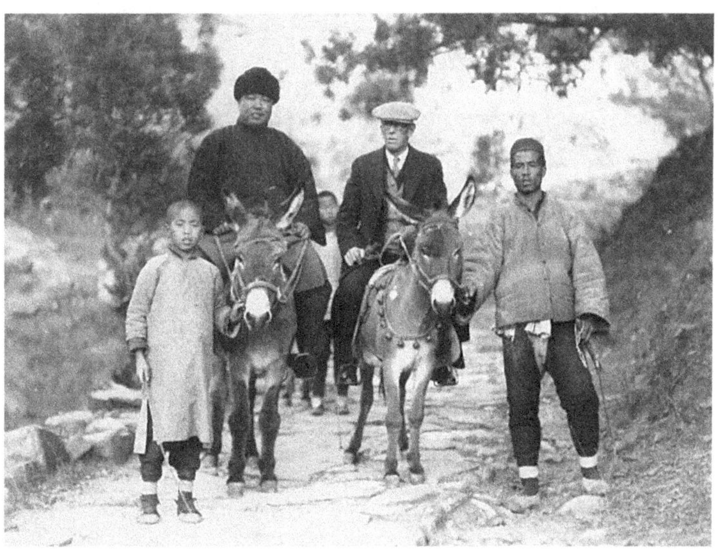

***46197A.** Near Pa Ta Chu, Western Hills, to the west of Peiping. P.H. Dorsett and his Chinese interpreter, Peter Liu, on the trail.*

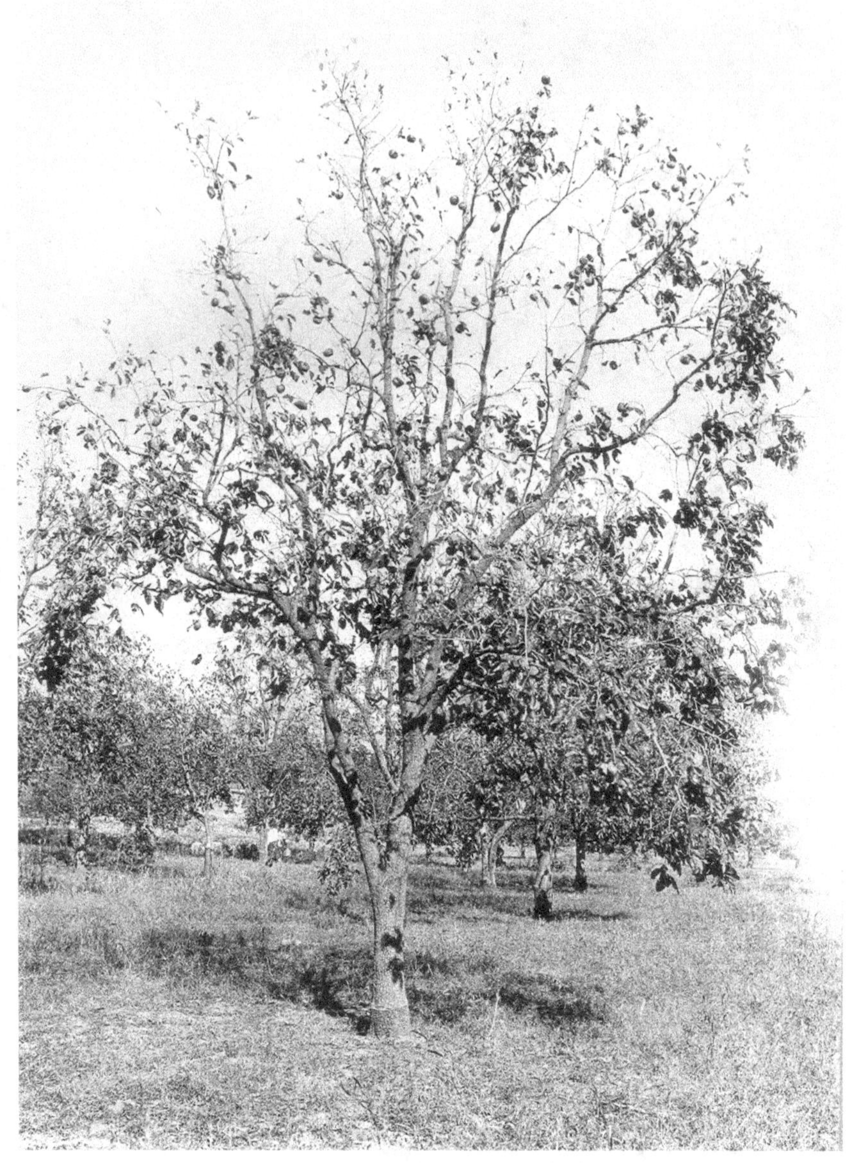

28487. *Oct. 8, 1924. Ming Tombs region. A close-up picture of a good tree of the large Chinese persimmon variety 25 yards or so from the old one shown in #29485.*

明陵 ming ling, Ming Tomb,
大柿子樹 Ta shih Tzu shu
Large persimmon tree

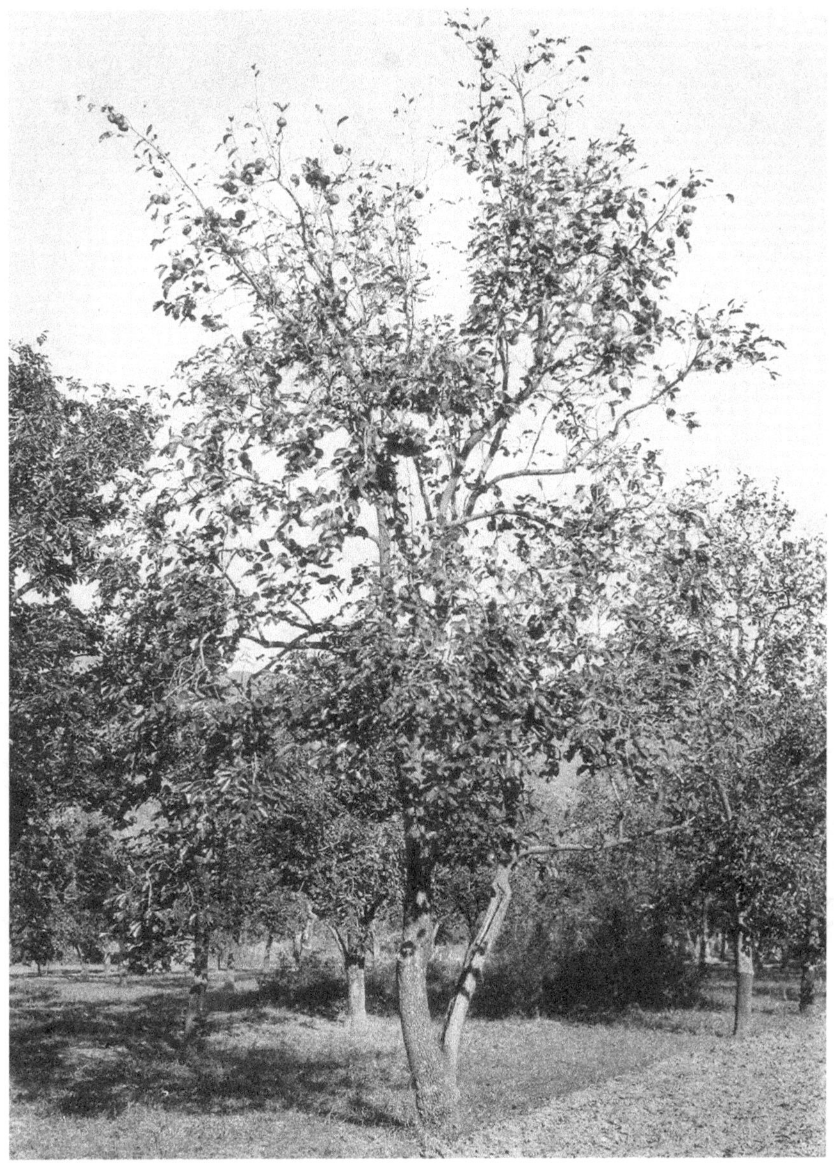

29478. *Oct. 8, 1924. Tai Ling Yuan village. A close-up picture of one of the trees of the large Chinese persimmon in an orchard.*

太陵園 village, Tai Ling Yuan
柿子園 Shih Tzu Yuan
Persimmon Orchard

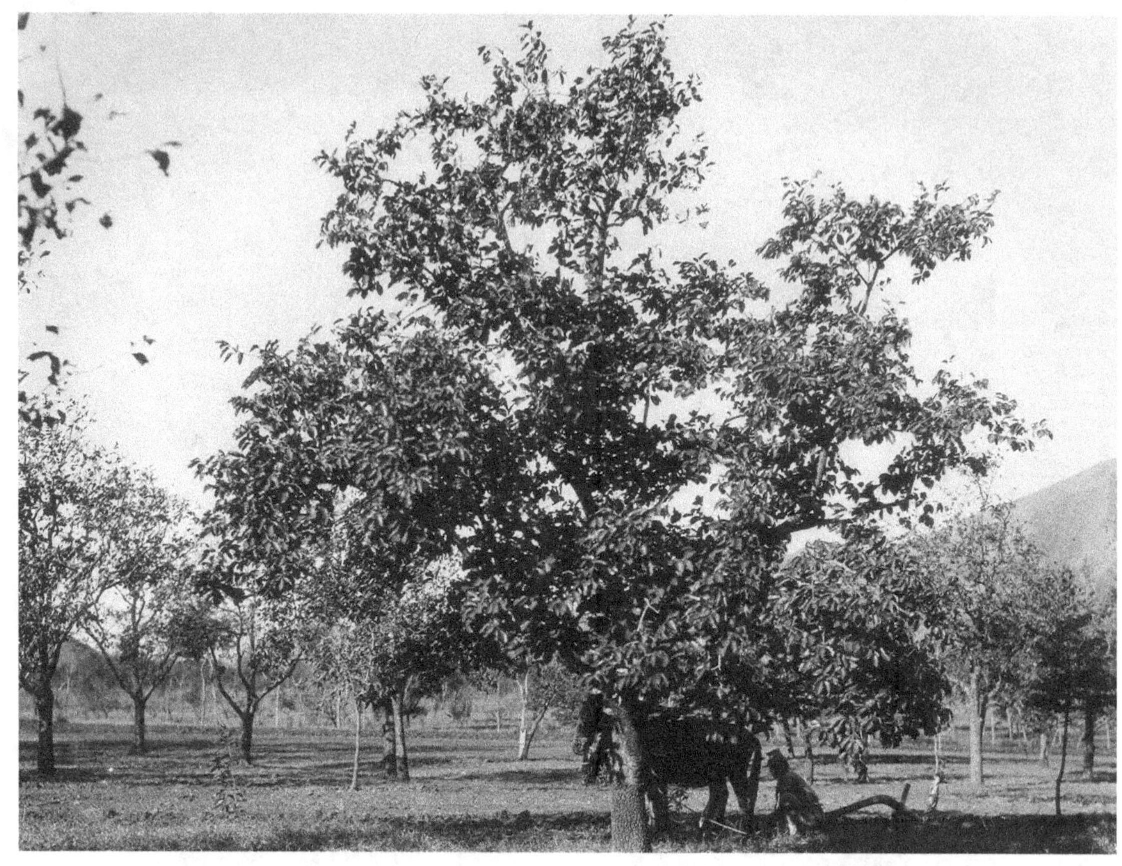

29477. *Oct. 8, 1924. Tai Ling Yuan village. View of persimmon orchard with field worker and mule under the tree.*

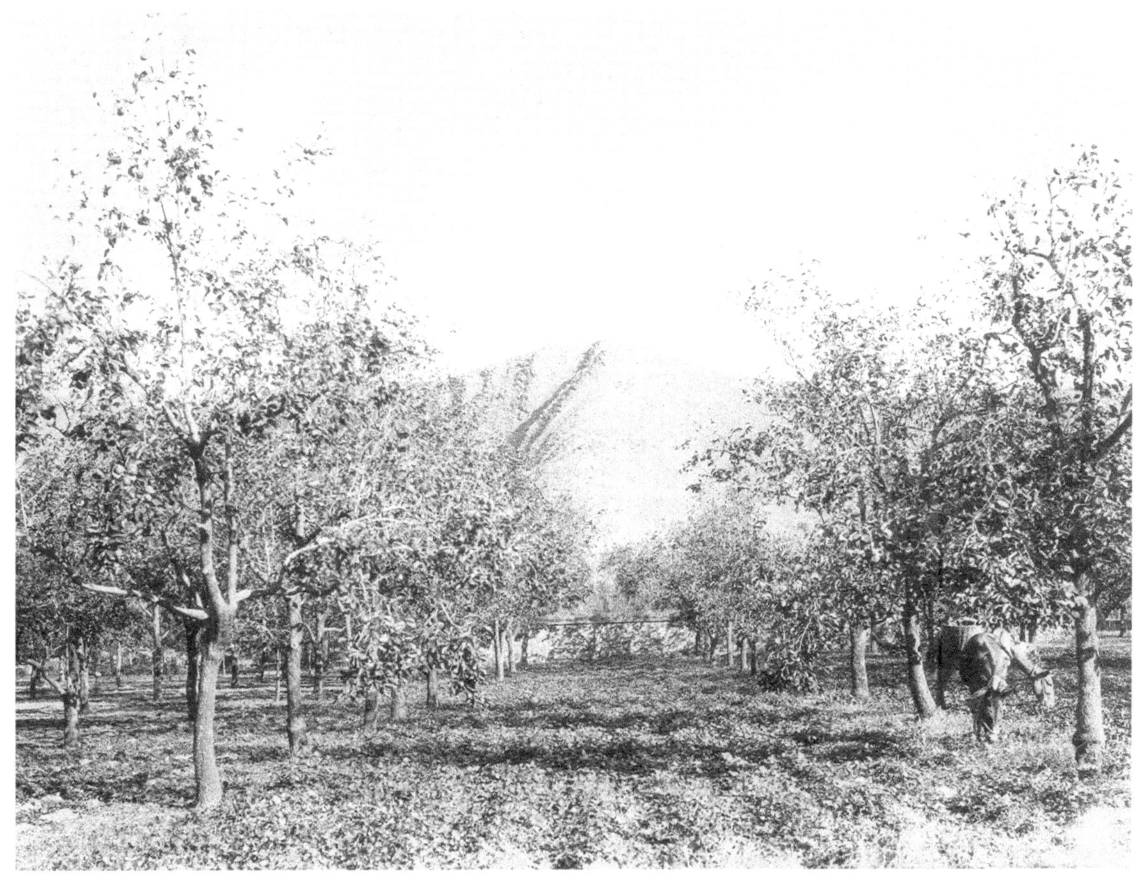

29476. *Oct. 8, 1924. Tai Ling Yuan village in the Ming Tombs region. View in the persimmon orchard of Mr. Sun Yen.*

太陵園 village Tai Ling yuan
柿子園 Shih Tzu yuan
Persimmon orchard

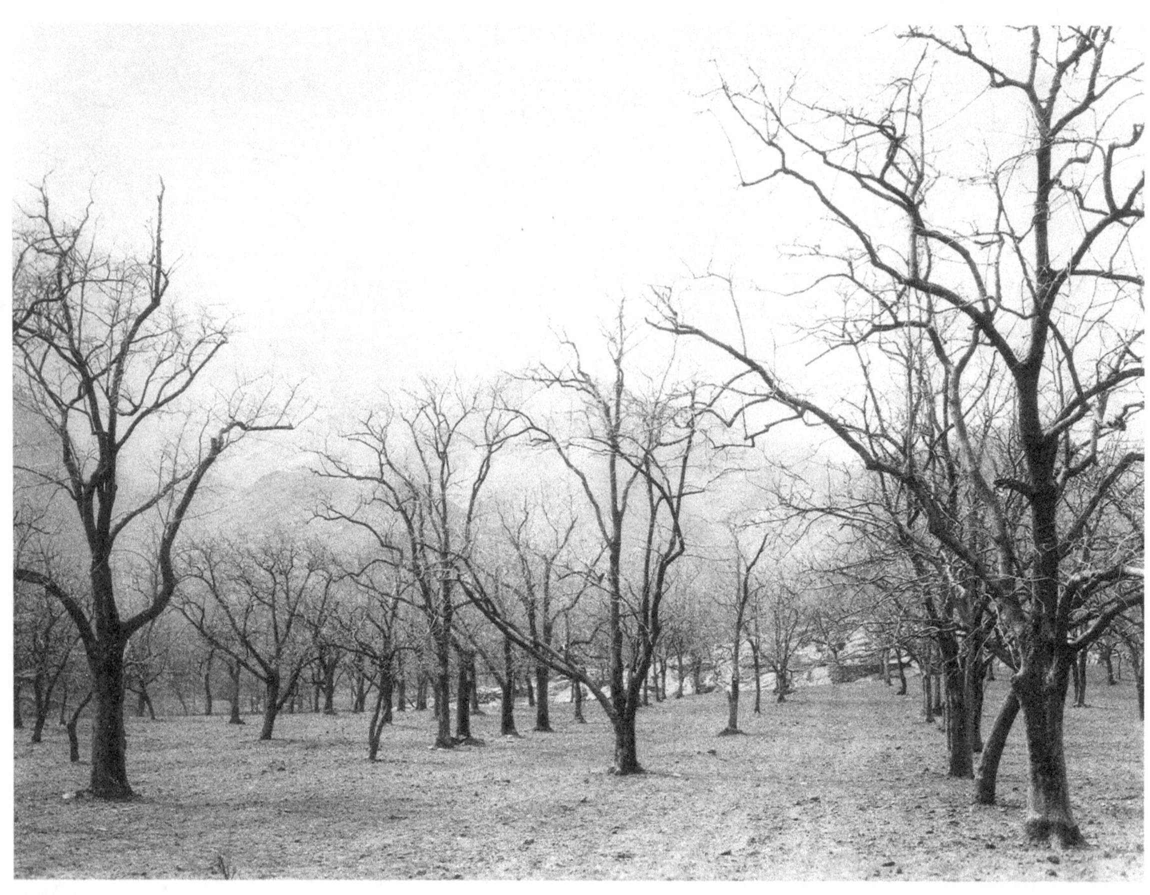

38500. *Mar. 8, 1925. Near Pan Pi Tien village. A picture from the east side of Mr. Li Yung Shen's persimmon orchard and looking west to the mountains.*

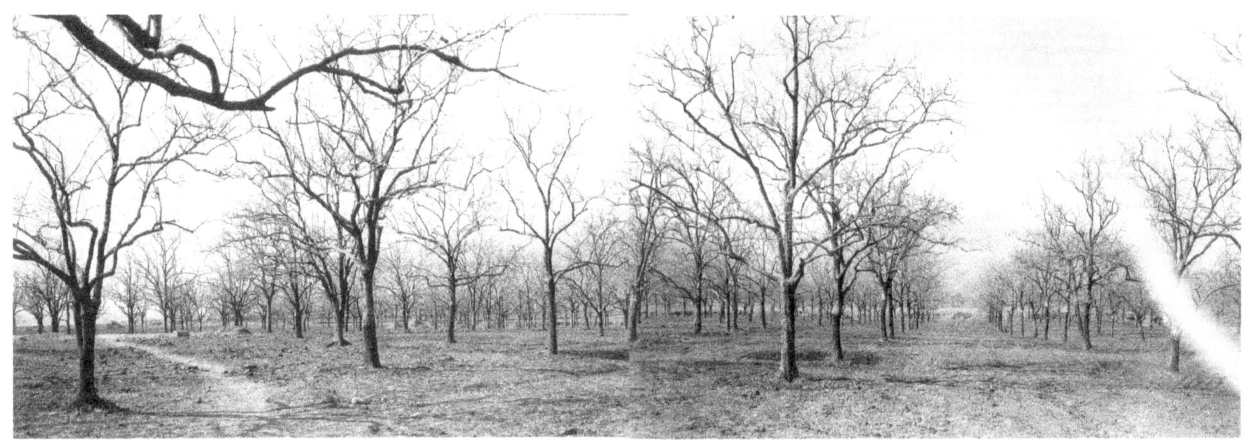

38475-7. *Mar. 7, 1925. Hsi Chung Tien village. A panoramic view of a persimmon orchard near the village.*

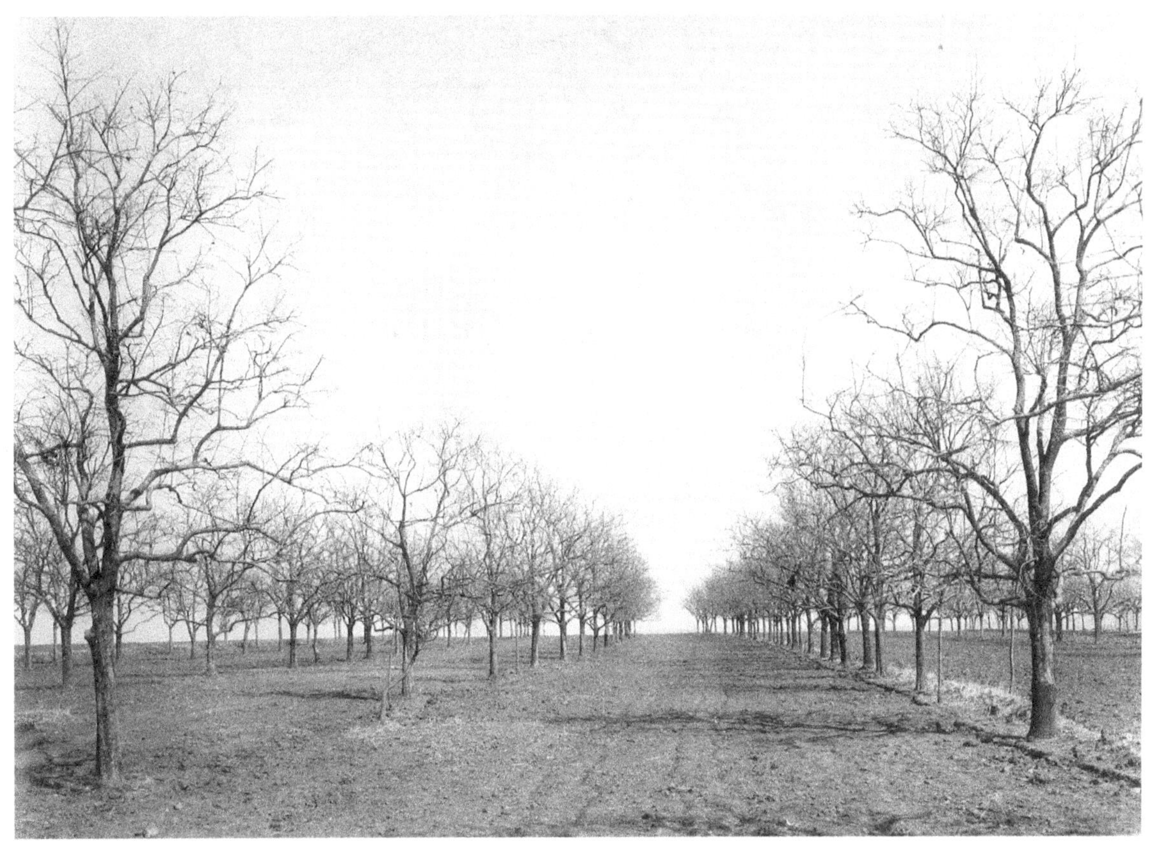

38474. *Mar. 7, 1925. Hsi Chung Tien village. A view of a persimmon orchard near the village, between Mentoukow and To Li.*

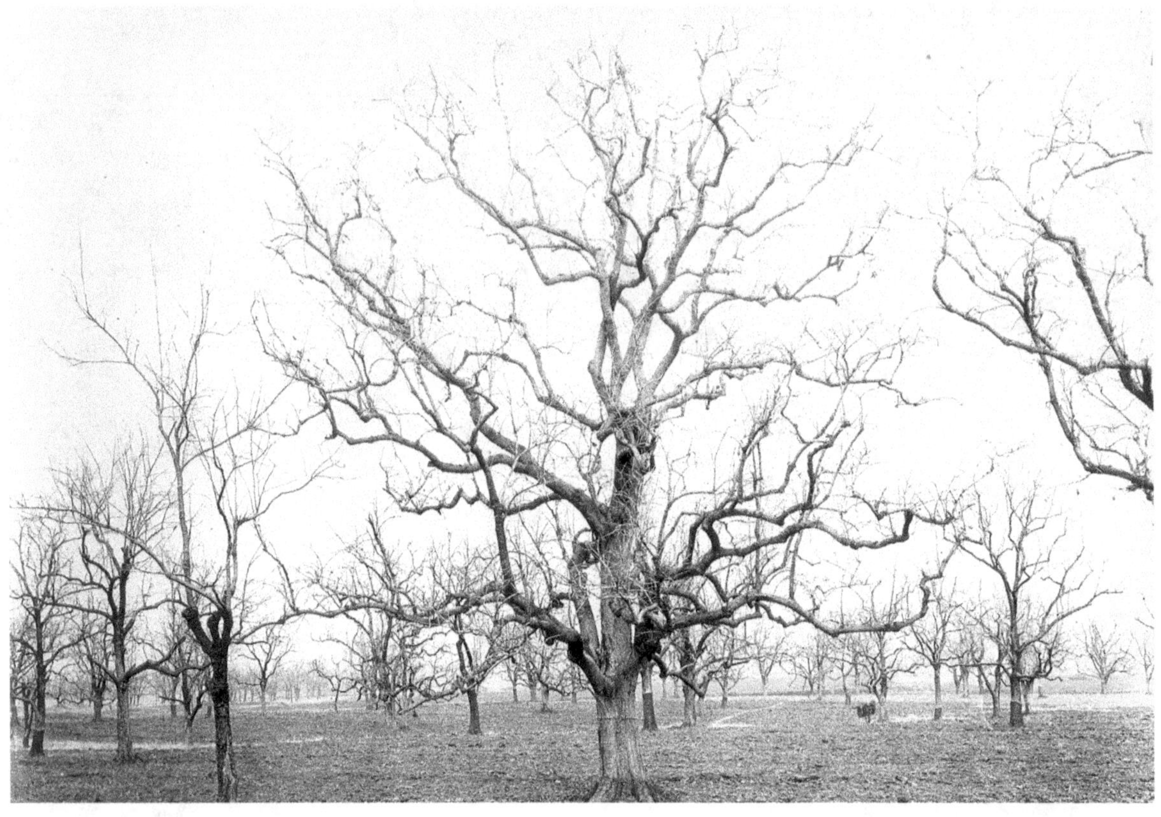

38049. *Nov. 28, 1924. Tai Ling Yuan. A nearby picture of a fine tree of the Lantern persimmon in an orchard near Tai Ping Chuang.*

太陵園 village, Tai Ling Yuan
燈籠柿子樹 Teng Lung Shih Tzu Shu
Lantern persimmon tree

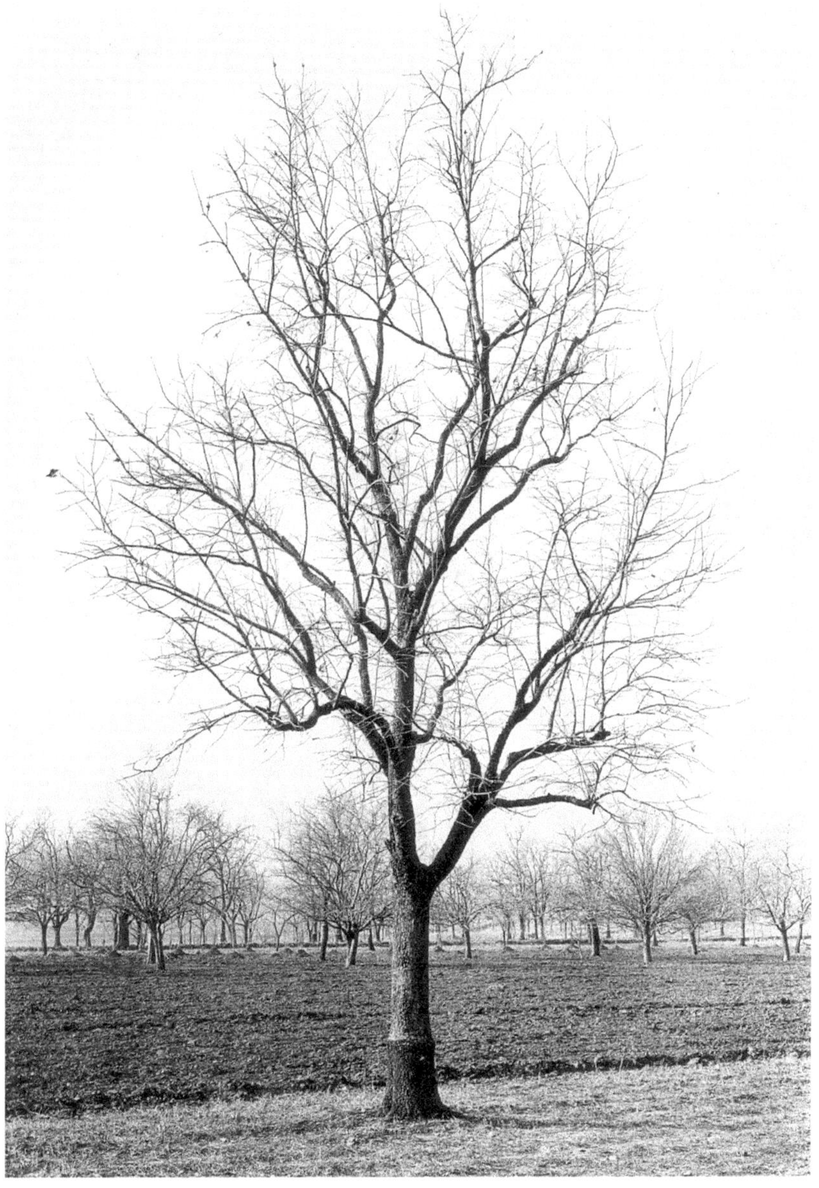

38040. *Nov. 28, 1924. Tai Ling Yuan. A close-up picture of a good average large-fruited persimmon tree in one of the large orchards in the district.*

太陵園 village, Tai Ling Yuan
柿子樹 Shih Tzu Shu
Large Persimmon tree

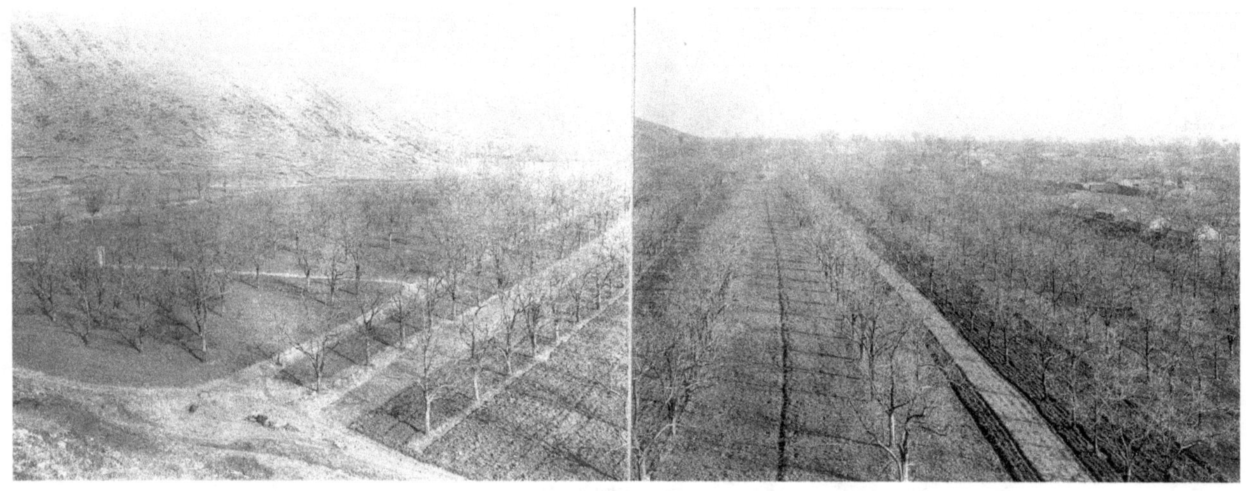

38038-9. *Nov. 28, 1924. Tai Ling Yuan. A panoramic view of two exposures in one of the large persimmon orchards.*

太陵園 village, Tai Ling Yuan
柿子園, Shih Tzu Yuan
Persimmon orchard

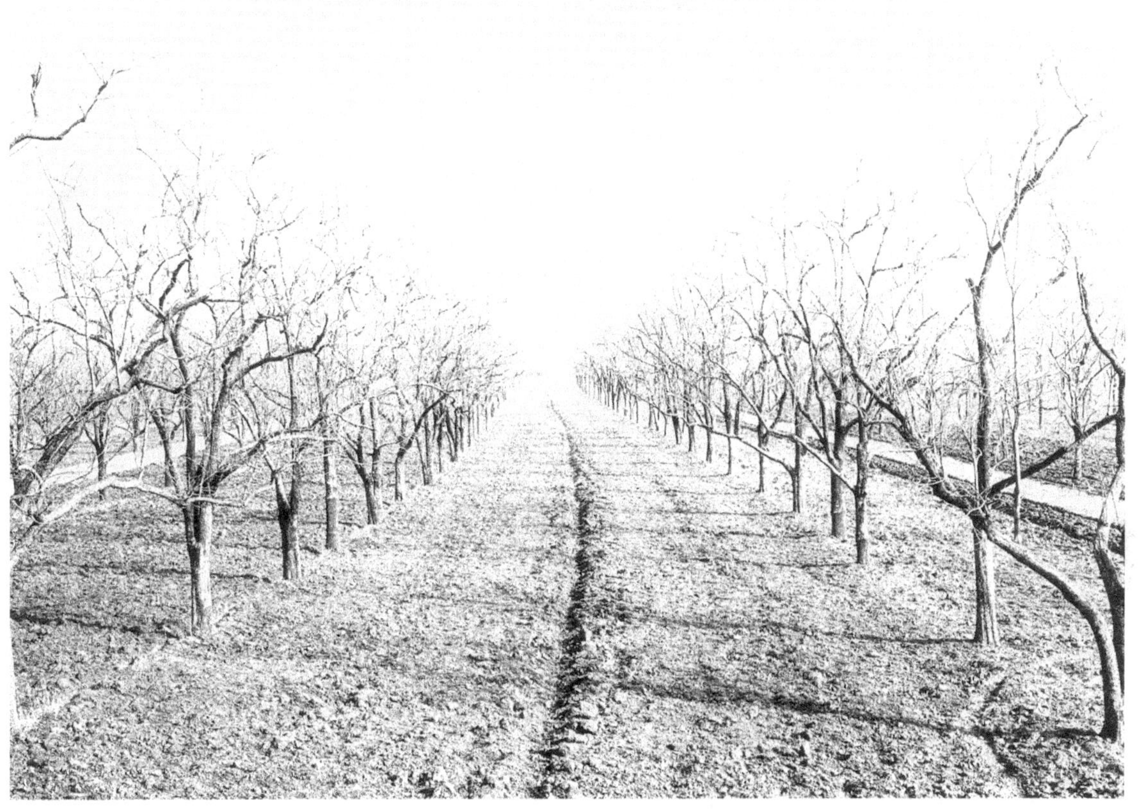

38037. *Nov. 28, 1924. Tai Ling Yuan. A view of one of the large persimmon orchards. The greater part of the orchard floor has been fall-plowed but not seeded.*

太陵園 village, Tai Ling Yuan
柿子園, Shih Tzu Yuan
Persimmon orchard

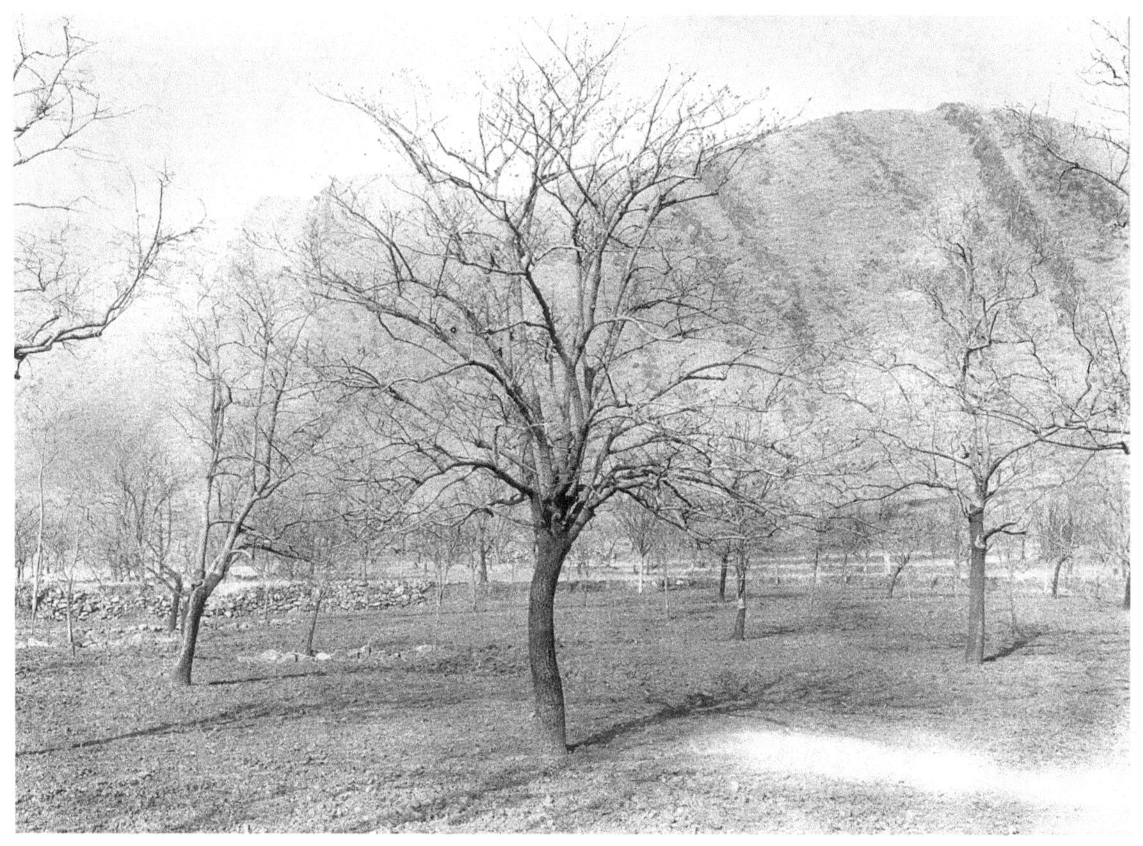

38035. *Nov. 28, 1924. Tai Ling Yuan, in the Ming Tombs region. A close-up picture of the black date tree shown in picture #29484 after the fruit we purchased for seed was picked and the leaves had fallen.*

太陵園 Village, Tai Ling Yuan
黑棗樹 Hei Tsao shu
Black Date tree

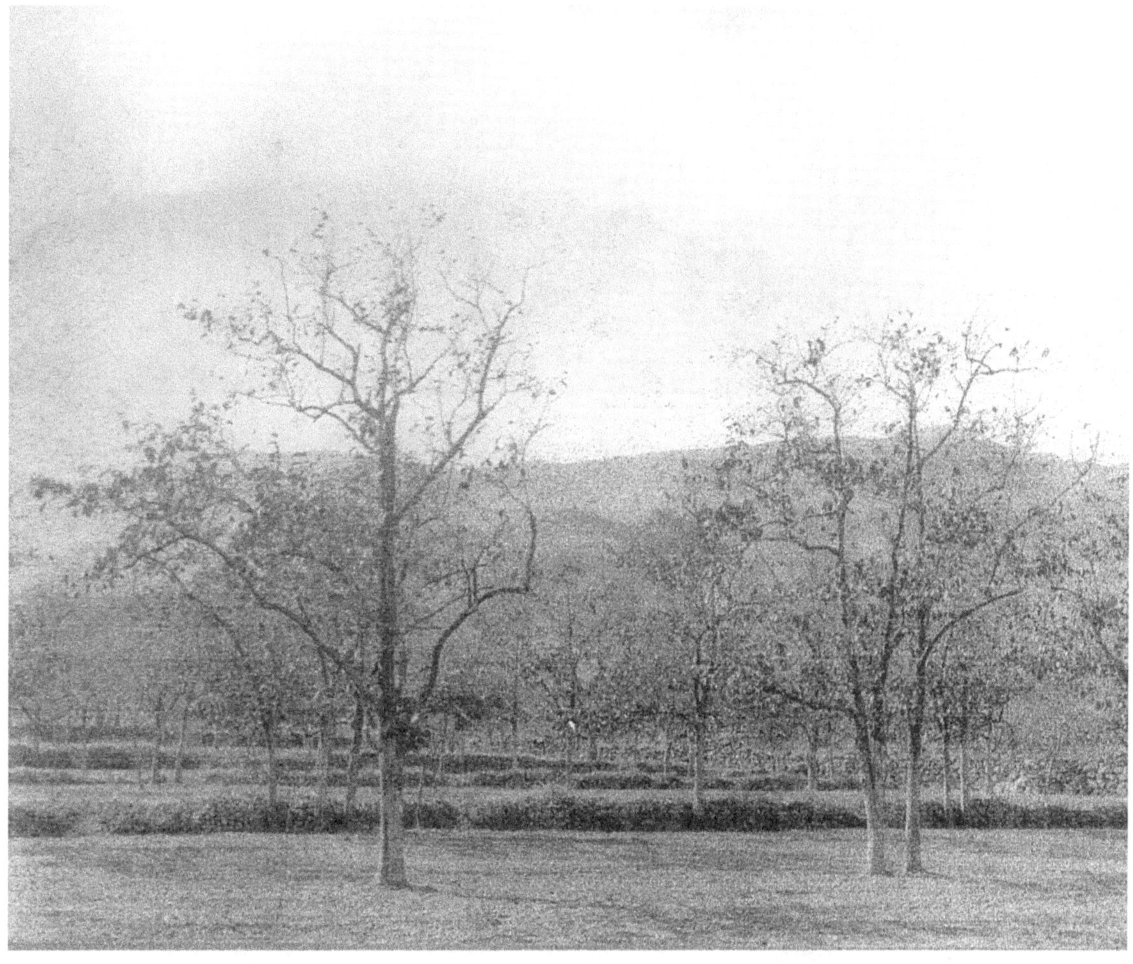

29623. *Oct. 21, 1924. La Chuch Ssu (Western Hill) near the Old Temple of Ta Kiao Ssu. A terraced large-fruited Chinese persimmon orchard some 40 or 50 miles to the northwest of Peking near the old Temple.*

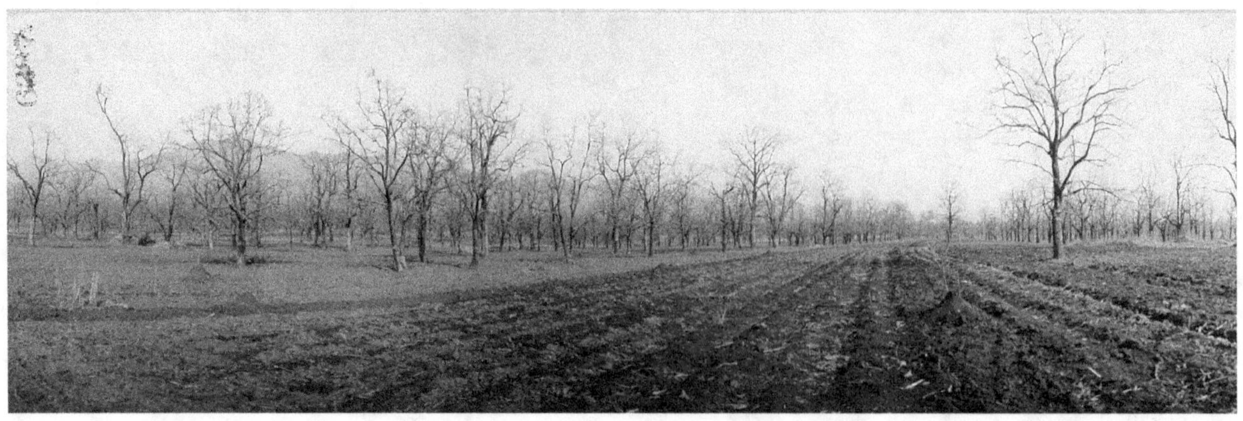

46187. *Near Hsiang Tang village. A panoramic view of a portion of a good-sized persimmon orchard near the village, some 25 miles to the north of Peiping. This view (and #46186) are typical of the persimmon orchards of that region and give a good idea of how they look at the winter season of the year.*

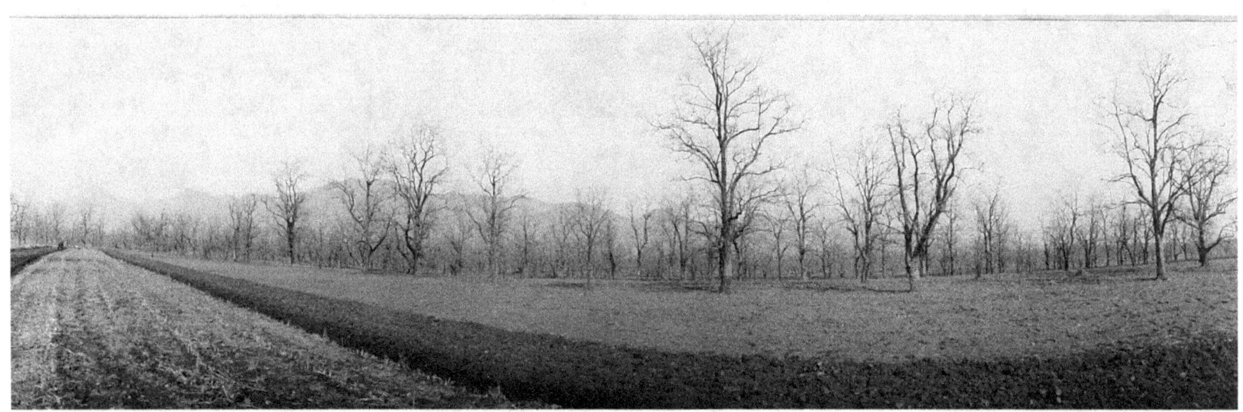

46186. *Near Hsiang Tang village. Panoramic view of a portion of a Chinese persimmon orchard near the village, some 25 miles to the north of Peiping. The orchards in this region, like those of other regions we have seen in China, are inter-cultivated to other crops.*

VARIETIES

Frank N. Meyer, after describing a number of persimmons that he procured and introduced, says, "in the Provinces of Shantung, Shensi, Honan, and Chekiang (and he should have included Chihli) there are many varieties of persimmons that are still waiting to be introduced."

In agricultural exploration in the vicinity of Peking only two species of persimmon were seen by the writers. One was *Diospyros lotus*, the small wild persimmon with many seeds, known generally among the Chinese as hei tsao (black date). The fruit of this species, both fresh and dried, is sold in Peking and other markets in considerable quantity, to children and to the poorer classes. The other species, *D. kaki*, is the commercial persimmon, embracing four types of fruit, only two of which are of any great economic importance in that part of China. From a commercial point of view there is little if any real difference in the two types of Chinese persimmons found in abundance in Peking and other markets in northeastern China, except in the size of the fruit and corresponding difference in price.

Of these types the one in greatest favor and most extensively grown is that known by the Chinese as Ta shih tzu (large persimmon). This is probably the same persimmon that Meyer introduced from near Peking, Chihli, China, as Ta mo pan shih tzu (large grindstone persimmon). The fruit is flattened, 2 to 3 inches long and 4 to 5 inches in diameter, with an equatorial constriction near the base, and is of a rich golden-yellow color, seedless, of excellent quality. However, it is astringent until fully ripe and soft.

The second is that known as Teng lung shih tzu (lantern persimmon). The fruit of this type, on account of its smaller size, sells in the orchards and at the storage grounds for about one-half the price asked for the larger-fruited type. This fruit is also astringent until ripe and soft, and it too has an equatorial constriction.

The third type, like the first, is also known as Ta shih tzu (large persimmon). The fruits of this type, which were seen by the writers but rarely in the markets and only once in the orchards, and then only as a bud sport on branches of the ordinary large fruited form, were more flattened than the large commercial type but otherwise identical with it..

The fourth type was found in an orchard near the village of Lung Tze Ting, but not in any of the markets visited. This fruit is small, oblong, 1 to 1 ½ inches is diameter and 2 to 2 ½ inches in length, with an equatorial constriction near the base, seedless, and of a golden orange-yellow color. The fruit in general appearance resembles a large bur acorn and is very attractive. The specimens procured by the writers were still astringent and not yet ripe enough for judging flavor and quality.

The soil in the orchard from which the last two types of fruit were procured was a rather heavy, friable, reddish yellow clay.

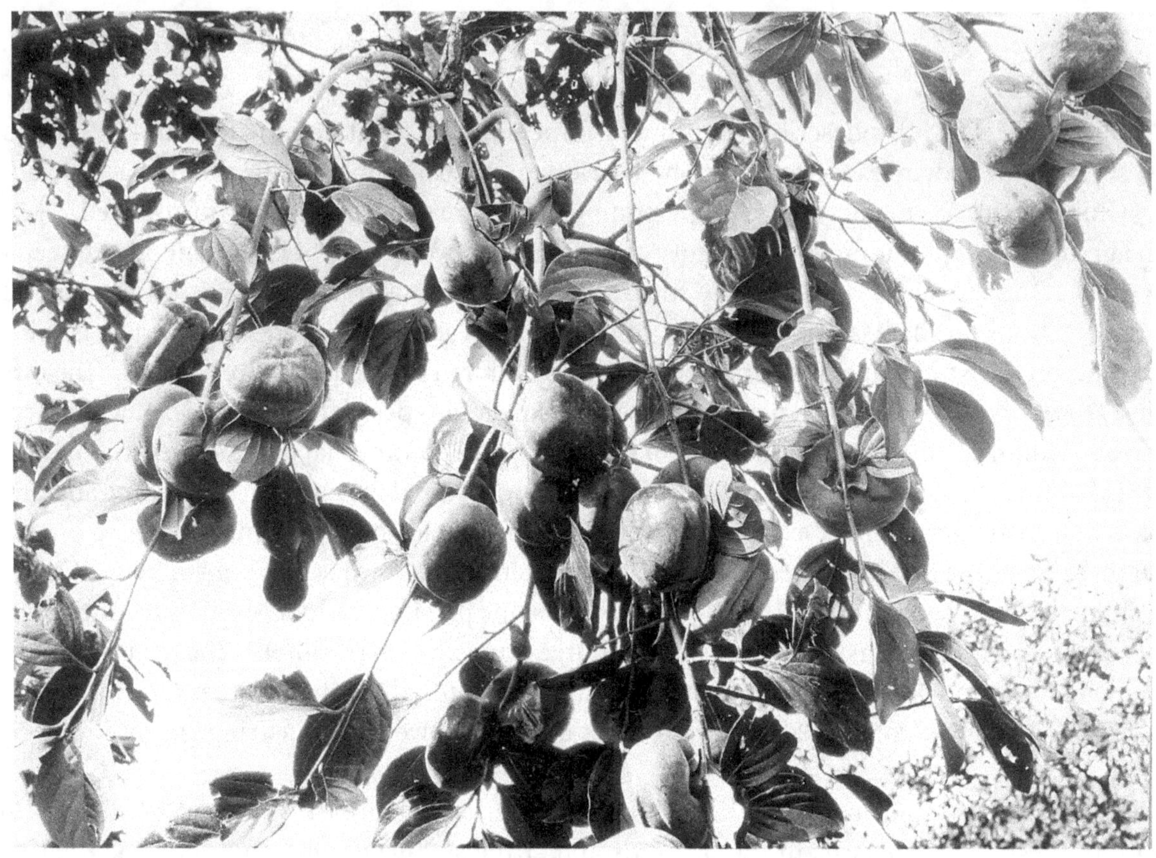

29536. *Oct 10, 1924. Lao Chun Tang village. Fruiting branches of Ta shih tzu, the large Chinese persimmon, in an orchard near the village in the Ming Tombs region north of Peking. This variety is now fruiting in the United States under the name of Tamopan.*

老君堂 village, Lao Chun T'ang
大柿子樹 Ta shih Tzu shu
Large persimmon tree

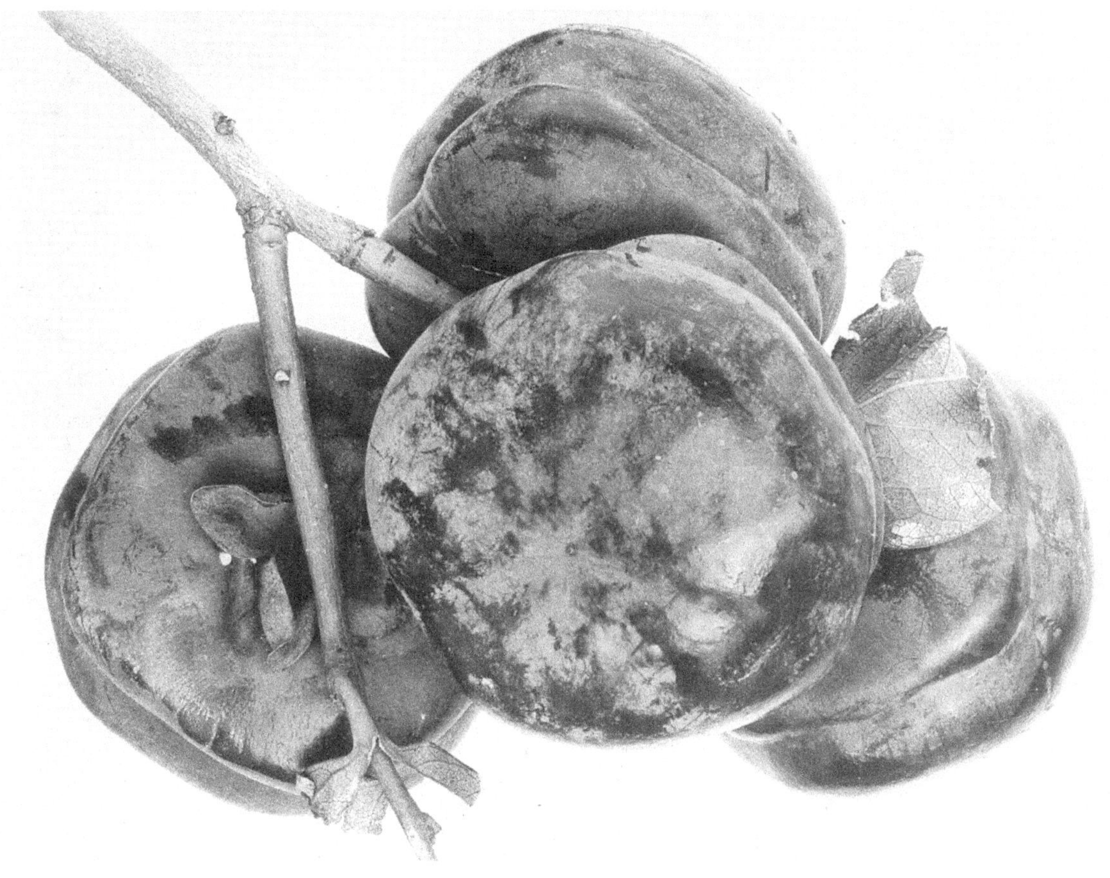

29630. Oct. 22, 1924. Nan An Ho village northwest of Peking. A three-quarter size picture of a cluster of the large Chinese persimmon from which we secured scions.

南安河 village, Nan An Ho
大柿子, Ta shih Tzu
Large persimmon

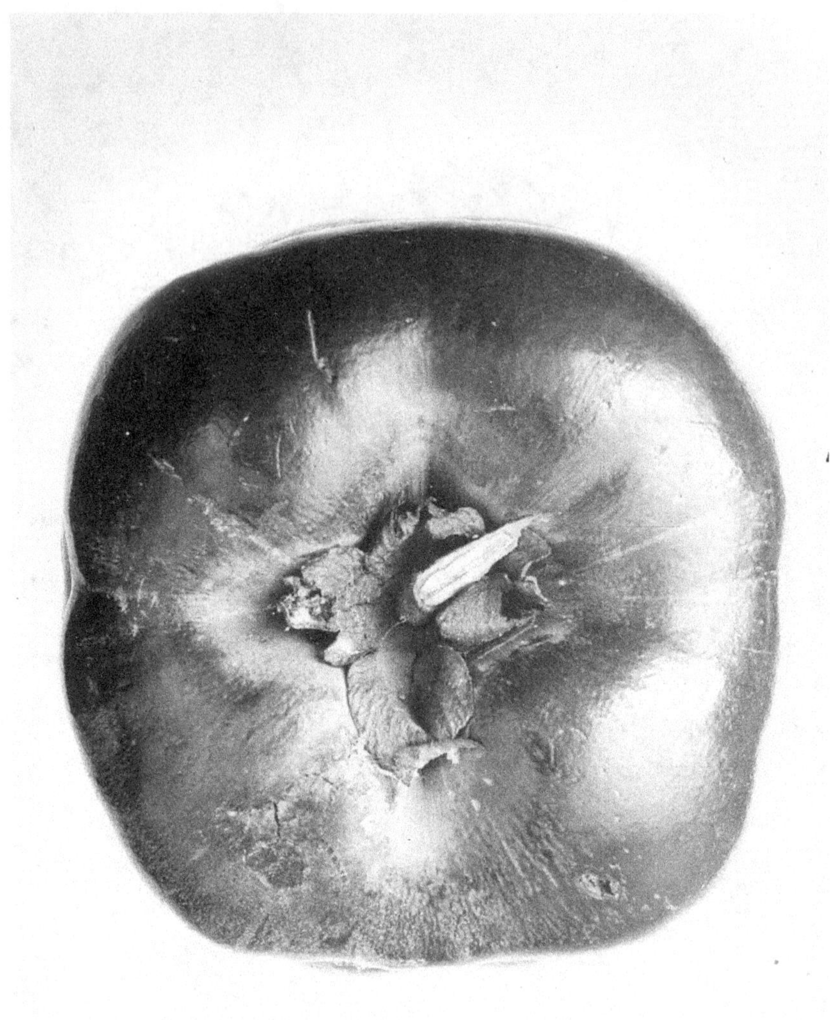

29436. *Sept. 29, 1924. A life-size picture of the stem end of the same persimmon shown in #29435.*

大柿子 TA Shih Tzu
Large persimmon

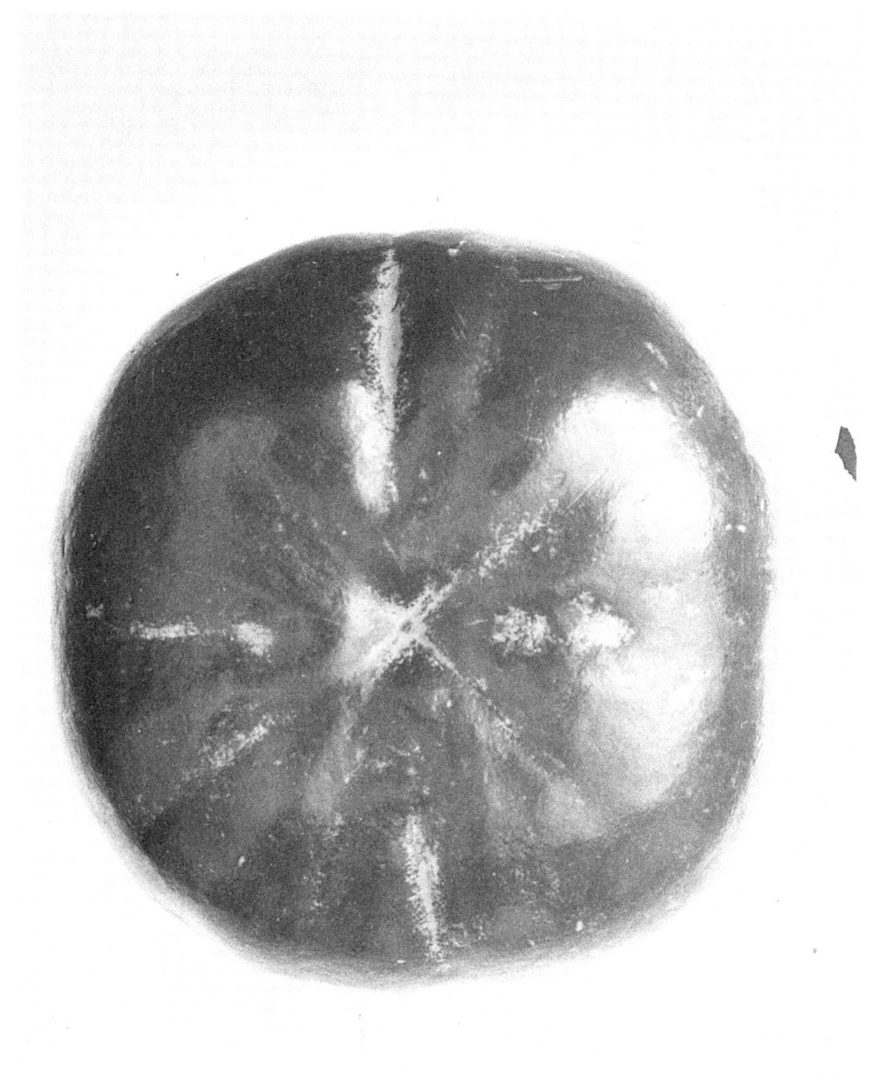

***29435.** Sept. 29, 1924. A life-size picture of the blossom end of a large 4" Chinese persimmon. See # 29438.*

大柿子 TA Shih Tzu
Large persimmon

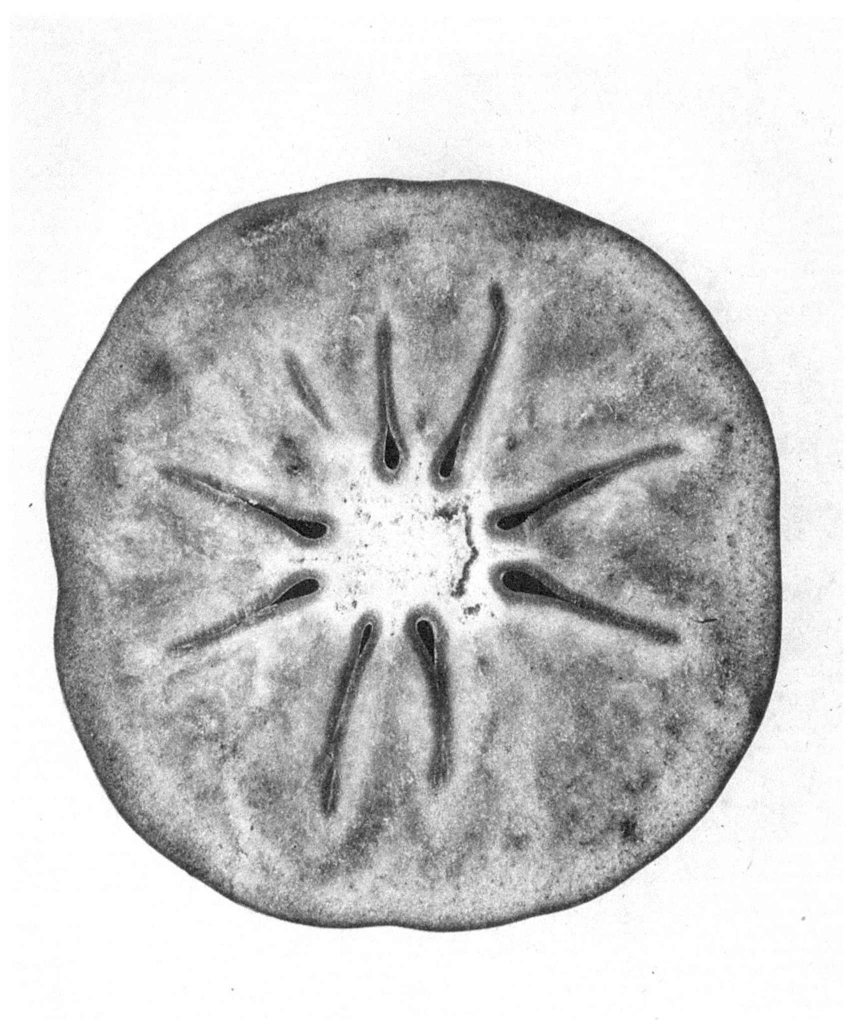

29438. *Sept. 29, 1924. A full-size picture of a cross section of the large 4" Chinese persimmon shown in # 29436.*

大柿子 TA Shih Tzu
Large persimmon

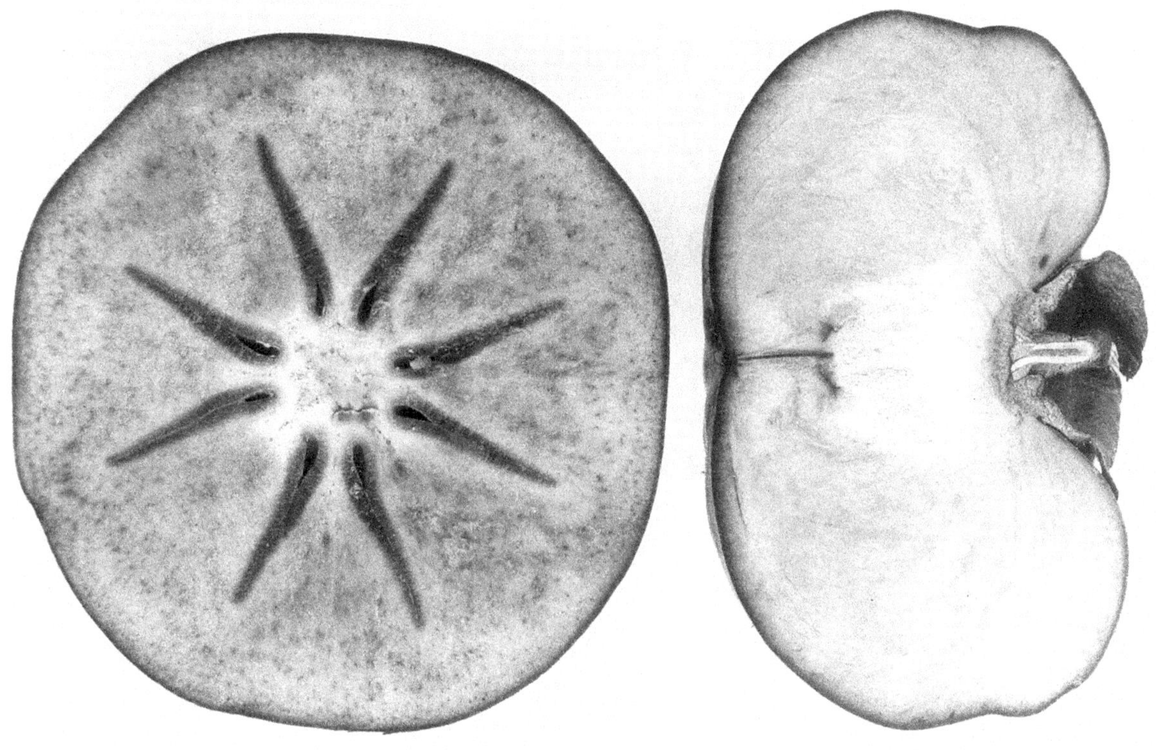

***29635.** Oct. 22, 1924. Nan An Ho village. A full-size picture of two of the large persimmon fruits after they were cut in half.*

大柿子 Ta shih Tzu
Large persimmon

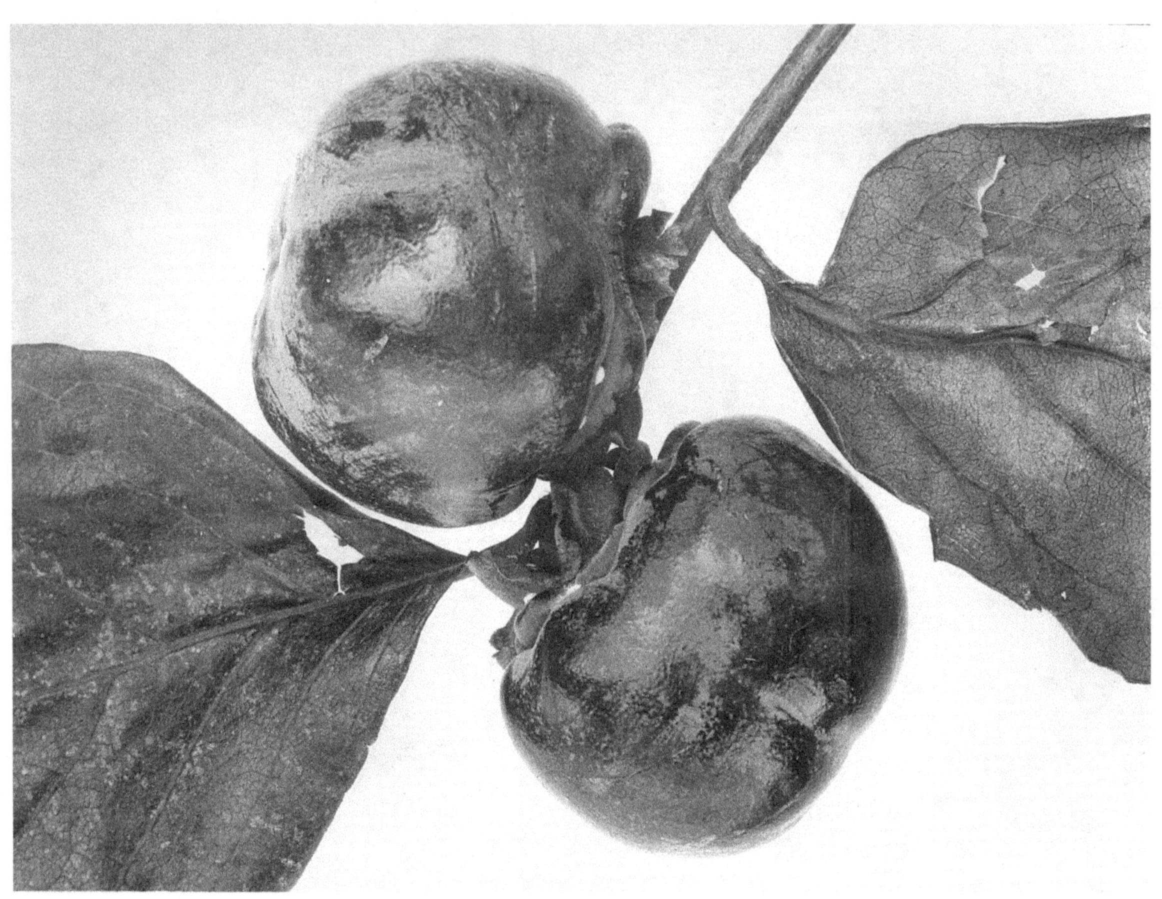

29632. *Oct. 22, 1924. Nan An Ho village. A life-size picture of a fruiting branch of the Chinese Lantern persimmon, a tree from which we cut scions.*

南安河 village, Nan An Ho
燈籠柿子 Teng lung shih tzu
Lantern Persimmon

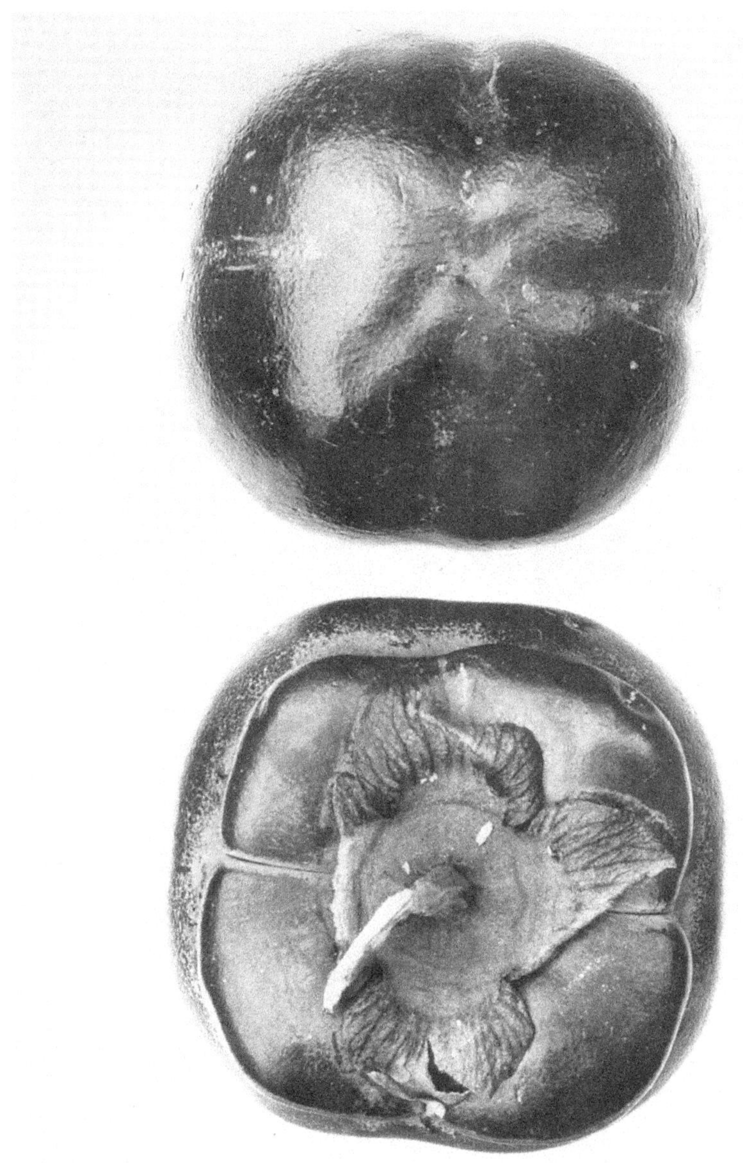

29459. *Oct. 6, 1924. Life-size picture of stem and blossom ends of Lantern persimmons. See #29460.*

燈籠柿子 Tenglung Shih Tzu
Lantern persimmon

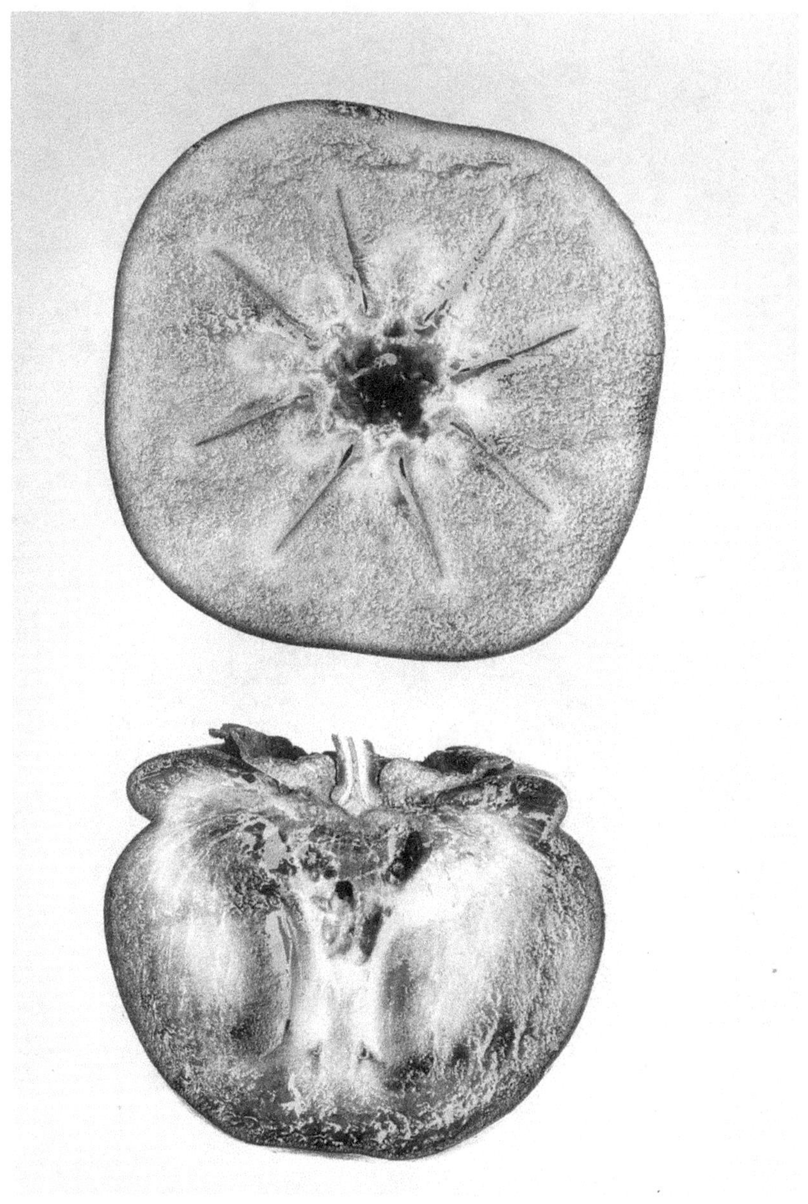

29460. *Oct. 6, 1924. Life-size picture of Lantern persimmon shown in picture # 29459.*

燈籠柿子 Tenglung Shih Tzu
Lantern persimmon

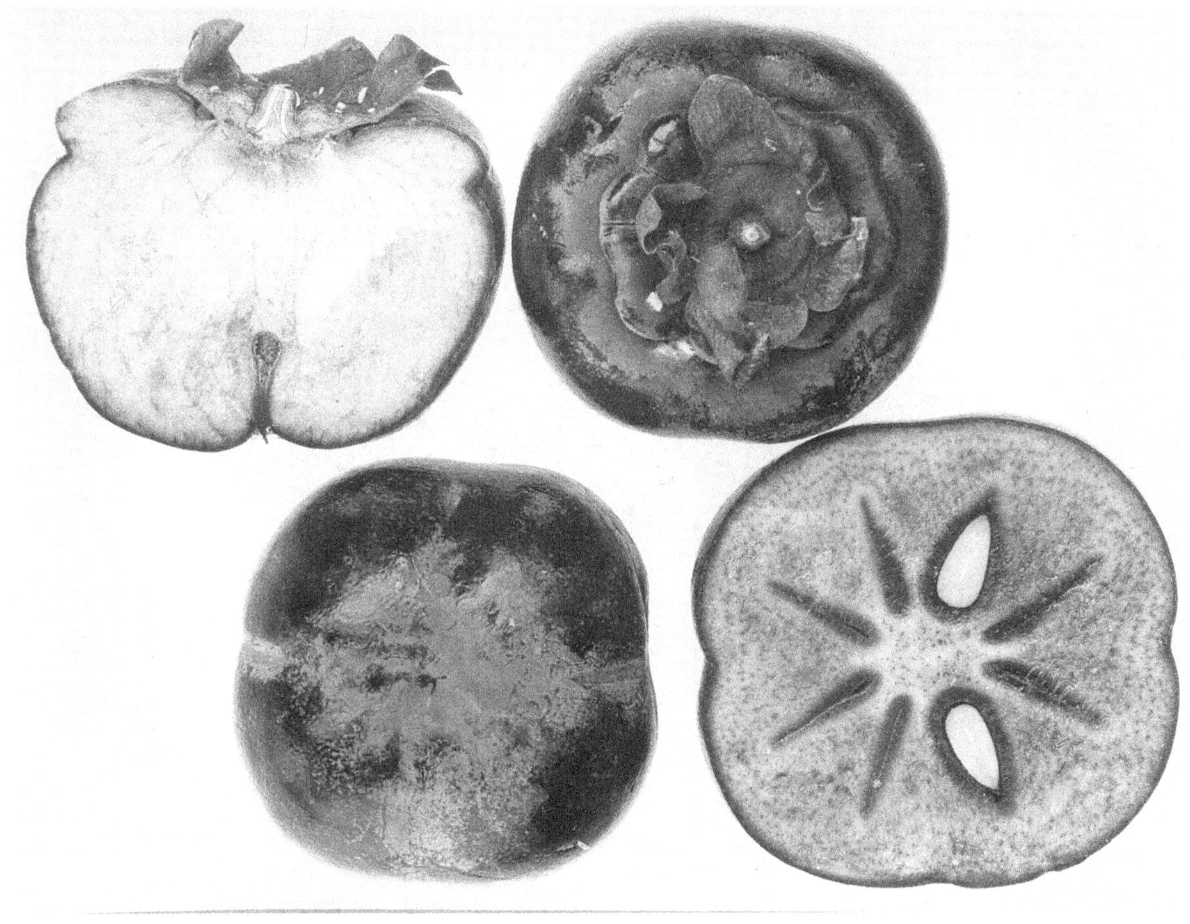

29634. *Oct. 22, 1924. Nan An Ho village. A full-size picture of Lantern persimmons, showing stem and blossom ends as well as section views.*

燈籠柿子 Teng Lung shih Tzu
Lantern persimmon

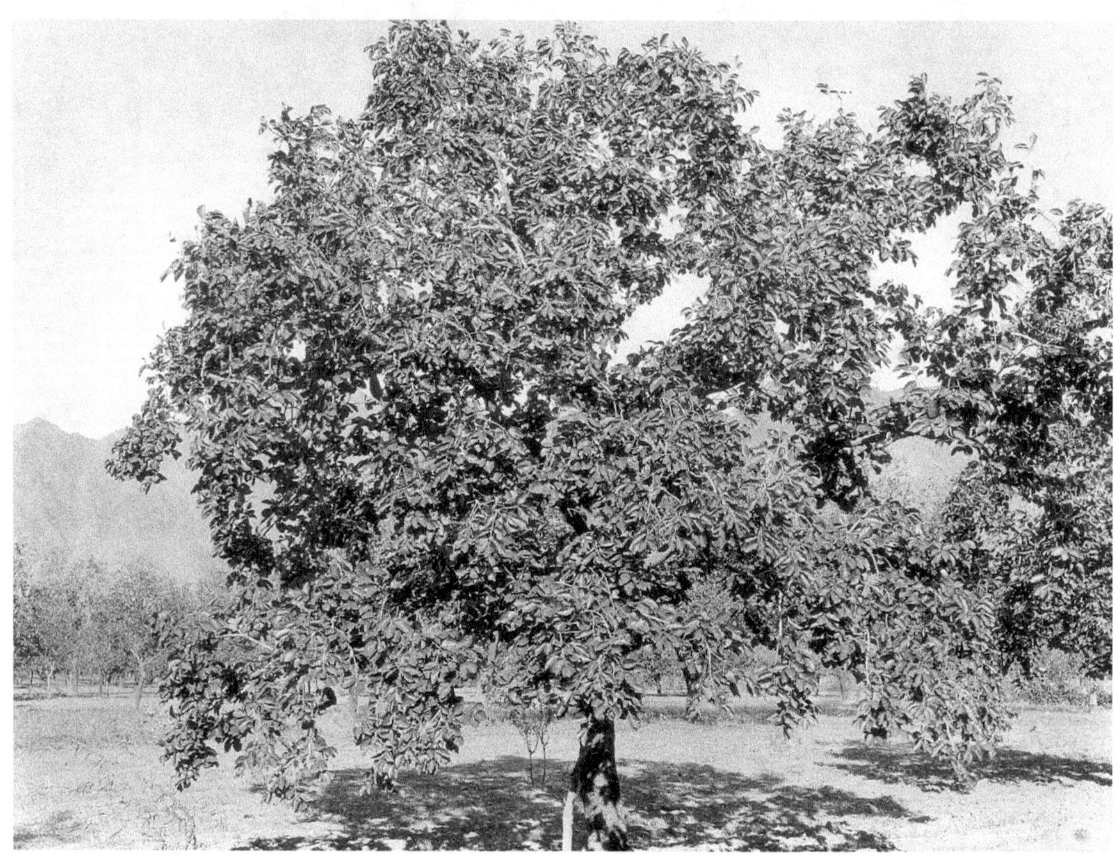

29479. *Oct. 8, 1924. Tai Ling Yuan village. A close-up picture of a good tree of the Lantern persimmon. (See picture #29480 for close-up picture of fruiting branch.)*

太陵園 village Tai Ling yuan
燈籠柿子樹 Teng Lung shih Tzu shu
Lantern persimmon tree

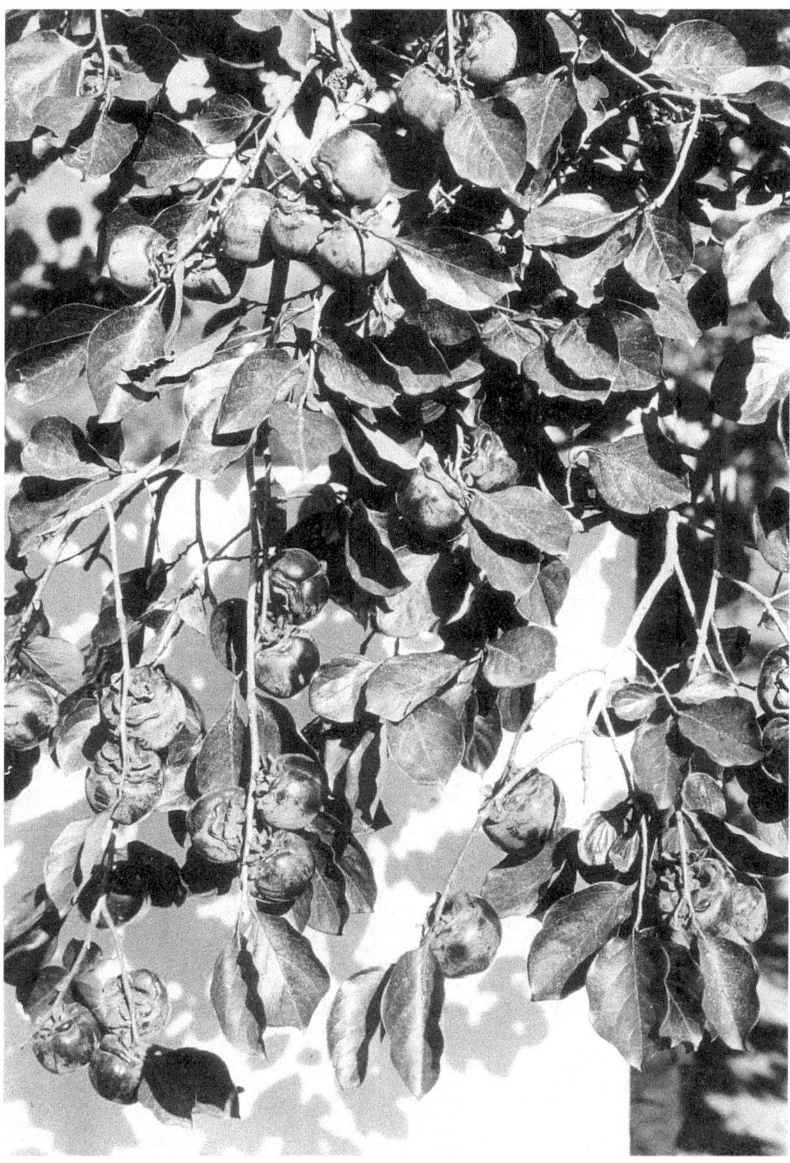

29480. *Oct. 8, 1924. Tai Ling Yuan village in the Ming Tombs section. A close-up picture of fruiting branches of Lantern persimmons.*

太陵園 village, T'ai Ling Yuan
燈籠柿子樹 TENG LUNG shih Tzu shu
Lantern persimmon

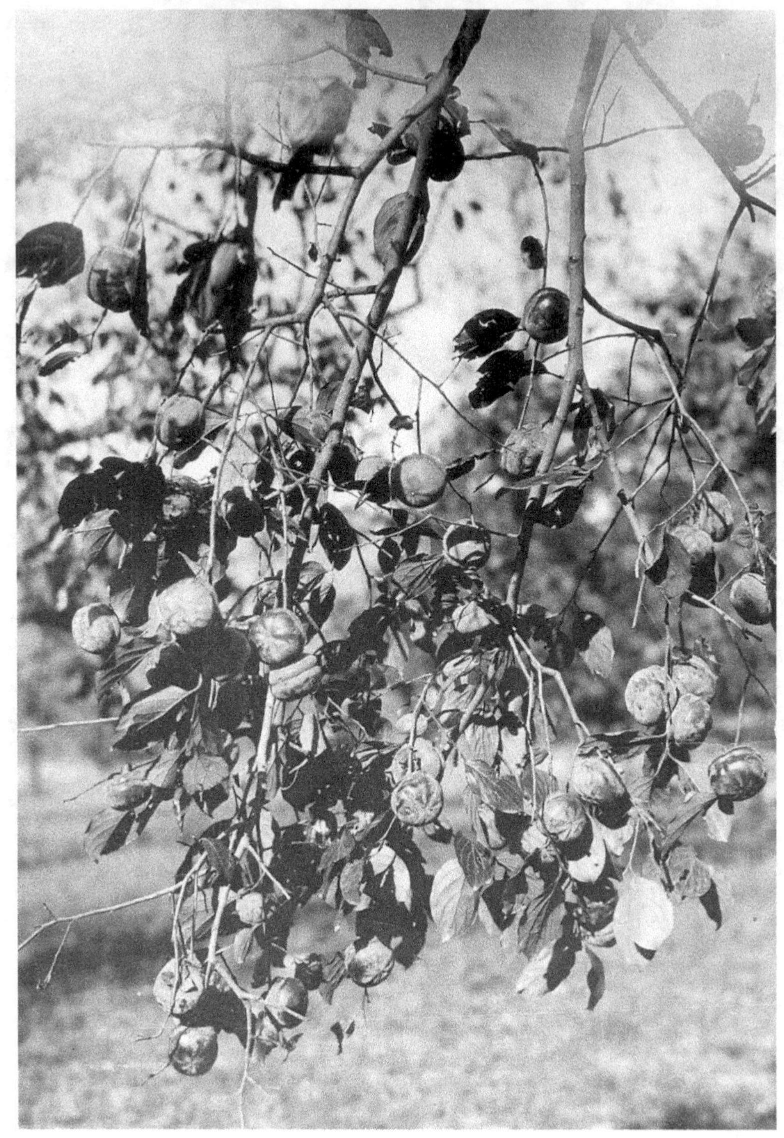

***29488.** Oct. 8, 1924. Ming Tombs region. A close-up picture of fruiting branches of Lantern persimmon shown in #29480.*

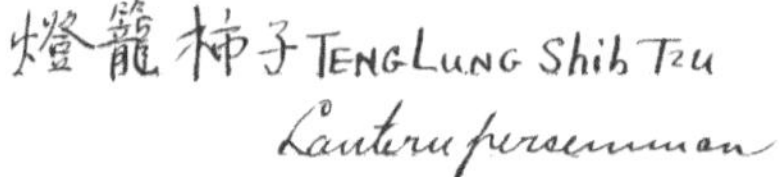

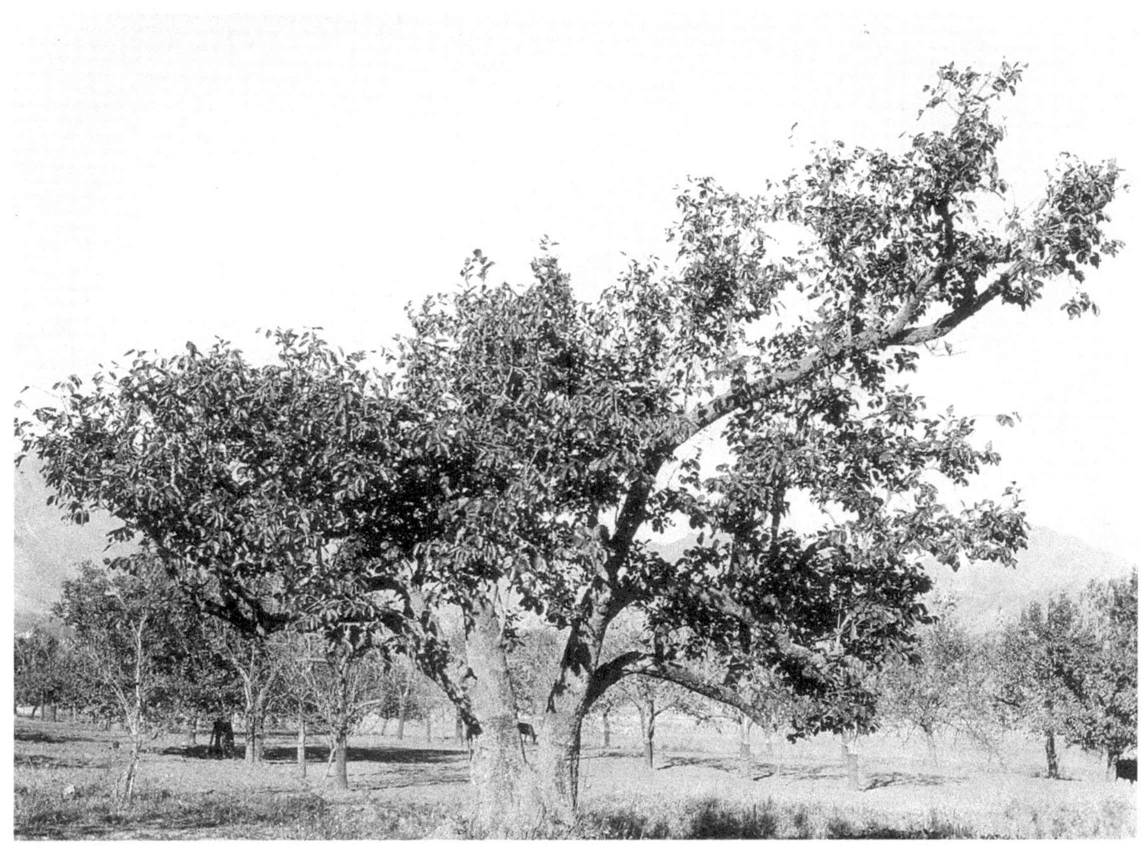

***29489.** Oct. 8, 1924. Ming Tombs region. A close-up picture of one of the large and supposedly 300- to 400-year-old Lantern persimmon trees.*

明陵 MING TOMB, Ming Ling
燈籠柿子樹 TENG LUNG shih Tzu shu
Lantern persimmon tree

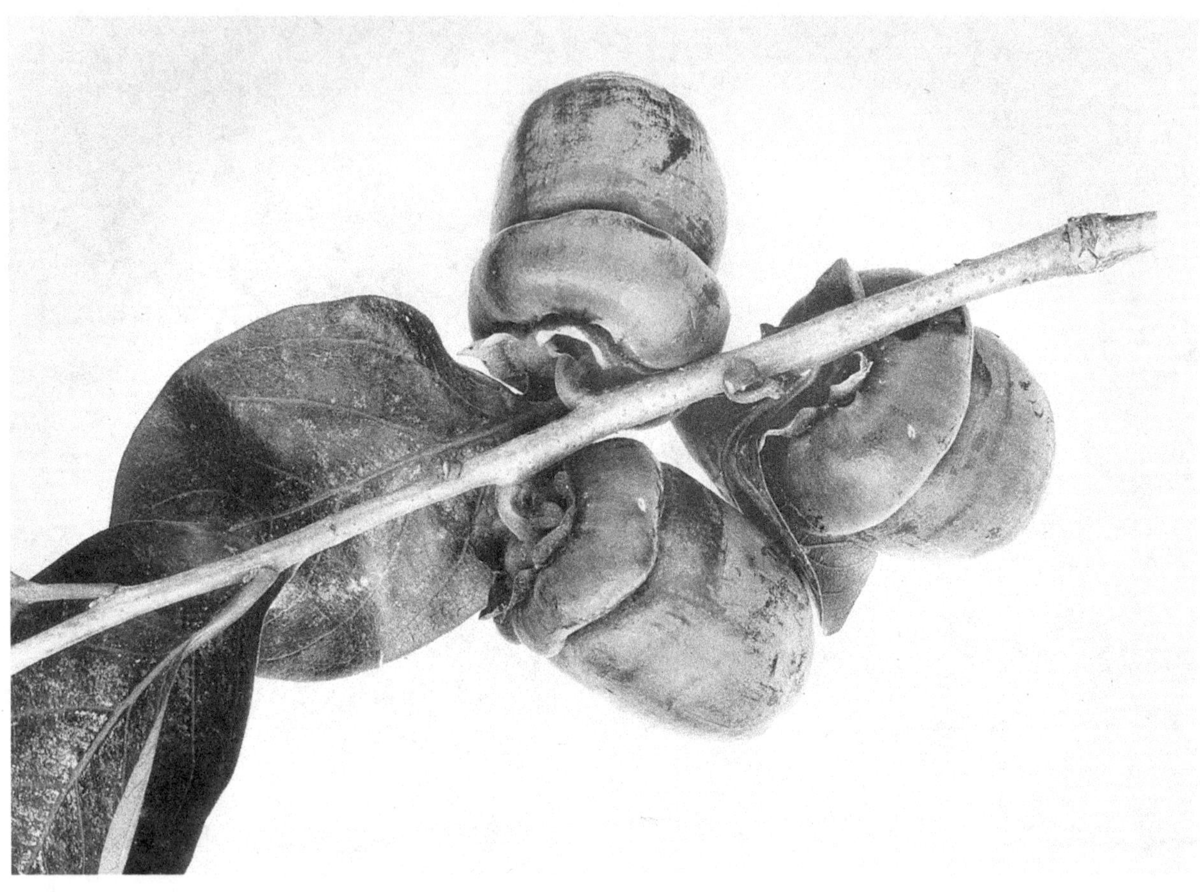

***29575.** Oct. 12, 1924. Lung Tzu Ting village. A full-size picture of a fruiting branch of a small slender quite long persimmon, reminding one of a large acorn.*

籠子頂 village, Lung Tzu Ting
小柿子, Hsiao shih Tzu
small persimmon

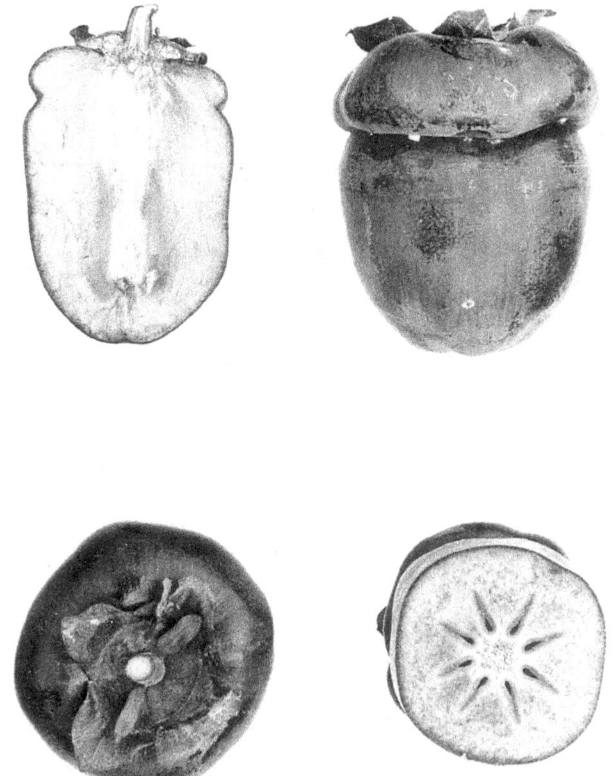

29576. *Oct. 12, 1924. Lung Tzu Ting village. A life-size picture of what we call "Acorn persimmon" showing side and end view, also section views.*

燈籠柿子 TENG LUNG SHIH TZU
Lantern persimmon

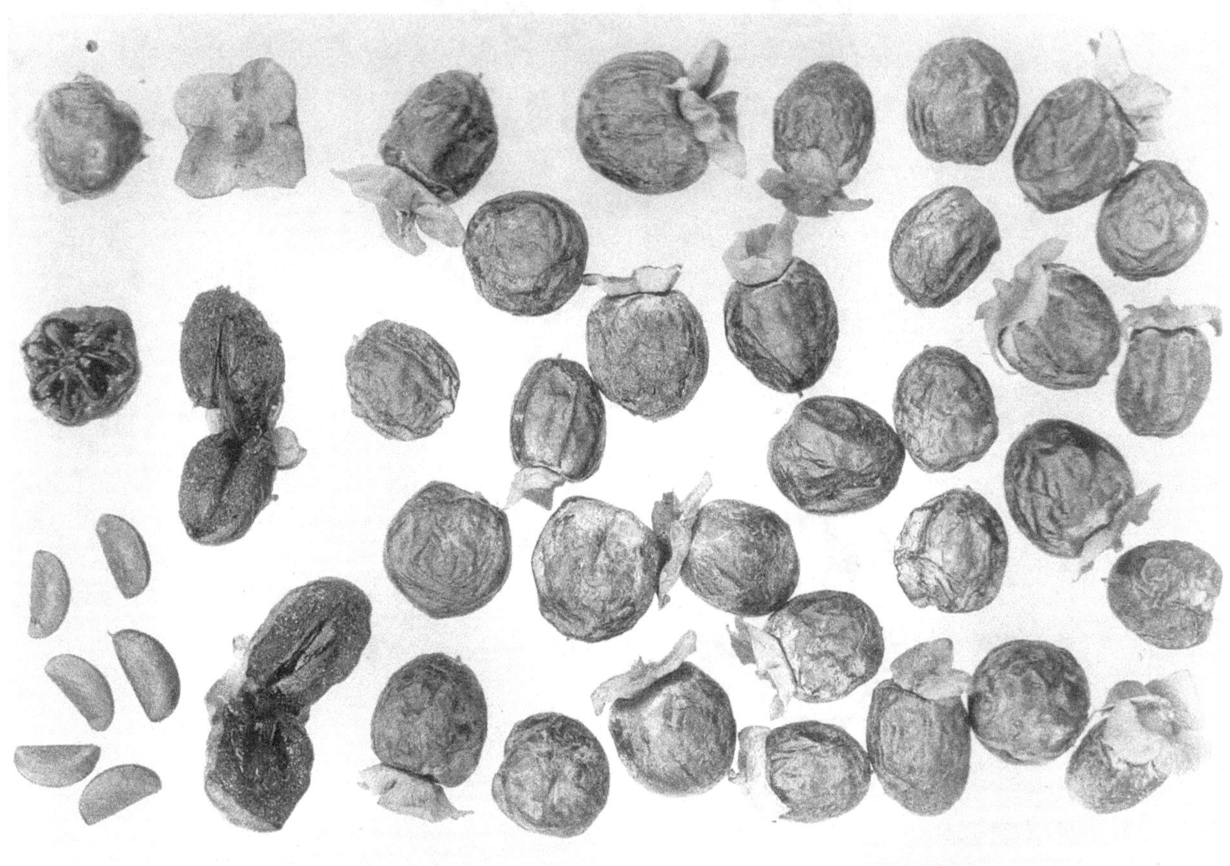

***29975.** Nov. 20, 1924. Peking. A life-size picture of ripe fruit of what the Chinese call "black dates". This species (D. lotus) is used as the Chinese (under)stock for their cultivated persimmons.*

黑棗 *Hei Tsao*
Black date

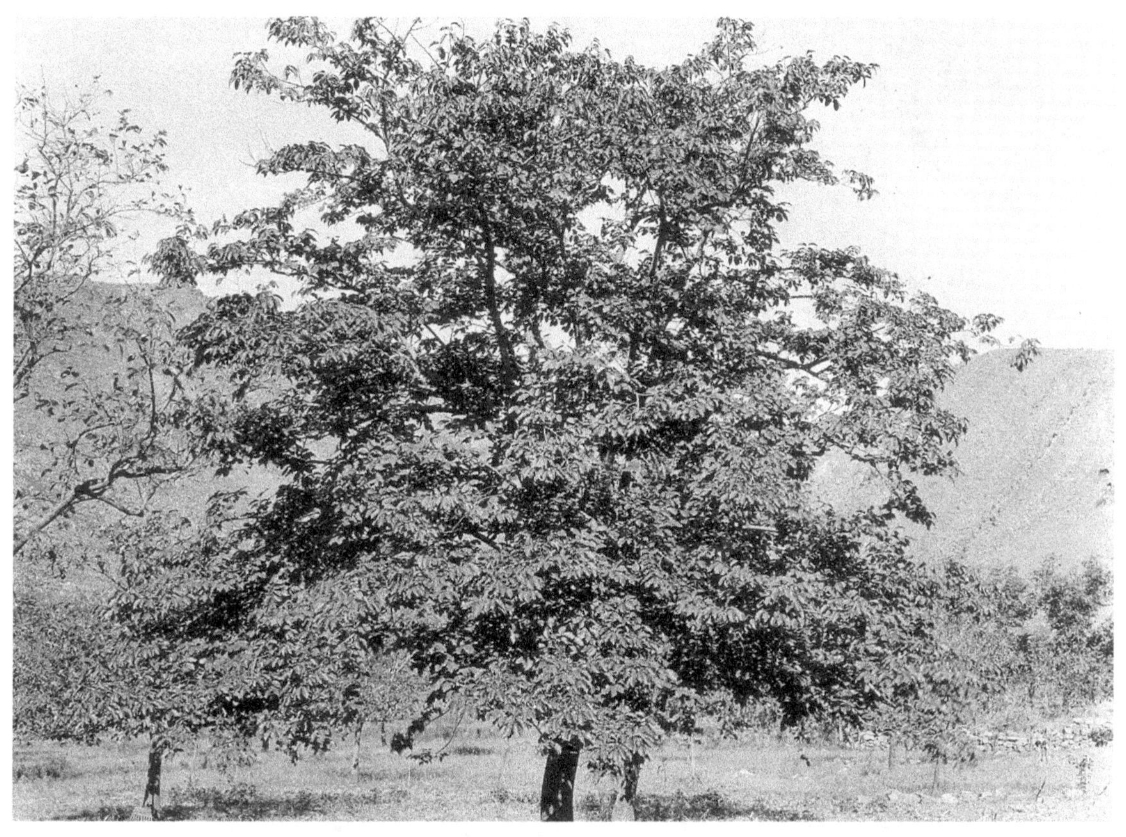

29484. *Oct. 8, 1924. Tai Ling Yuan. A close-up picture of a good young tree of Chinese black date (**Diospyros lotus**) near the village. We purchased the crop of seed from this tree.*

黑棗樹 HEI TSAO Shu
Black date tree

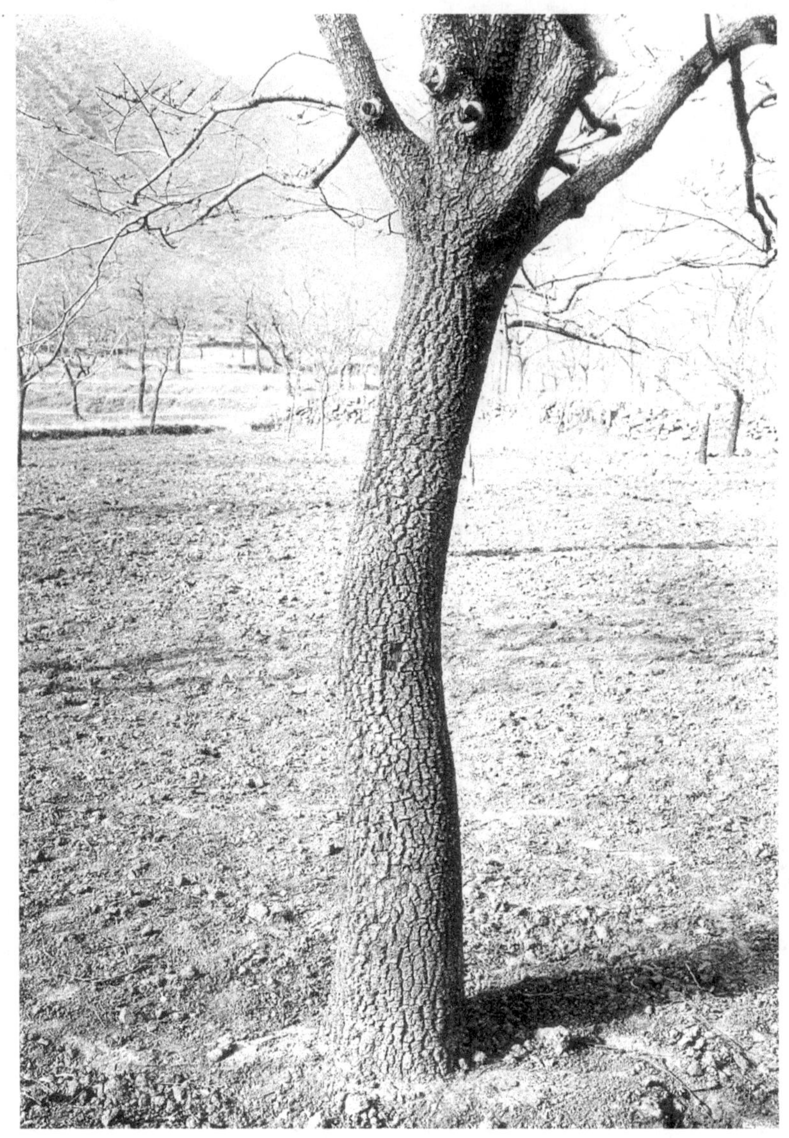

38036. *Nov. 28, 1924. Tai Ling Yuan. A close-up picture of the trunk and a portion of the large branches of the black date tree shown in #29484.*

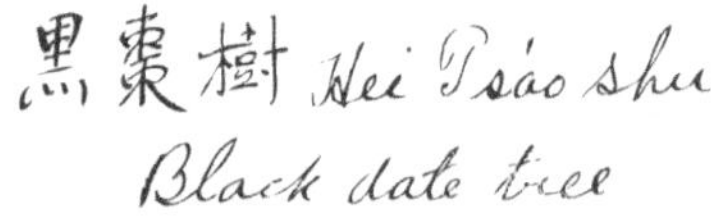

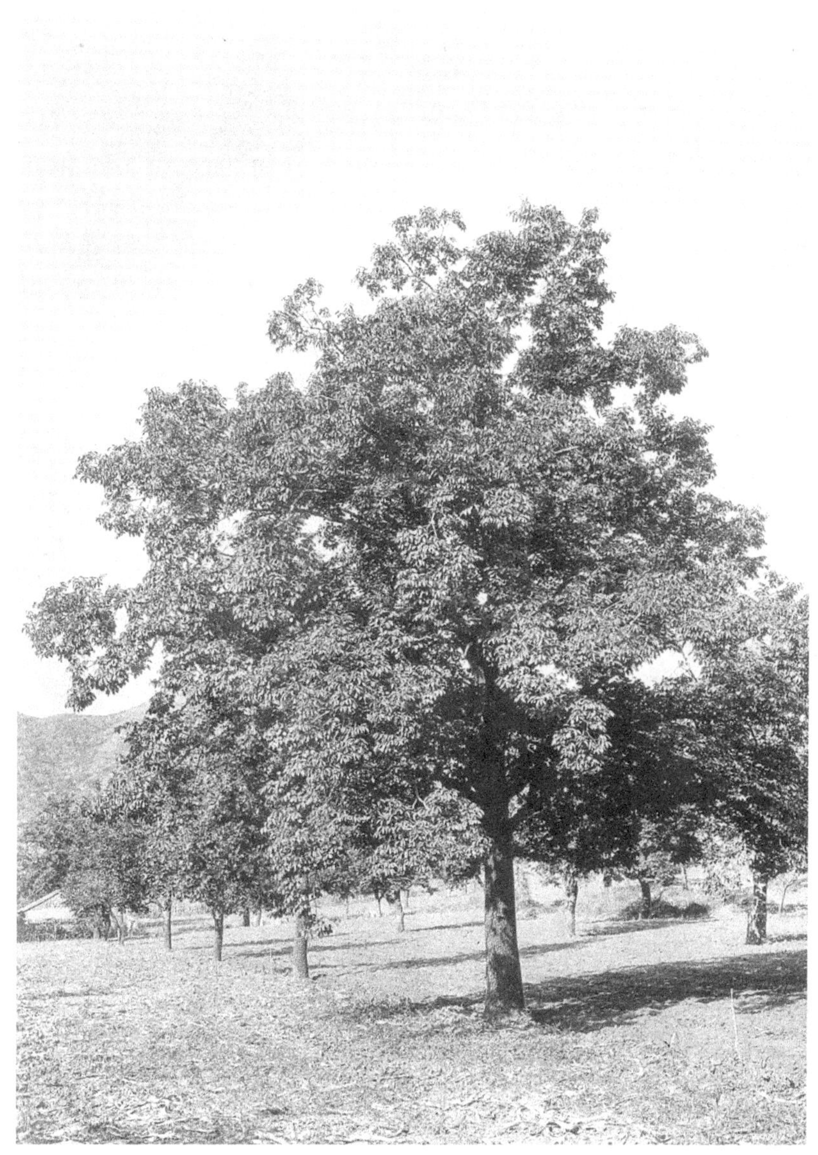

***29537.** Oct. 10, 1924. Lao Chun Tang village. A close-up picture of a good tree of the Chinese black date.*

黑棗樹 Hei Tsao shu, Black date tree
老君堂 village, Lao Chun Tang

DISEASES AND INSECT PESTS

The persimmon orchards in the vicinity of Peking were apparently free from diseases, and in only a few instances were infestations of mealybugs observed on the fruits and branches. In these instances this pest was rather abundant and doing some damage. So far as could be learned, no precautions or treatment of any kind were being used to destroy or control this pest.

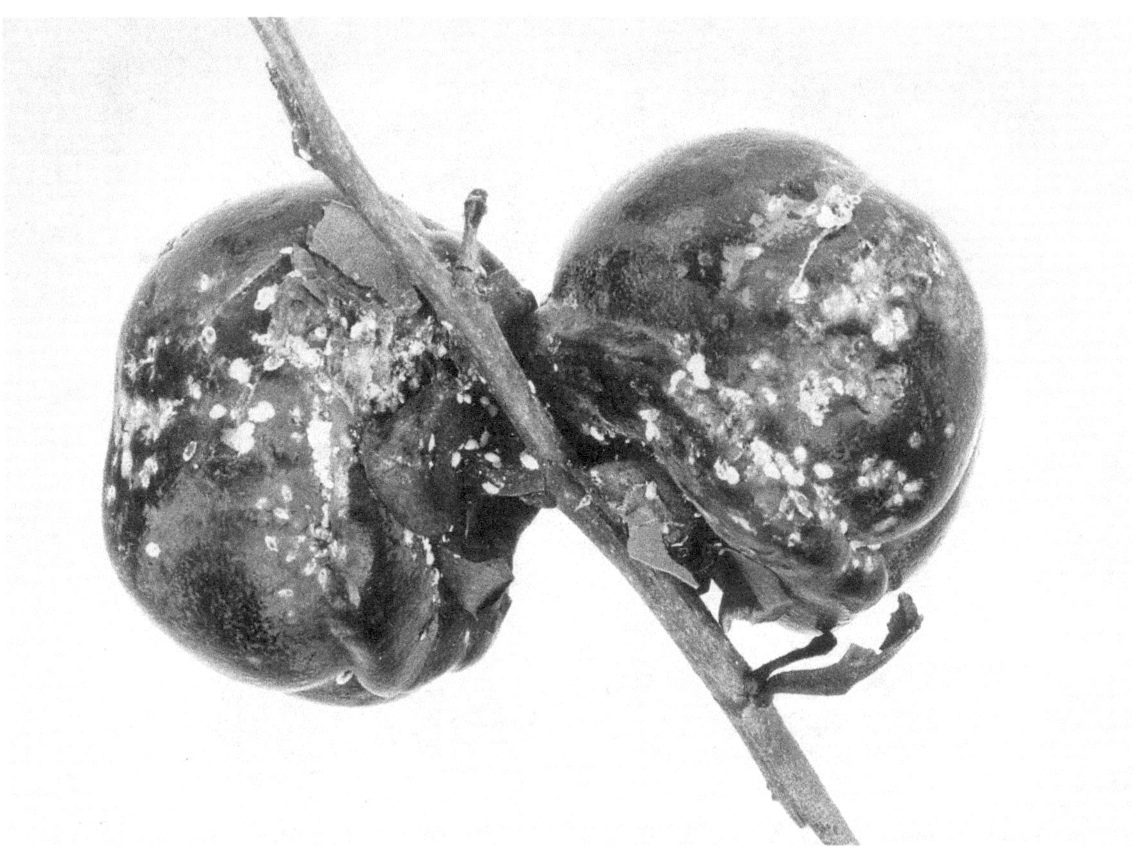

29633. *Oct. 22, 1924. Nan An Ho village. A full-size picture of 2 Lantern persimmon fruits badly infested with mealy bug.*

燈籠柿子 Teng Lung shih Tzu
Lantern persimmon

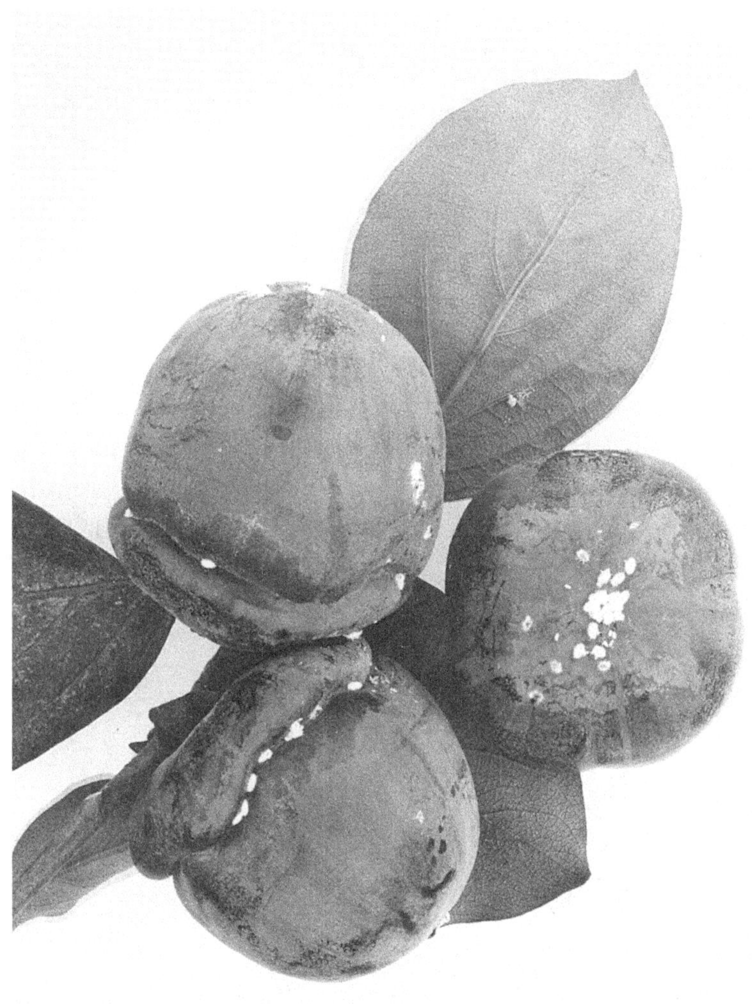

***29577.** Oct. 13, 1924. A life-size picture of a fruiting branch of Lantern persimmon. These fruits are below average size and pretty badly infested with mealy bugs.*

Lantern persimmon
燈籠柿子 Teng lung shih tzu

GIRDLING

The fruit growers of northeastern China often practice girdling to induce shy-bearing plants to produce larger crops and sometimes to increase the size of the fruits. A number of girdled trees of the tsao or Chinese jujube *(Zizyphus jujuba)*, a promising new fruit now being established in the southeastern United States, were seen. Trees of the Teng lung shih tzu (lantern persimmon), while much more vigorous than the large-fruited form (Ta shih tzu, Tamopan or large persimmon), are apparently not always good bearers, since numerous trees were seen with girdle marks around the trunks and frequently around the larger branches. However, no trees of the Tamopan type with such marks were noticed.

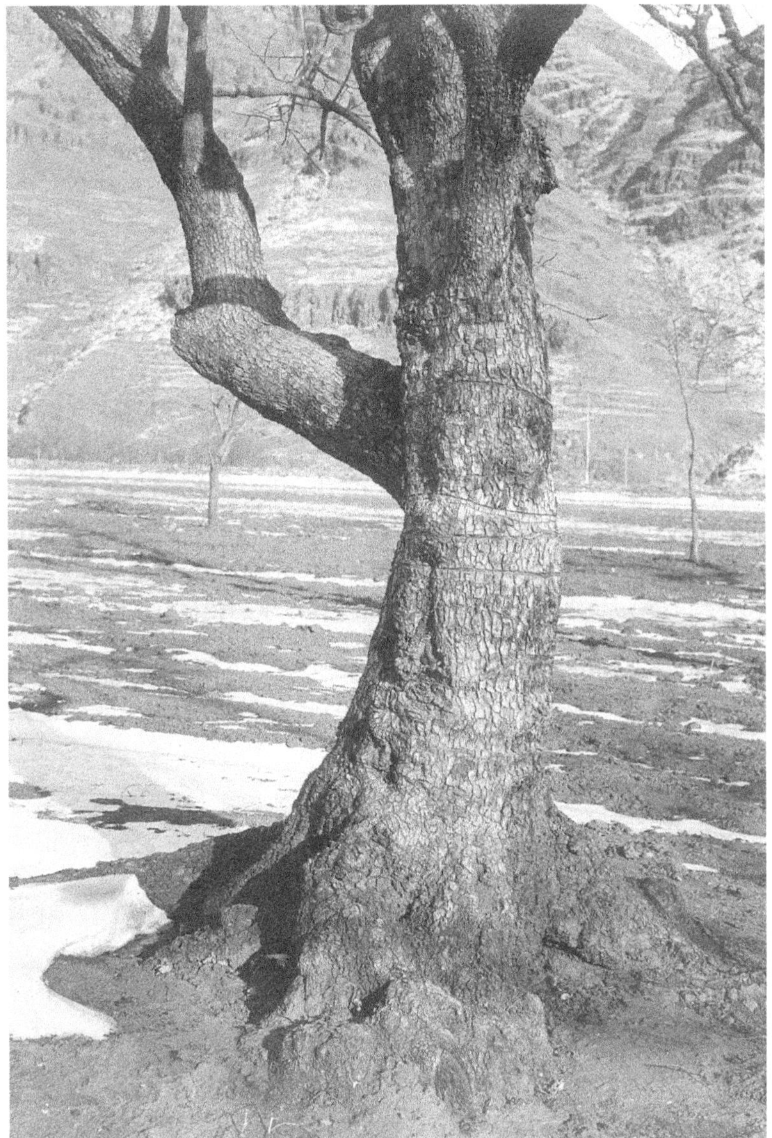

38191. *Jan. 1, 1925. Between Hsai Chuang and Shaho. A close-up picture of the Lantern persimmon tree, showing girdling marks and the over-growing of the stock.*

下庄 village, Hsia Chuang
燈籠柿子樹 Teng Lung shih Tze shu
Lantern persimmon tree

GRAFTING

The trees of the commercial varieties in the orchards visited were all ring budded or grafted, usually the former, on seedling trees of what is commonly known among the Chinese as hei tsao (black date), *Diospyros lotus*, which is found to be growing wild in the mountains. Frequently one or two trees are grown in the orchards to supply seed for stock purposes. As a rule the young seedlings are planted in place in orchard form and budded or grafted the second year after setting. The trees are worked at irregular heights from the ground, which may be due primarily to the fact that the practice of budding, as explained to the writers, necessitates selecting the stock of the same size as the scion, so that the ring containing the bud can be slipped from the scion to the stock without splitting the ring, as is usually done in ring-bud propagation in the United States.

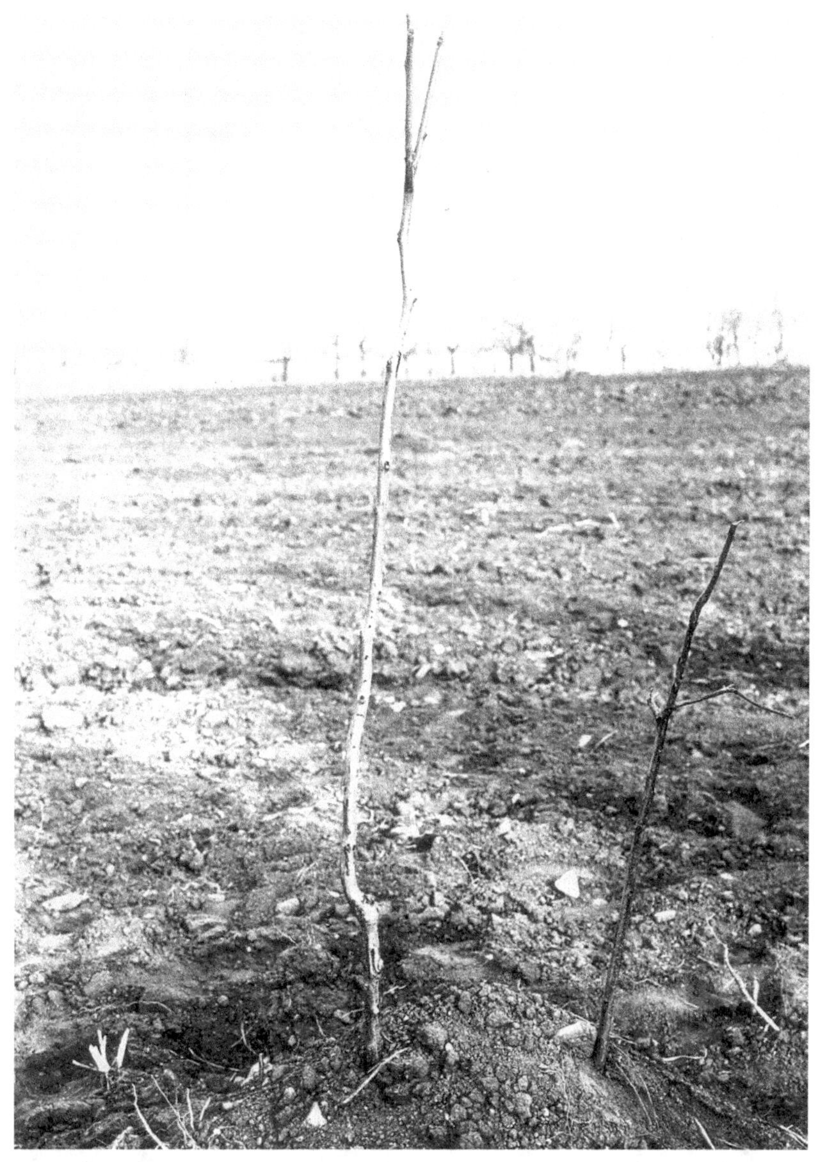

38048. *Nov. 28, 1924. Tai Ling Yuan. A close-up picture of a black date tree worked by a peculiar ring-bud method of grafting.*

黑棗樹, Black Date
套筒結 TÁO TÚNG Chieh
Ring bud grafting method

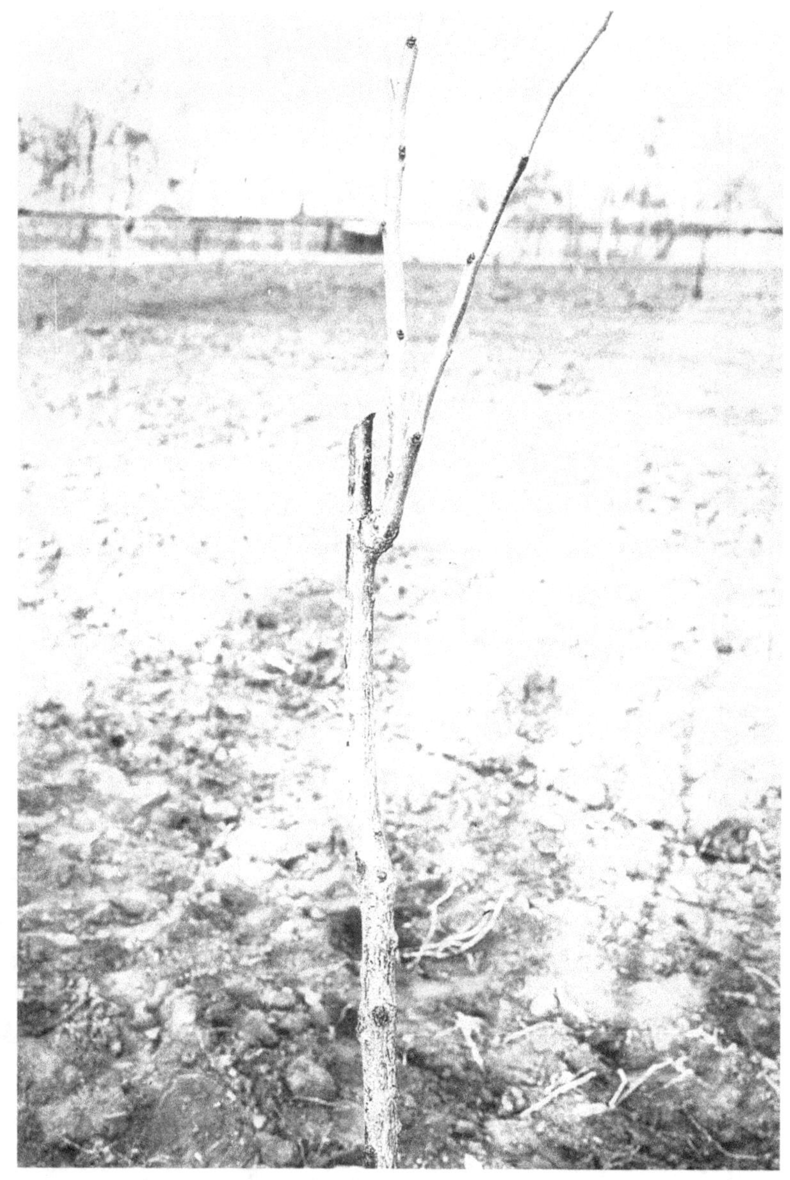

38047. *Nov. 28, 1924. Tai Ling Yuan. A nearby picture of a young black date tree that is shield-budded.*

太陵園 village, Tai Ling yuan
黑棗樹 Black Date
粘皮結 Chan Pi Chieh
sticking bark grafting
Shield budded

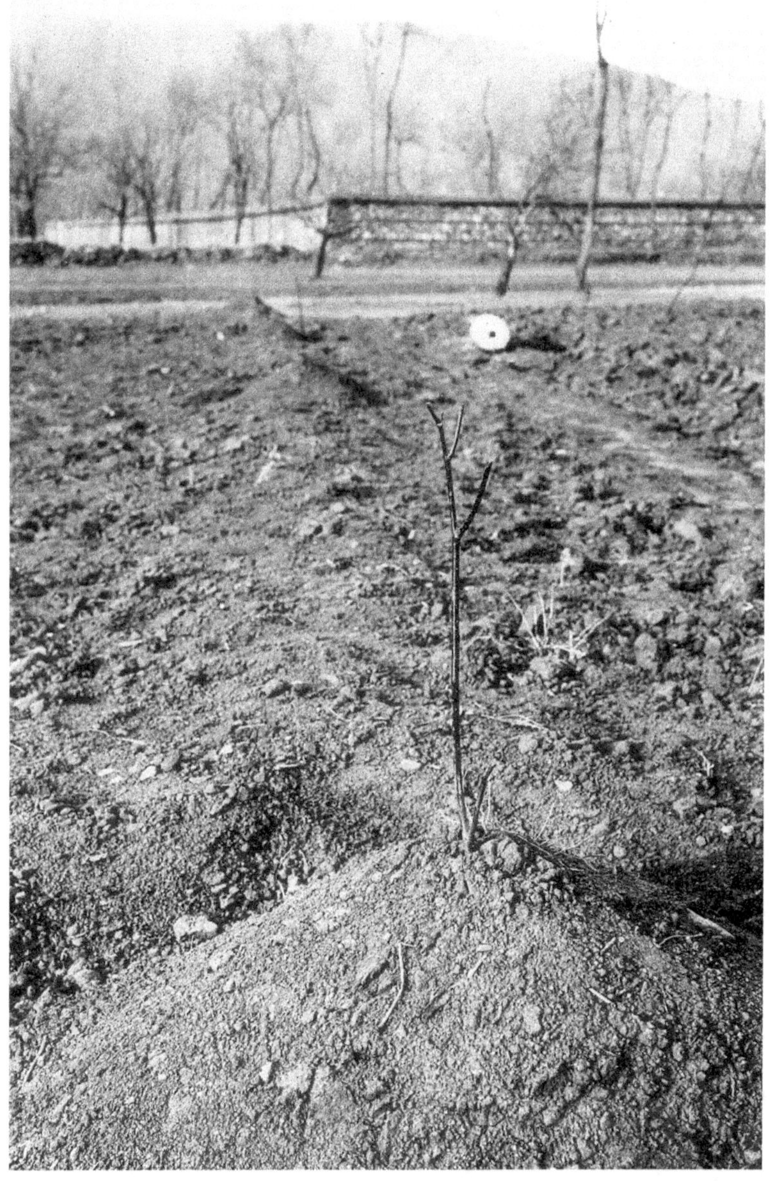

***38046.** Nov. 28, 1924. Tai Ling Yuan. A nearby picture of a small plant of black date in an orchard, intended to be understock for grafting.*

太陵園 village, Tai Ling Yuan
黑棗樹, Hei. Tsao Shu, black date

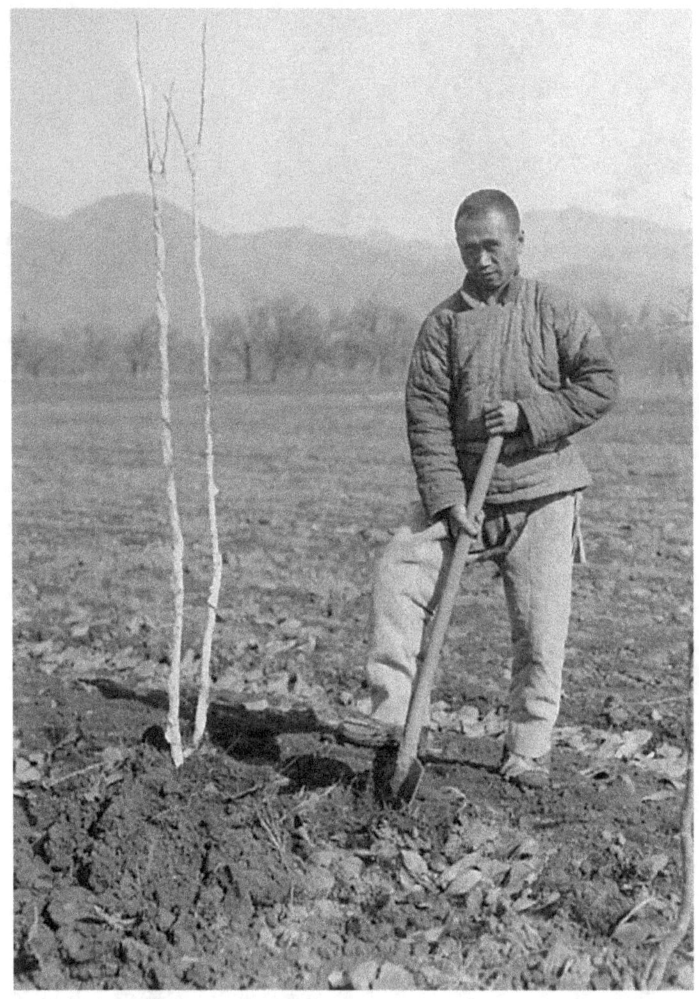

46168. *Near the village of Hsiang Tang, a few miles to the northwest of Tang Shan. This shows a Chinese farmer mounding, for winter protection, two young persimmon tree sprouts of one year's growth from the bud. The trees have also been wrapped with paper as a winter protection.*

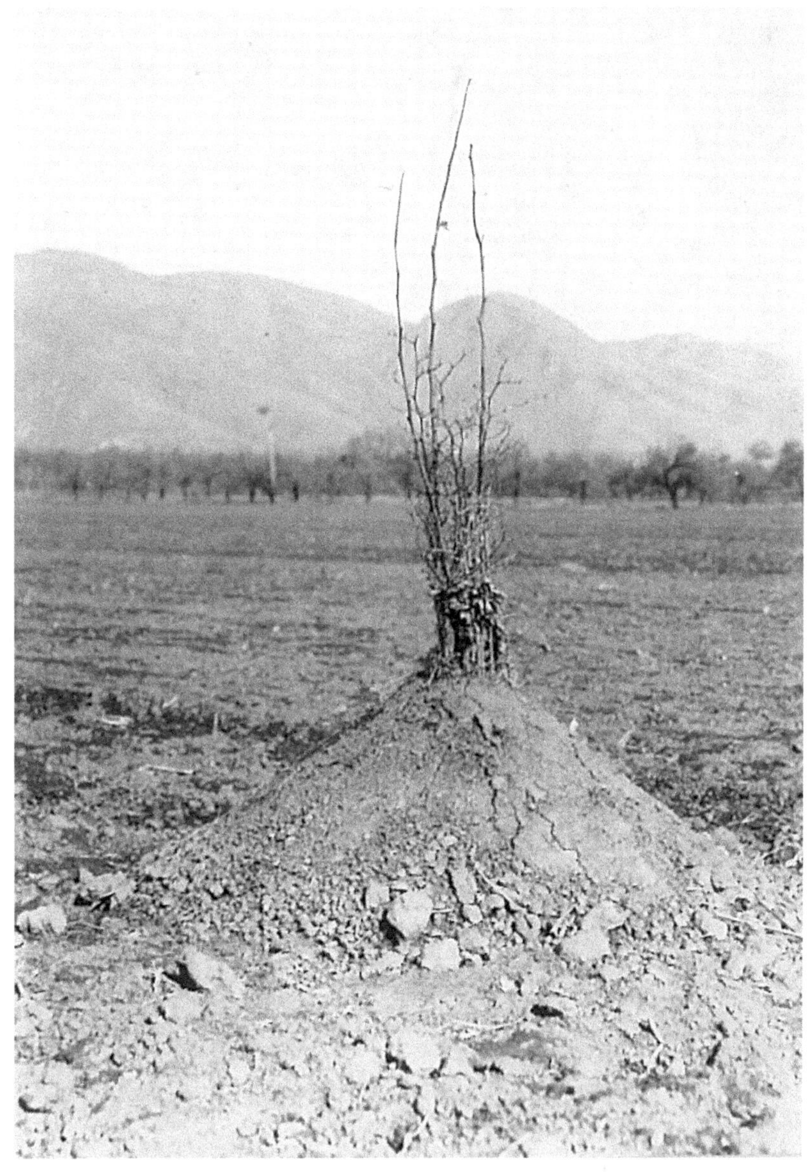

46169. *Near the village of Hsiang Tang, a few miles northwest of Tang Shan. Three young persimmon trees (perhaps from buds or grafts on the same stock) protected by thorny Jujube branches and mounded for winter protection against cold.*

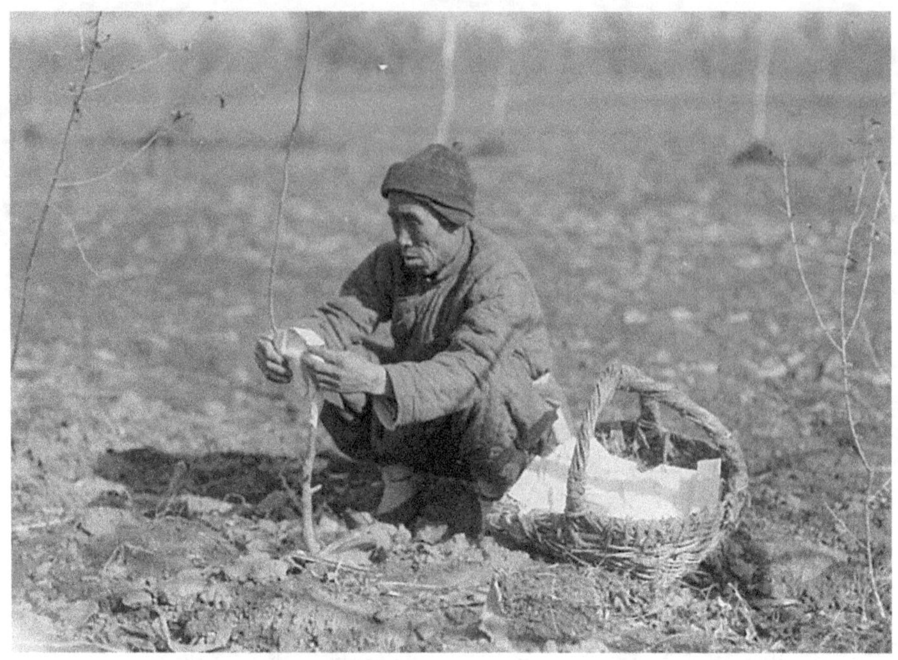

46166. *Near the village of Hsiang Tang. A farmer wrapping, with old newspaper, one-year buds. We understand they are only protected in this way the first year.*

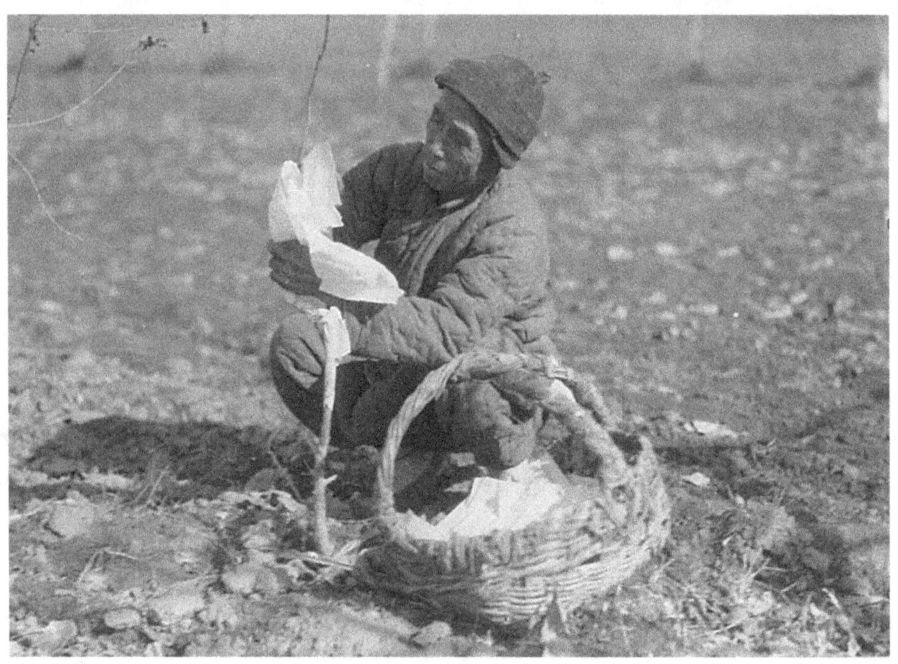

46167. *Near the village of Hsiang Tang. A slightly different view showing the wrapping of persimmon buds.*

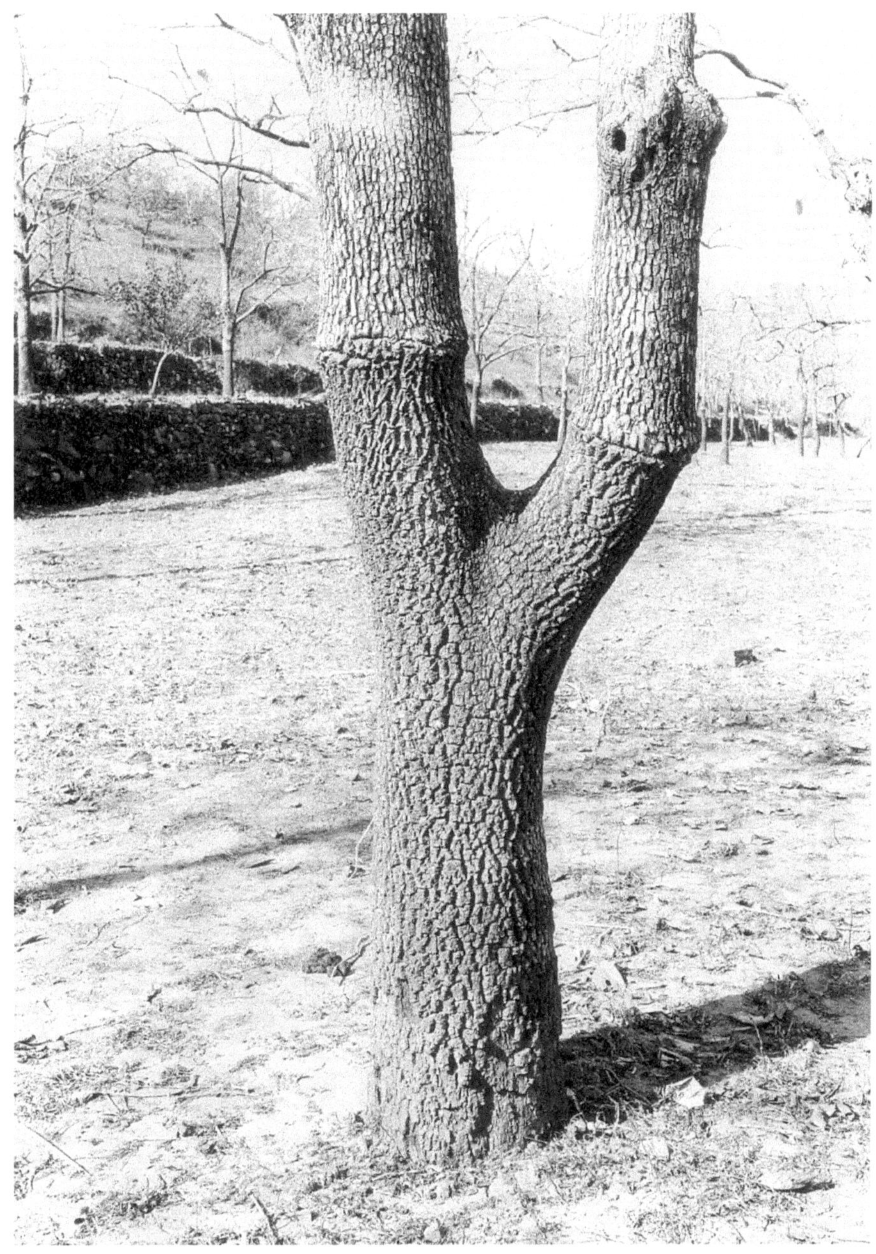

29850. *Nov. 6, 1924. Chia Yü K'ou. A close-up picture of the trunk and 2 grafted main branches on a persimmon orchard tree.*

賈峪口 village, Chia Yü K'ou
柿子樹 shih Tzu shu, Persimmon tree

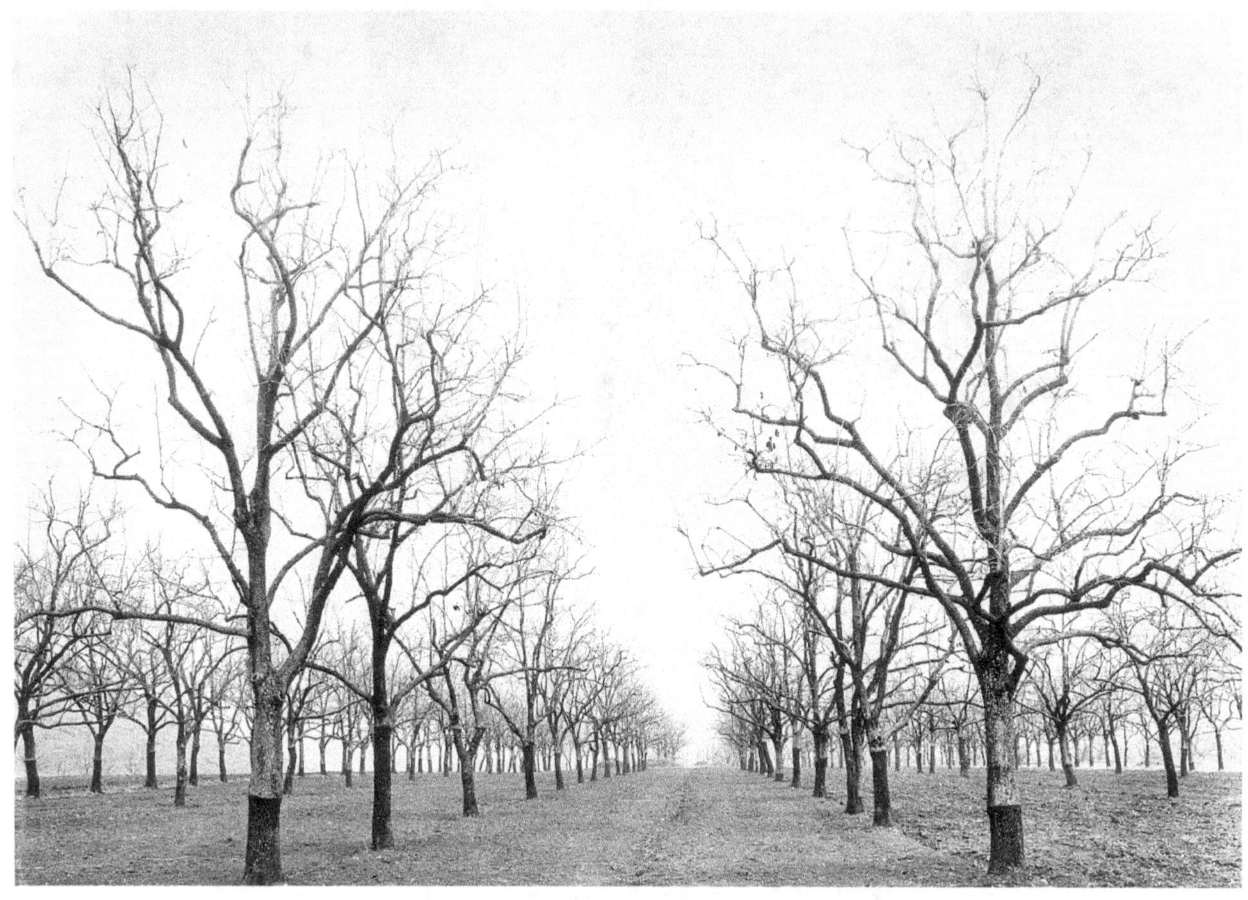

38050. *A commercial persimmon orchard northwest of Peking, in winter condition. Note the freedom of the ground from litter or any weeds, which is characteristic of the orchards at this season of the year, and also notice the union of the stock and scion at various distances from the surface of the ground.*

太陵園 village, T'ai Ling Yuan
柿子園 Shih Tzu Yuan
Persimmon Orchard

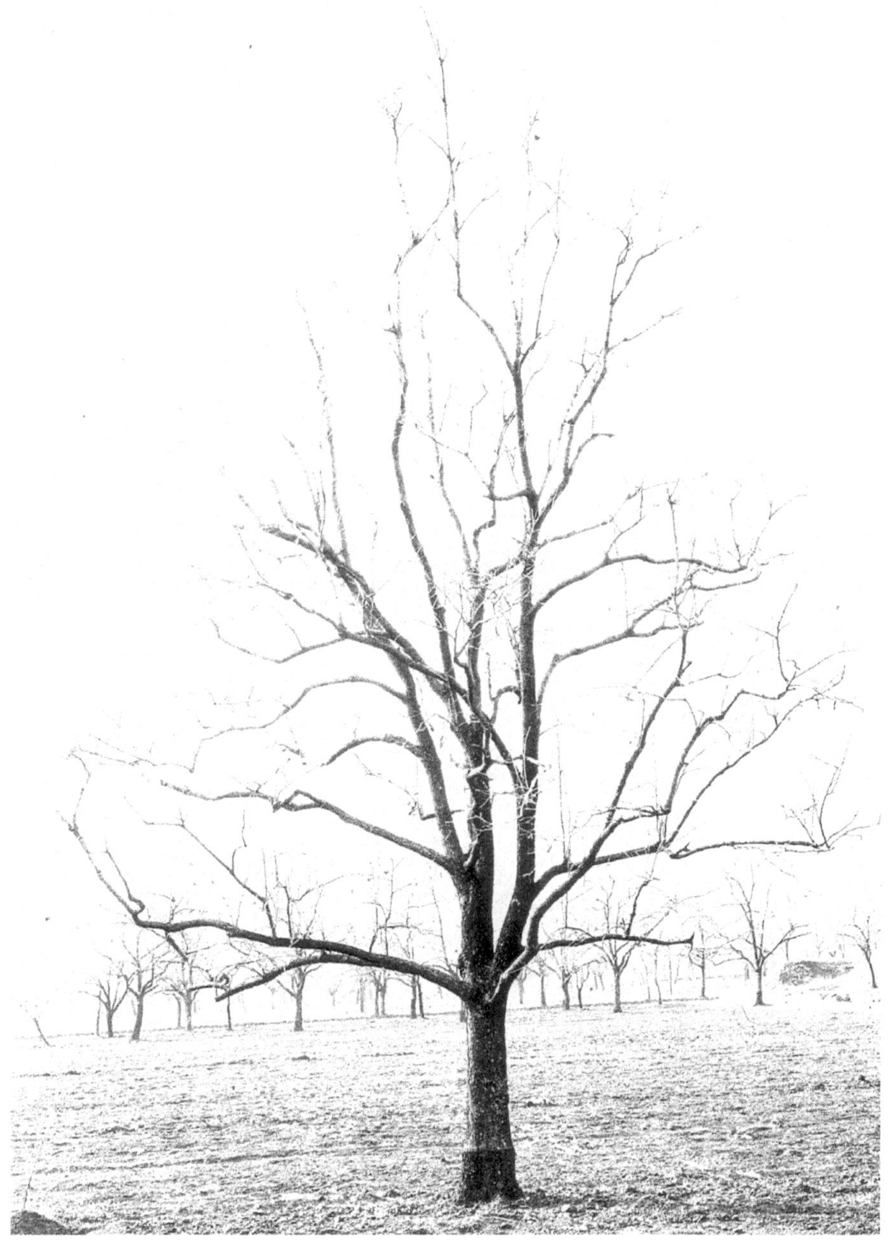

38041. *Nov. 28, 1924. Tai Ling Yuan. This is another good tree of the large Chinese persimmon in one of the orchards. Note the distinct demarcation between stock and scion on the trunk.*

太陵園 village, Tai Ling Yuan
柿子樹 Shih Tzu Shu
Large Persimmon tree

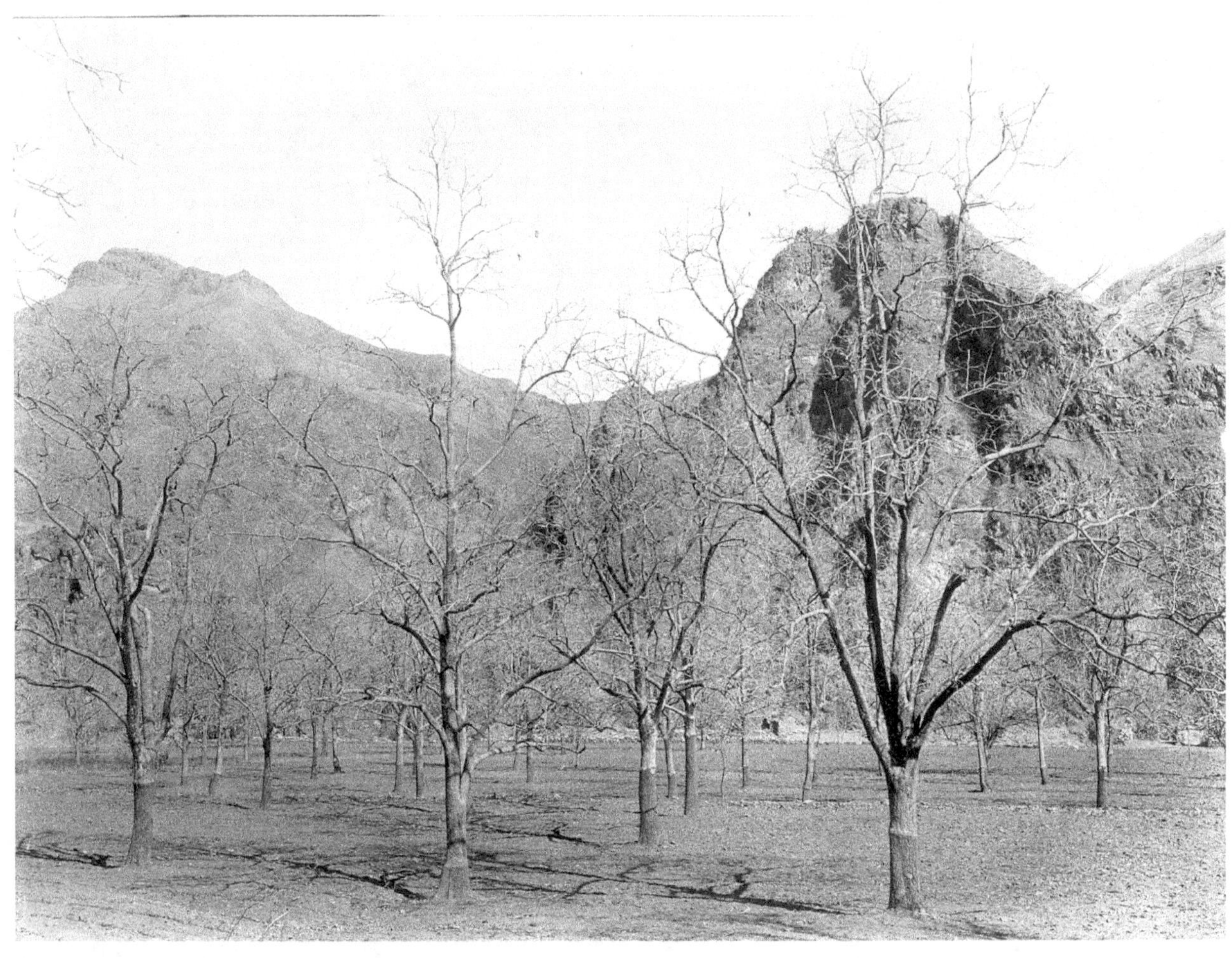

29849. *Nov. 6, 1924. Chia Yü K'ou. A general view in a large and good persimmon orchard near the village. Note the distinct demarcation between stock and scion on the trunks of several of the trees.*

PRUNING

As far as could be learned, the Chinese persimmon growers do not practice pruning as do American orchardists with their deciduous fruits, except to remove dead limbs. However, the common practice of harvesting with special hooks results in severe pruning that removes adjacent short branches along with stems having fruit buds, thereby reducing the yield of fruit for the following season's crop. The pruning resulting from these methods of picking perhaps accounts for the trees not being pruned otherwise.

[Ed.: It should be noted that trees of *D. kaki* (and especially *D. virginiana*, our U. S. native) are considered to be rather noticeably self-pruning. These trees very readily shed all growth that is weak or unproductive, and in early spring the ground under these trees can be littered with self-discarded limbs and twigs.]

HARVESTING AND HANDLING

The fruit begins to ripen early in October, and by the middle of the month harvesting is well under way. Harvesting is done by means of hand picking, and it appears that each region follows its own practice and uses its own special equipment. In the Toli district a bamboo pole, 8 feet or more in length, with one end split, is used. The picker operates this tool from the ground or up in the tree. The split end of the pole is slipped astride the small twig near the fruit, and the picker, with a sudden twist of the pole, breaks the twig. He then slips the pole down through his hand, removes the twig and the attached fruit, and places them on the ground or in a basket in case he is in the tree. When the basket is full it is lowered to the ground by means of a grass rope, and the fruit is emptied into a pile upon the ground. It is not uncommon to see two pickers working together, one up in the tree and the other on the ground. In the Ming Tombs region an iron hook attached to a pole, 4 to10 feet in length, is the tool used in picking persimmons. A man with the short pole climbs up into the tree and places the iron hook over the small twig to which the fruit is attached and with a sudden twist, as with the split bamboo pole, breaks the twig. Both twig and fruit fall and are usually caught by a man with a short piece of gunny sacking attached to two short sticks. A man with an 8- or 10-foot pole can pick many fruits from the ground, but the falling fruit still needs to be caught to prevent bruising.

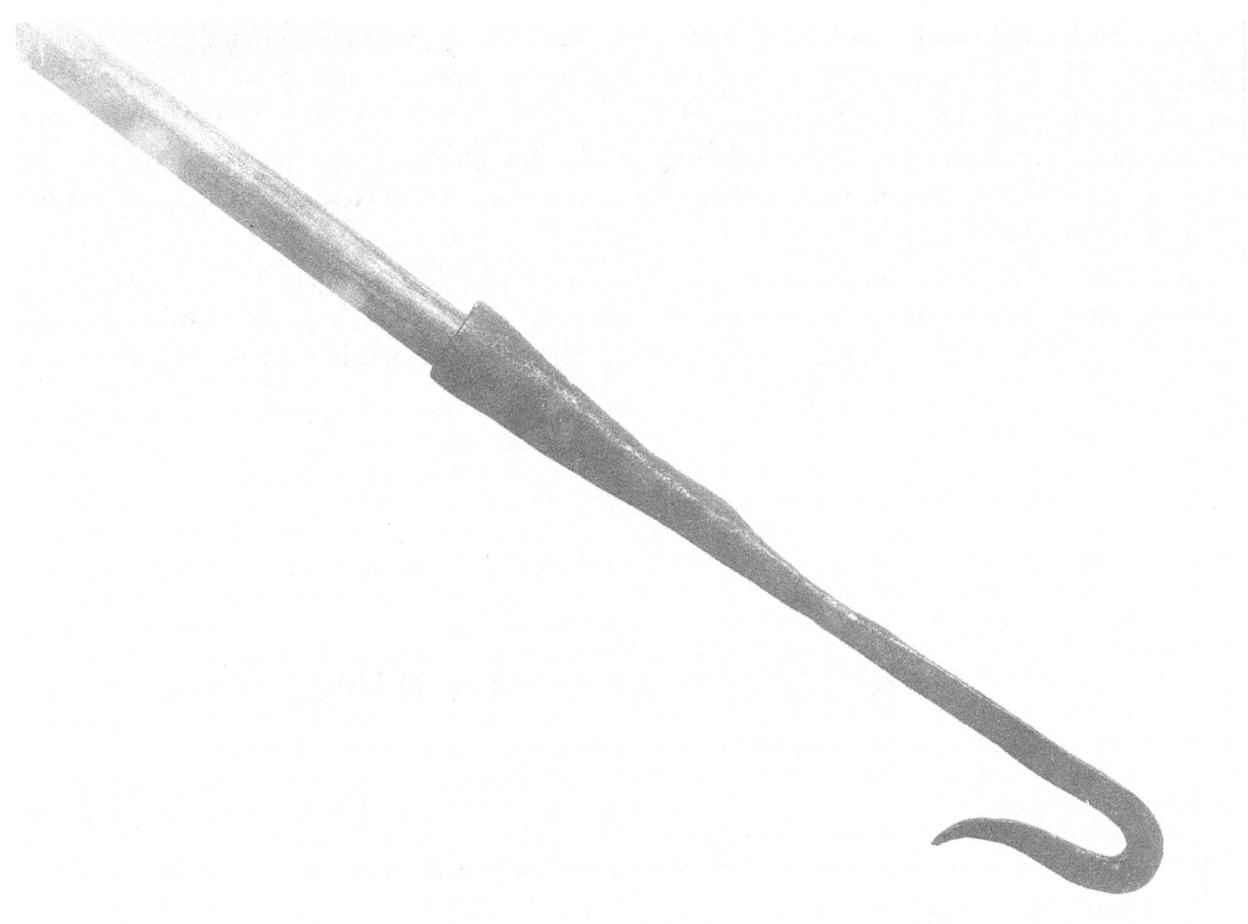

38051. *Nov. 28, 1924. Tai Ling Yuan. A half-size picture of an iron hook used in harvesting persimmon fruits. This picture shows a portion of the 8- to 10-foot pole. [Ed.: Harvesters also used a long bamboo pole with a slit in the end to hook the stem above the fruit and break the stem off. Both methods of harvesting resulted in severe pruning of branch tips.]*

柿子鈎子 Shih Tzu K'ou Tzu
Hook for picking persimmon

PROCESSING

[Ed.: The persimmon varieties chosen by the Chinese in North China for commercial orcharding and marketing happen to have the characteristic of astringency ("pucker") in the fruits until they are fully ripe and soft. To remove astringency before the fruits soften requires manipulation of the fruits by chemical or physical means, and the Chinese devised a rapid astringency removal system that allowed them to handle and market the "depuckered" fruits before they became soft.]

The Chinese hot water method of processing persimmons in Peiping is simple, unique, fascinatingly interesting, comparatively inexpensive, and exceptionally efficient. Briefly, persimmon fruits are immersed in hot water and allowed to remain overnight; by morning they are ready for market.

This practice of treating persimmons to remove their astringency is in operation for some two months in early fall, from about the middle of September until about the middle of November, but of course varying, more or less, depending on the season. As a rule, at this latter date or thereabout, the hot water processed persimmons are replaced by fruit from the open-air winter storage beds from which the astringency has been removed by nature's process of ripening and freezing.

Persimmons are processed in specially constructed kilns which are used only for this purpose. This hot water "depuckered" fruit supplies the market demand from about the middle of September to the middle of November, after which fruit from the open-air storage beds makes its appearance.

We have seen only two types of kilns: one with six containers, the other with eight having two containers in front and below the level of the other six. These kilns are made of adobe brick plastered over with chopped rope, lime, and earth mortar.

The containers within the kilns are glazed earthenware jars of varying sizes, the walls of which are about two inches in thickness. They are usually 21 to 30 inches across at the top and from about 30 to 36 or 40 inches in depth.

There is a rather broad shallow metal pan in front of the kiln and at about ground level. This is between the fire pit and the kiln, and directly over the firing space. This pan is used for heating the water (for the containers into which the persimmons are submerged) up to the desired temperature, which is routinely determined by a "rule of thumb" method.

The fire pit is connected with a flue running to the back wall of the container where it continues with a hole in the ground 10 inches across and 24 to 30 inches in depth. We understand that a kiln cannot be successfully operated without this underground chimney.

There are two small draft openings in front near the top of the kiln, and similar openings on each side near the top at the back of the kiln. When the kiln is fired, which is two or three times during the night (depending on the season and ripeness of the fruit), these drafts are unplugged, and when the fire is checked, the openings are replugged.

The temperature of the water in the containers into which the persimmons are put varies according to the ripeness of the fruit and the time of the season, from perhaps (as far as could be reckoned) 40C in early fall with unripe fruit, to 15 or 20C later in the season when the fruit is considerably more ripe.

The containers are, as a rule, filled in the forenoon, and in the early season, if fired three times, the first fire is started about dark and continued for about an hour. The second fire is started about 10 or 11 PM and continued for about the same length of time, and the third fire is started about 3 AM and is continued for about one hour.

If the kiln is only fired twice during the night, the first fire is started about 6 or 7 PM, and the second at about 3 AM. At both times the firing continues for about an hour. By about 6 AM, the fruit is "depuckered" and is ready for sale and distribution. The total processing requires 16 to 18 hours to effect the "depuckering" of the fruit.

At the curing yard where we were, the kilns were fired with old reed-grass matting, and the fires were light and slow.

We noted that persimmon growers or their representatives rent a room at an inn for the persimmon season, and also space at the inn compound for storing their persimmons and on which to build a kiln. They rent the glazed earthen containers and build their own kiln, and when the processing season is over, they raze the kiln and return the containers to their owner.

The seasonal rental of these containers varies in proportion to their size, and is as follows: for the smallest size (about 20" wide and 30" deep) 80 cents Mex.; the next largest size (about 25" wide and 33" deep) $1.00 Mex.; and the largest size (about 30" wide and 40" deep) $1.50 Mex.

Adobe brick	$ 2.00
Line, rope, and the chopping of the rope	2.00
Labor for 2 men, 2 days each @ 0.90 each Per day for building kiln	3.60
Seasonal rental of a battery of 6 containers, 2 small, 2 medium, 2 large	6.60
Total cost of kiln complete	$ 14.20 Mex.

In this connection, it is believed that the following scaled drawing, showing in detail the construction of the 6-container kiln will prove of interest and value.

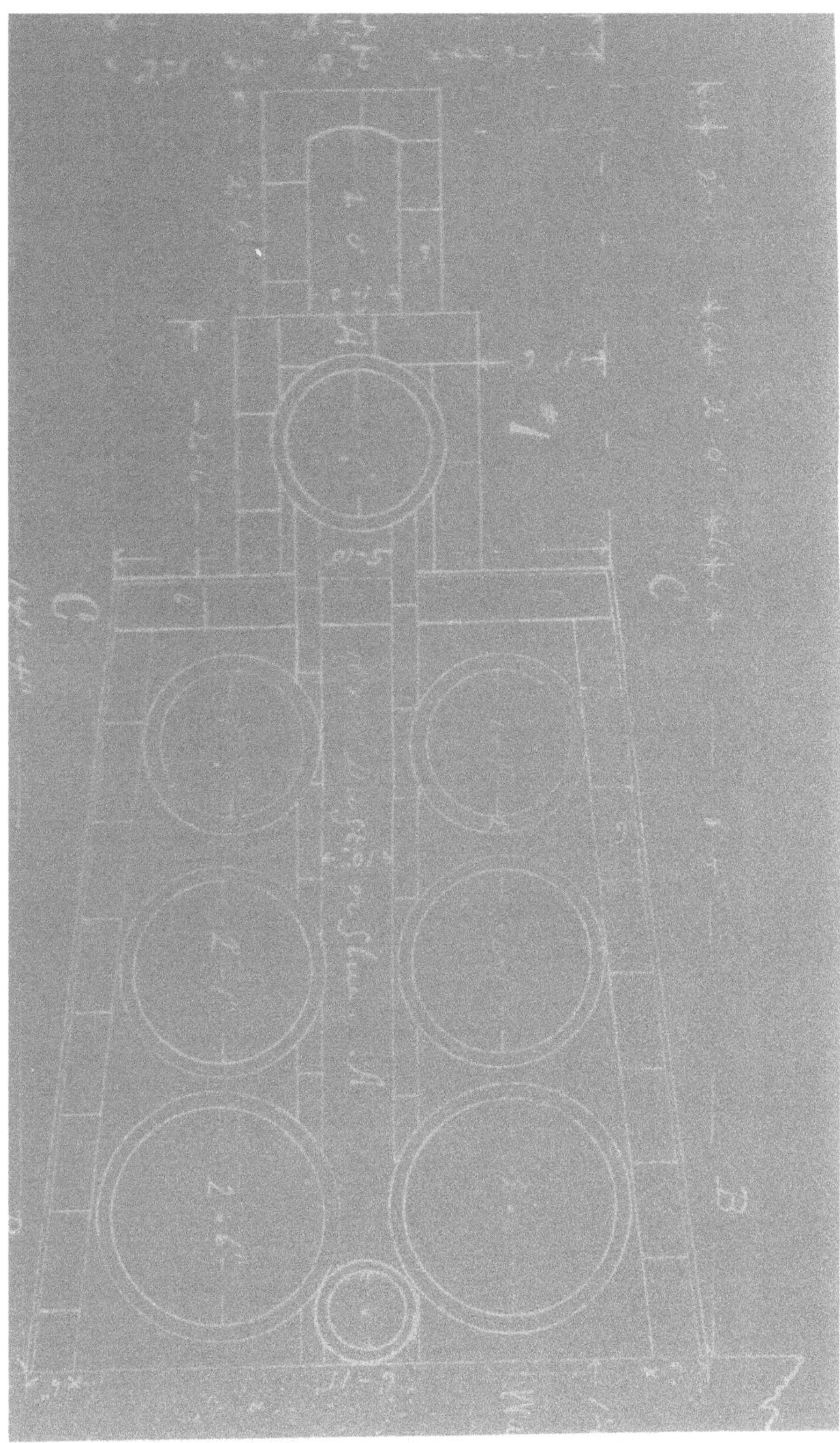

Blueprint: *Persimmon hot water processing kiln for use in the treatment of Chinese persimmons in Peiping and vicinity, from about September 20 to November 20 (seasonally) to remove their astringency. After November 20 this is accomplished through the natural means of ripening and freezing in open air storage beds, on the ground, in the persimmon-growing regions to the north and northwest of Peiping. #1 is a top view of a six-container kiln. #2 is a section through "A". #3 is a section through "B". #4 is a section through "C".*

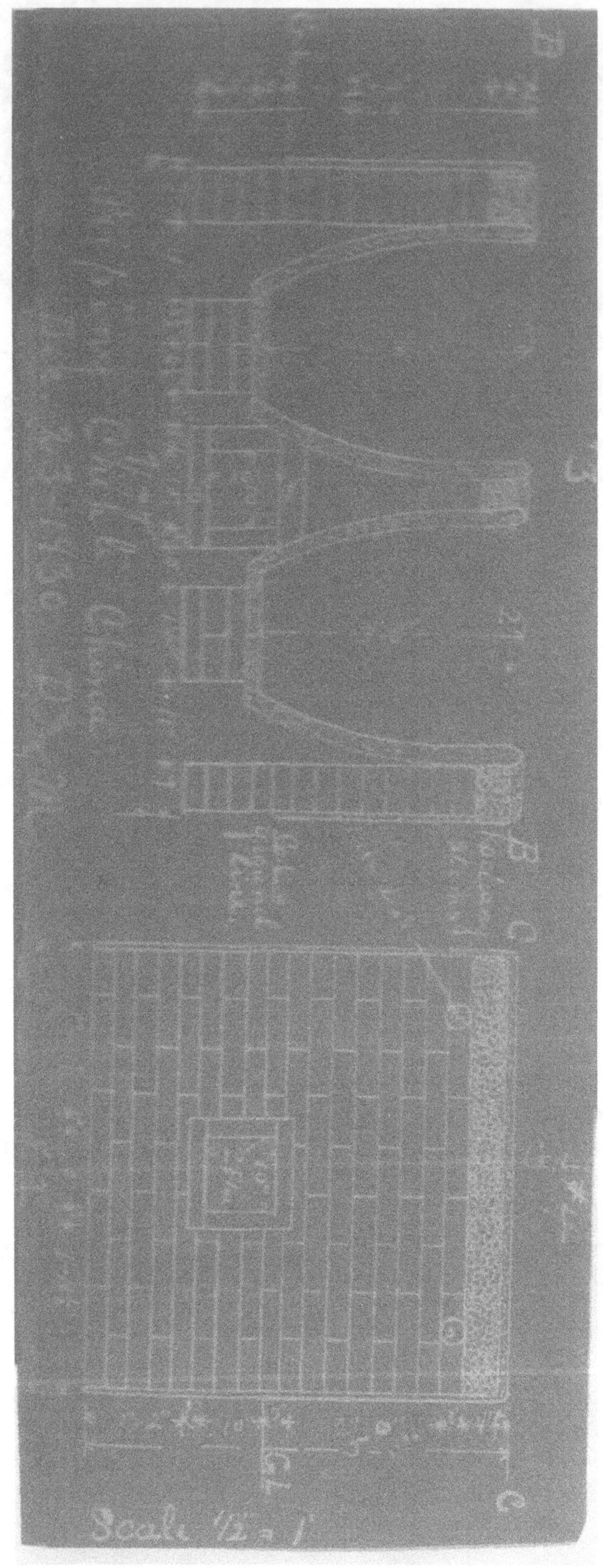
Scale ½" = 1'

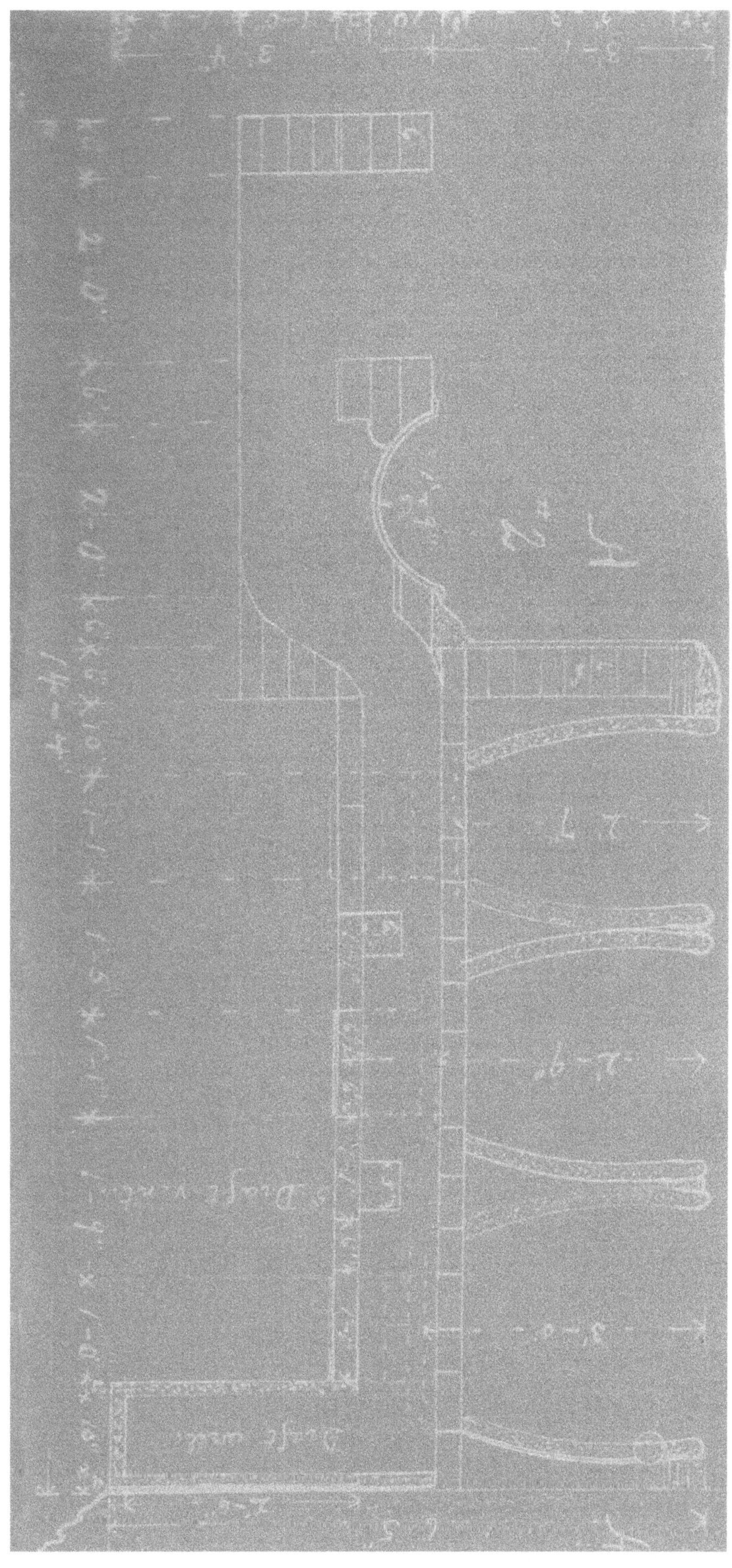

The average daily capacity of a 6-container kiln like that illustrated above is estimated to be 4,166 first grade large persimmons (Tamopan), and for the season (Sept. 20 to Nov. 20 - about 61 days) is 254,126 fruits. We were given an off-hand estimate of the seasonal run of a 6-container kiln as 250,000 to 260,000 large persimmons. If we take the average estimate of 650 large persimmons per day for each container in a 6-container kiln, we get a daily output of 3,900 and a seasonal output for 61 days of 237,000 fruits. The average of the 3 seasonal estimates is 249,000, which is probably somewhat less than the actual number of fruits actually kiln-processed per season.

We are advised that there are no less than half a dozen places in Peiping and its environs where persimmons in the early season of each year are hot water processed to render the fruit non-astringent. It is estimated that upward of 6,500,000 persimmons are annually hot water processed for the Peiping market during the season.

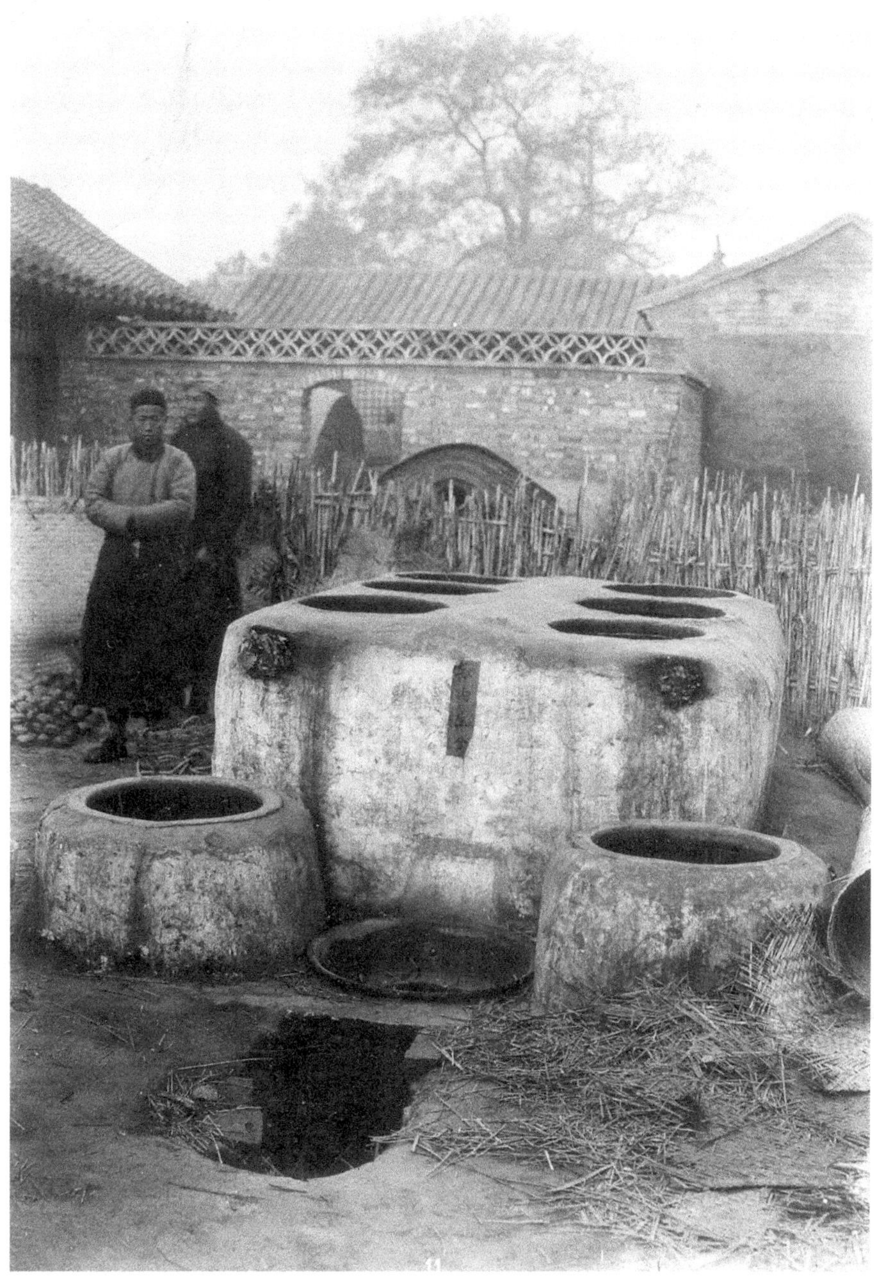

45209. *Nov. 11, 1930. Peiping. A nearby front view of an 8-container persimmon processing kiln in the Wan Shun Tien compound outside the city wall to the southwest. In the foreground to the right of the firing pit is some of the old grass matting which is used in firing the kiln. Just back of the firing pit and between the two low down containers is the broad shallow metal water pan. Note that it is directly over where the fire is built, and as a result, the water heats quickly. This extra heated water is used to temper the water in the containers into which the persimmons are placed. The view also shows the two small plugged flue openings in front and to each side and near the top of the kiln.*

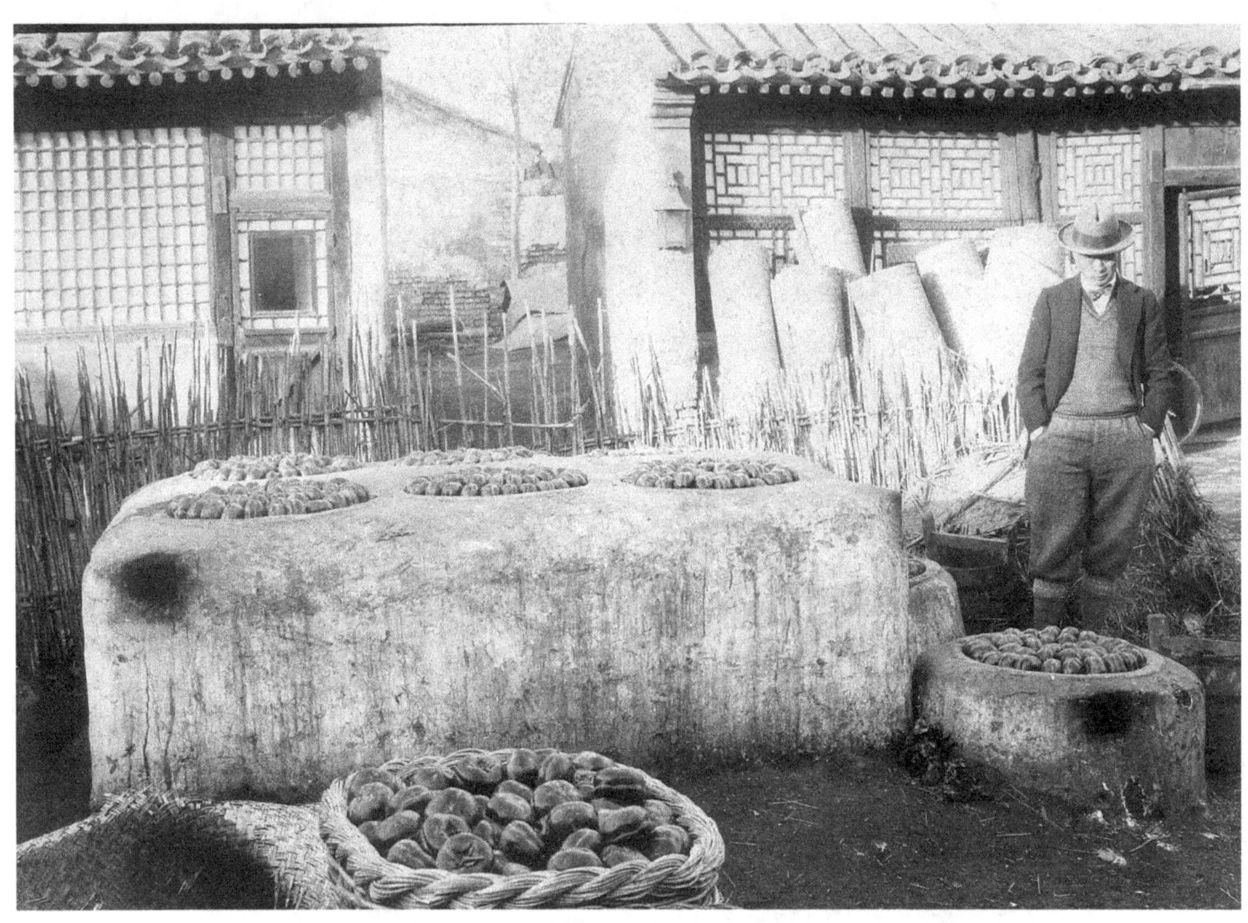

46164. *Nov. 4, 1930. Another view of the 8-container kiln from a little different angle.*

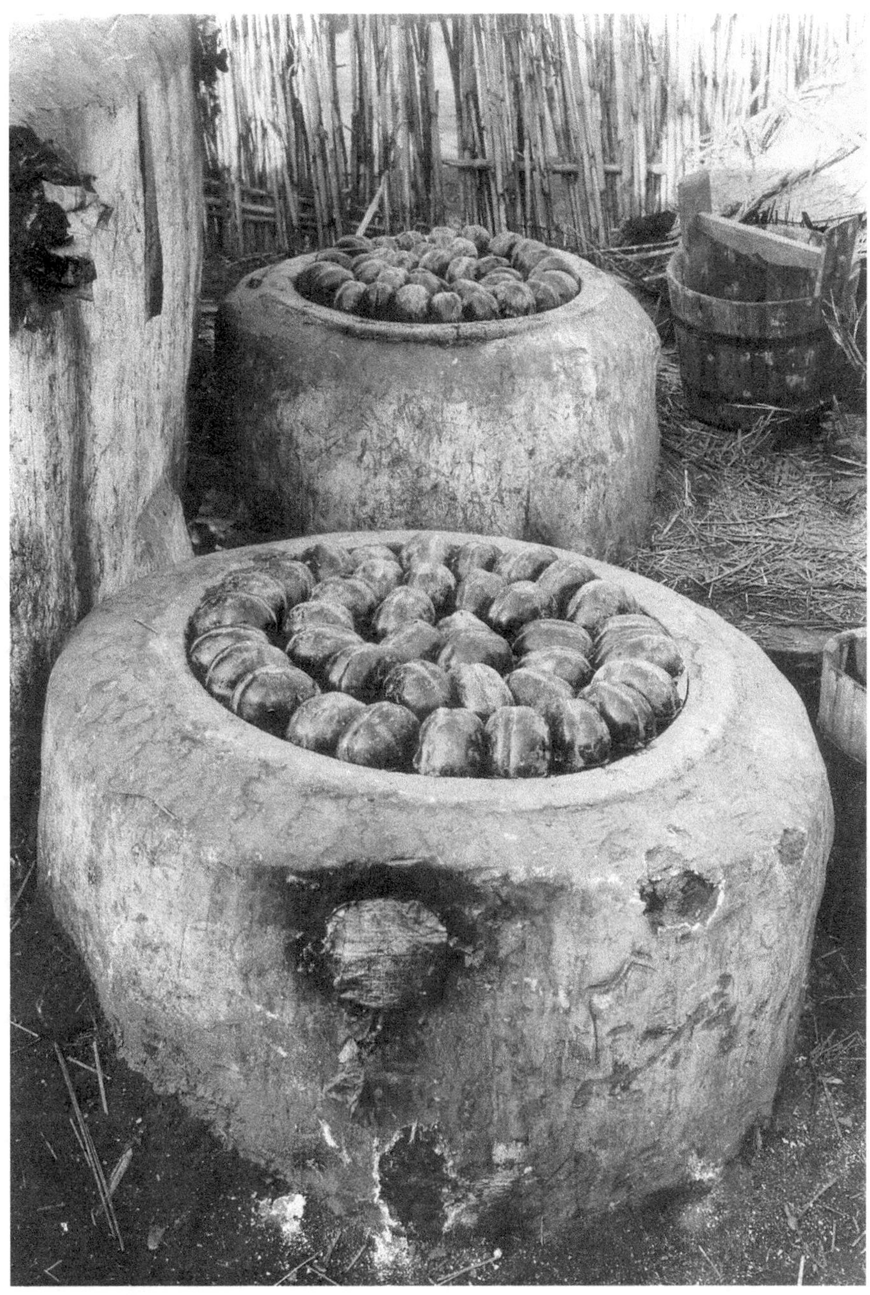

46165. *Nov. 4, 1930. A nearby side view of the two low down containers next to the wall of the rest of the kiln. It will be noted that the flue draft on the side near the top of the low down container in the foreground is plugged, and also that the top layer of persimmons are on edge and arranged evenly in circles.*

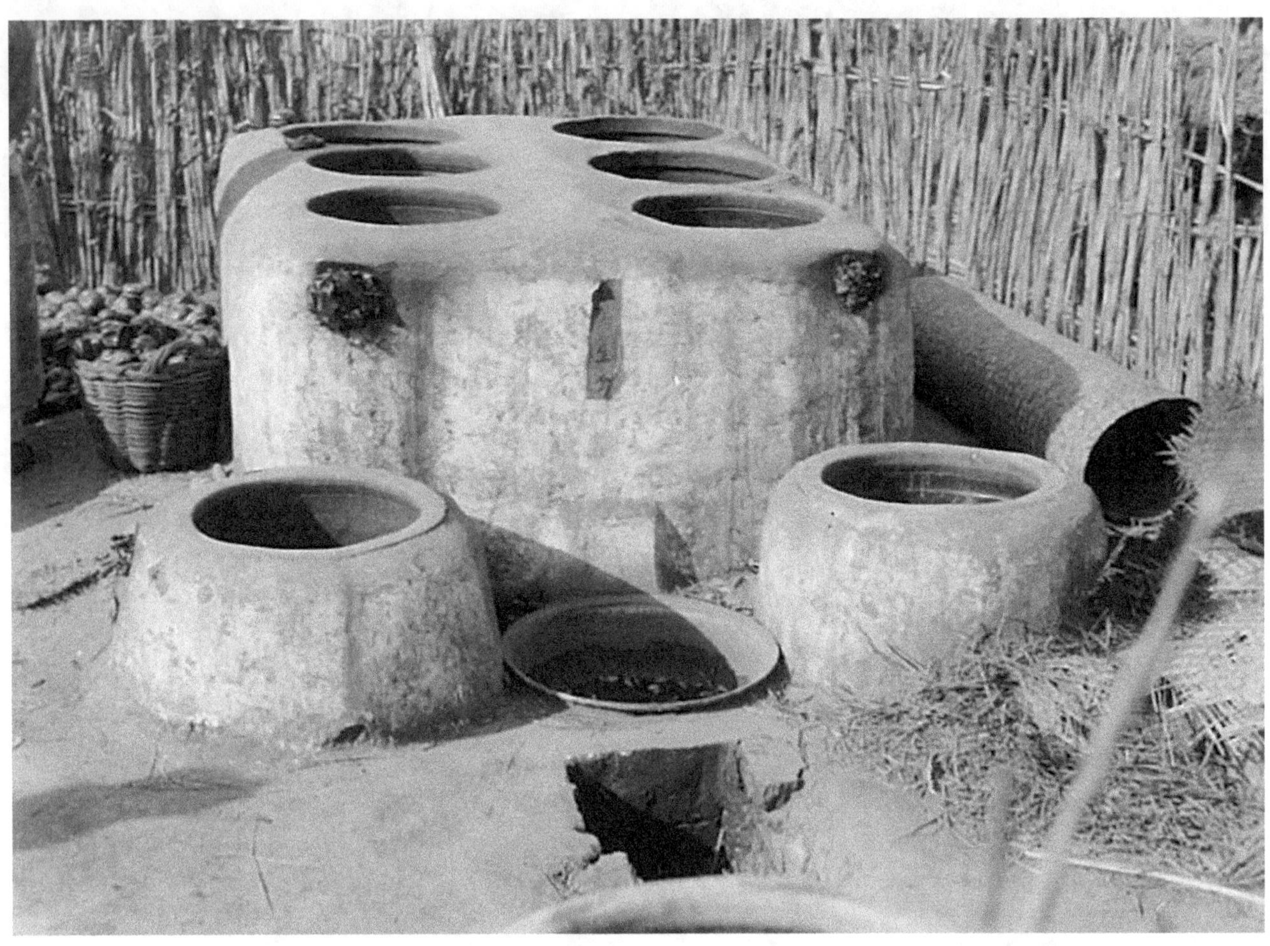

***46208.** Peiping. A fairly nearby view from in front of a hot water treating kiln for removing the pucker from persimmons. It is in use from early fall until the persimmons are naturally cured by freezing and ripening.*

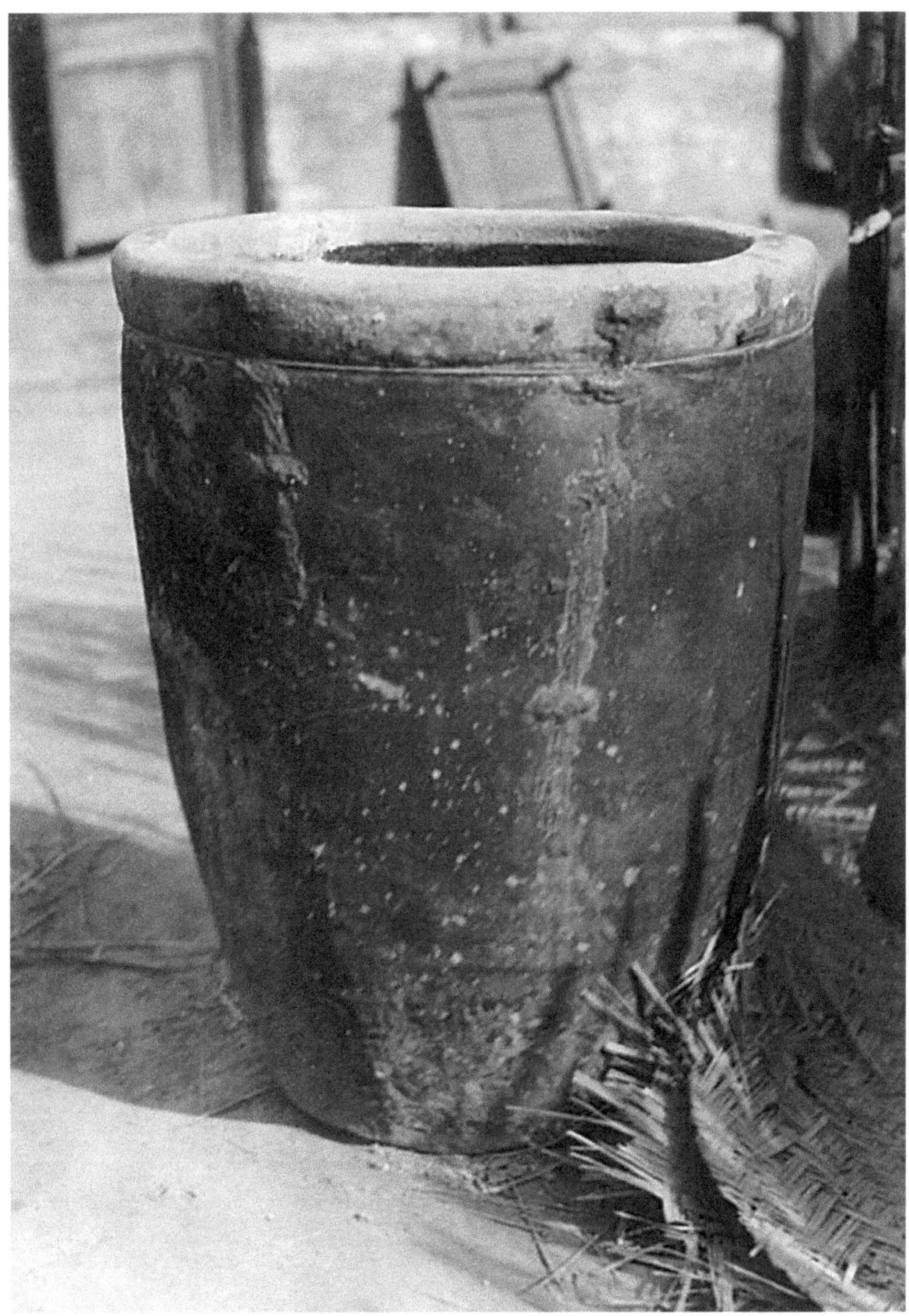

46216. *Nov. 11, 1930. Peiping. Glazed earthen container, similar to those used in the curing kilns for the hot water treatment of persimmon fruits to render them non-astringent. The containers are 20" or more across the inside and 30" or more in depth, and the walls are about 2" thick.*

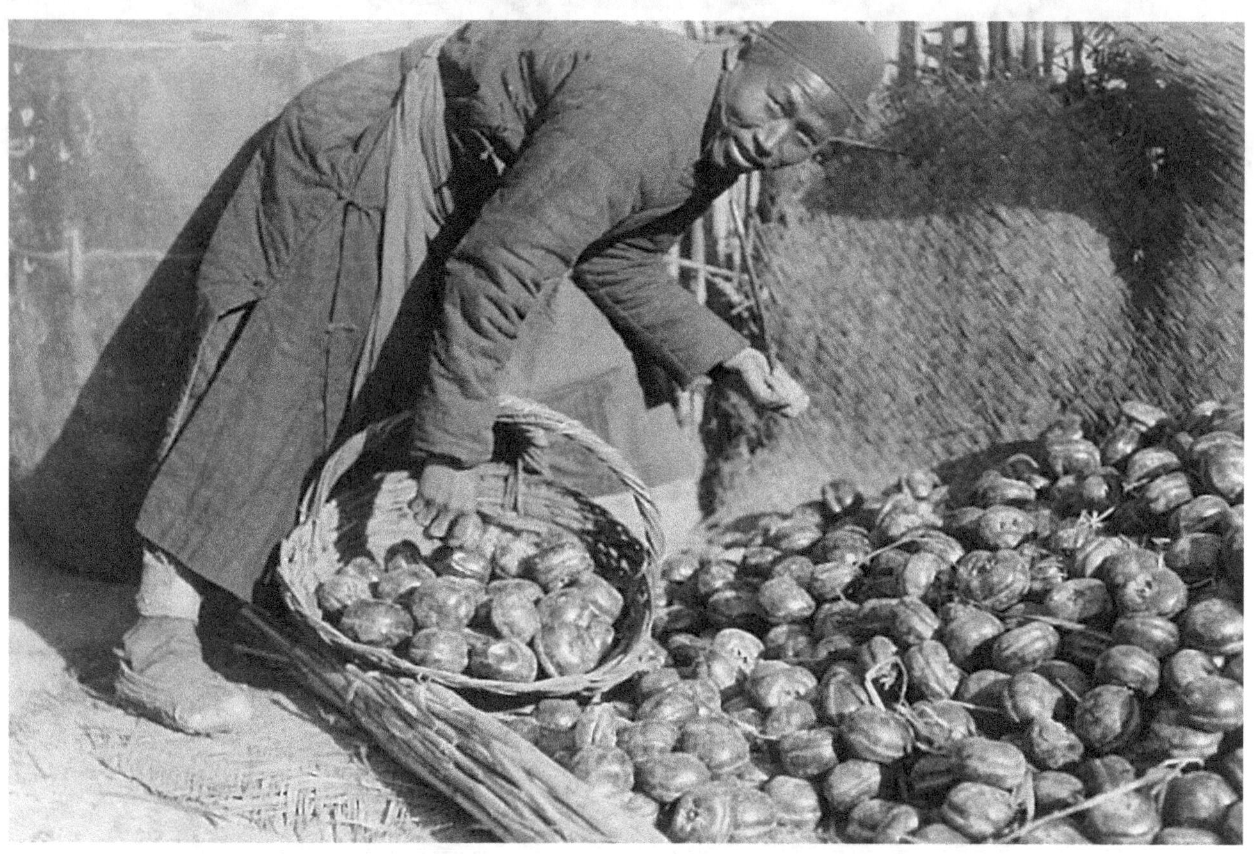

46206. *Nov. 11, 1930. Peiping. Selecting persimmons from a pile on matting on the ground, in the compound of the Wan Shun Tien Inn, for hot water processing. As a rule only firm fruit is processed. The soft or cracked fruits are put to one side and are sold as is, for whatever the owner can get for them*

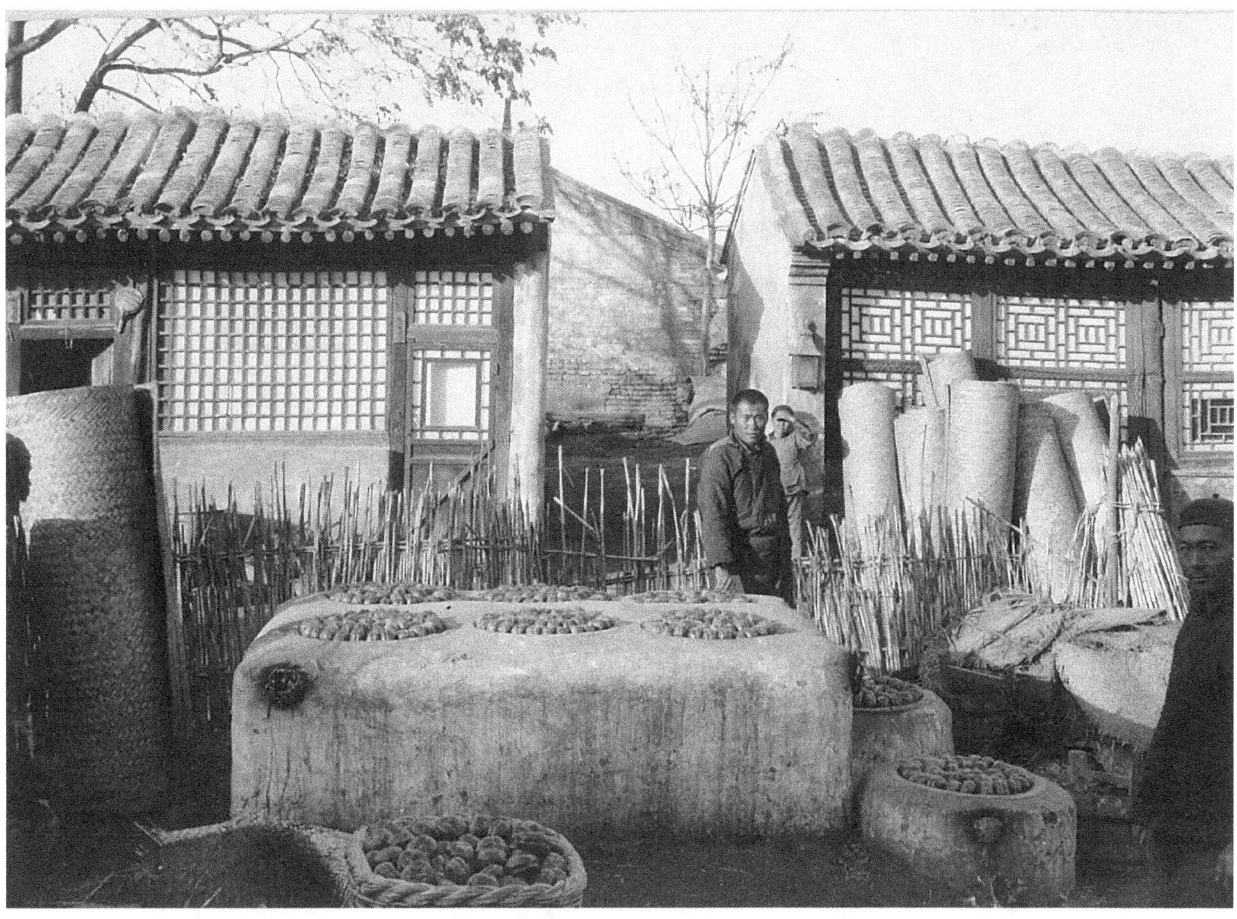

46163. *Nov. 4, 1930. Side view of an eight-container hot water processing kiln with all eight of the containers filled to their capacity, ready for processing. Note that the flue opening on the side of the low down container, and the one in front just above it, as well as the one on the side of the back of the main container, are all plugged. If all the containers are in use, all flues are opened when the fire is started, and all are plugged when the firing ceases. If these are not in use the flue openings are left closed.*

If in the main kiln the two first containers only are used, the two front openings are opened and the back ones are plugged. If, however, the middle and back containers or the back ones alone are used, the back flue openings are opened and the two front ones are left plugged.

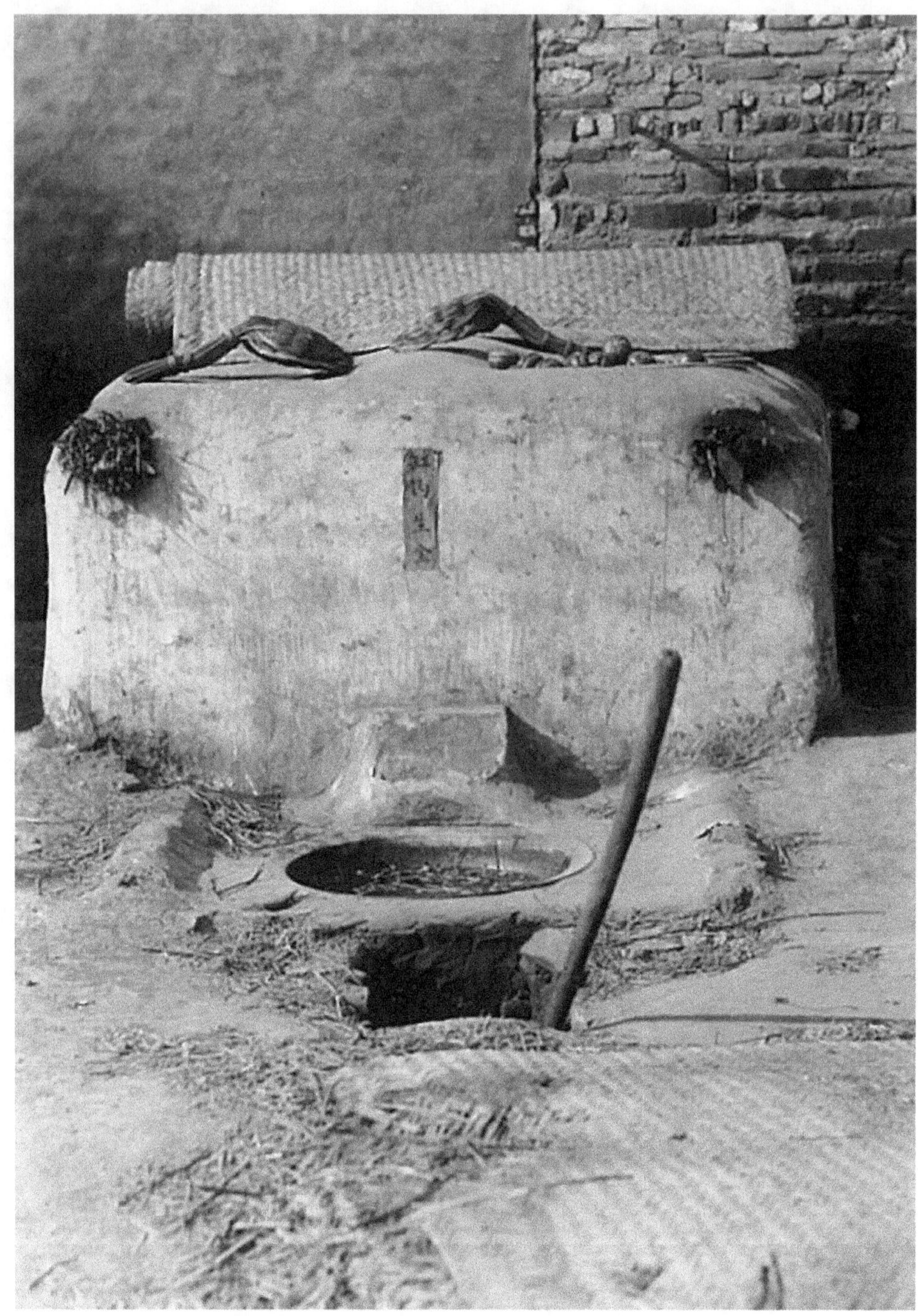

***46210.** Nov.11,1930. Peiping. A rather distant view of a 6-container hot water persimmon processing kiln at the Wan Shun Tien Inn compound on Hsuan Wume Street. Between the fire pit and front of the kiln is the rather broad shallow metal pan used in heating the water to temper that in the containers into which the persimmons are submerged.*

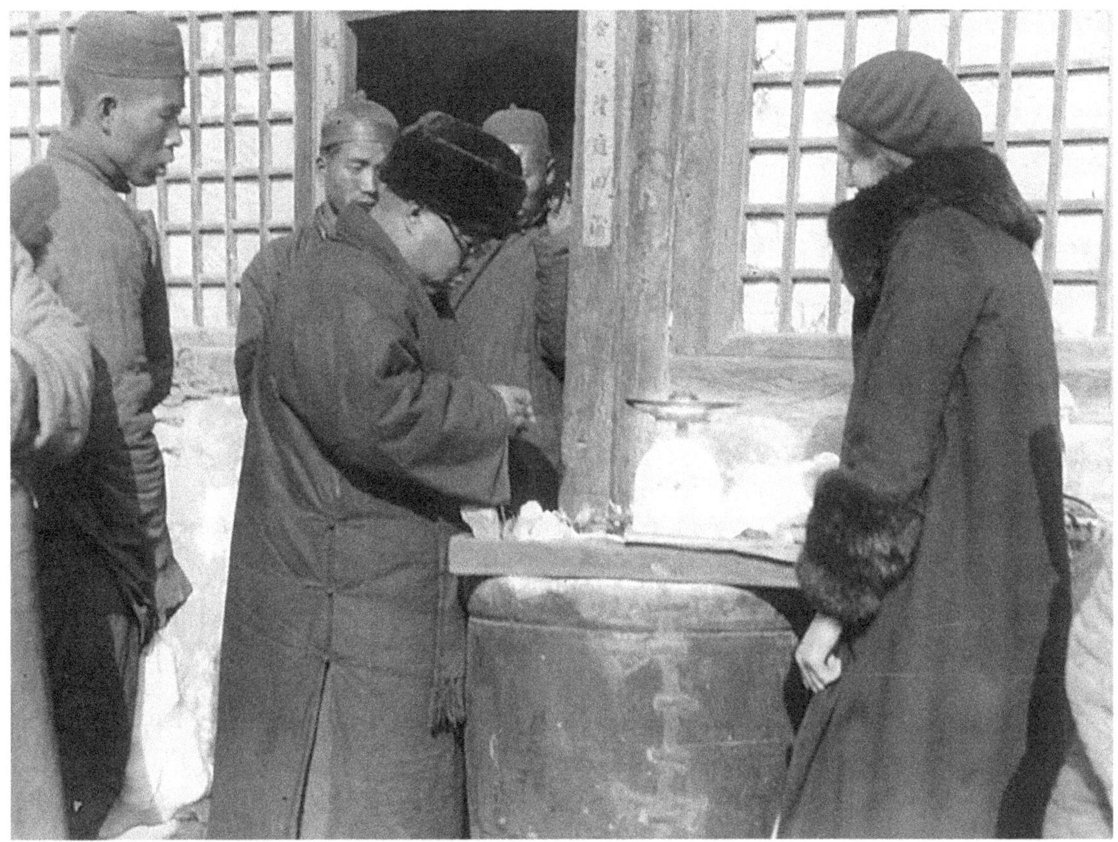

46218. *Peiping. Peter Liu is weighing numbered persimmons and recording their weights, with daughter-in-law Ruth B. Dorsett and Chinese kiln tenders looking on. The fruits were weighed before and after processing, but there was found to be no significant difference in weights.*

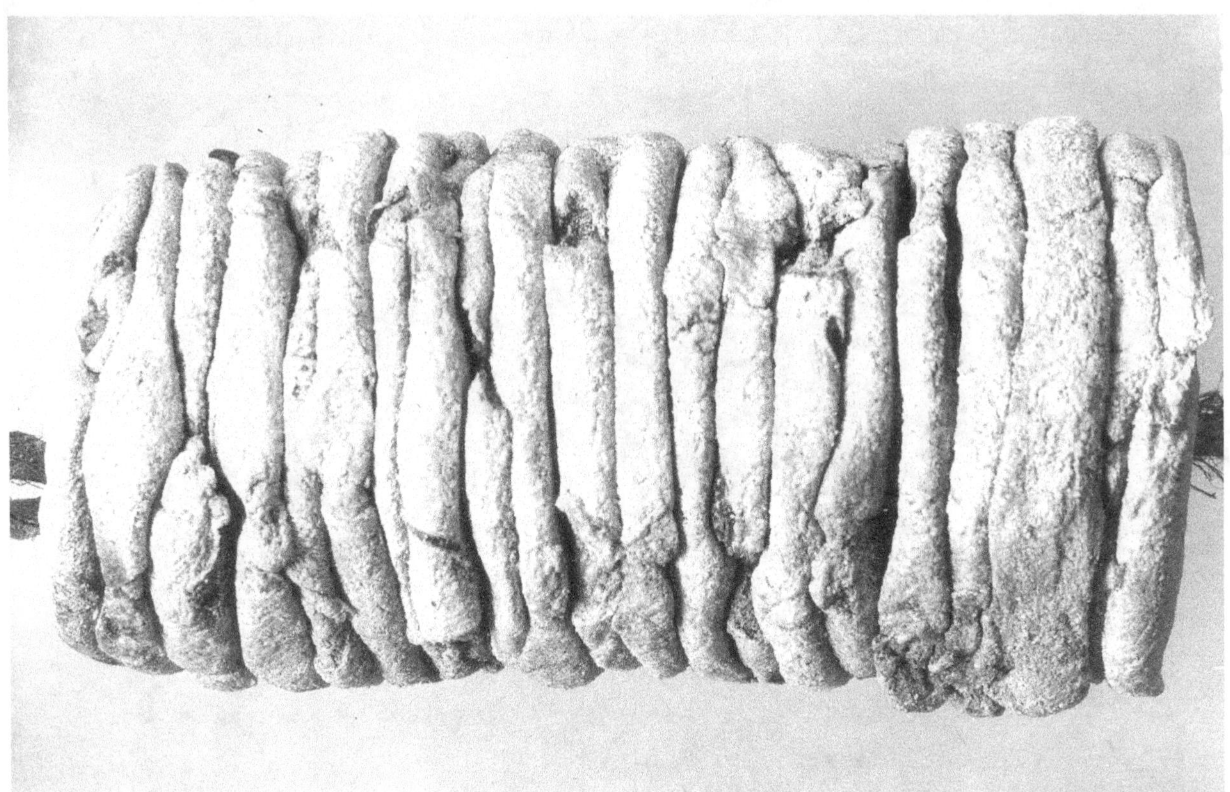

***38203.** Jan. 7, 1925. A life-size picture of a 10-fruited caltic string of large dried persimmons shipped in from Ho Nau. They cost 16 cents Mex. per caltic. (Ed.: Drying of persimmon fruits consisted of peeling off the outer skin of ripened non-astringent fruits, air-drying them for a period of time on long cords, then assembling them into saleable quantities of, say, ten fruits, and pressing them together to make a caltic. Although interested in dried persimmons, Dorsett apparently did not include photographs of the drying process in his collection of persimmon-related photos. However, F. N. Meyer photographed the process elsewhere in China. J. R. Smith, in his book on Tree Fruits, used Meyer's photo {below} with the following legend: "Long strings of peeled persimmons hanging from a pole set up on the mud roof of a house at Siku Kansu near the Tibetan border of West China.")*

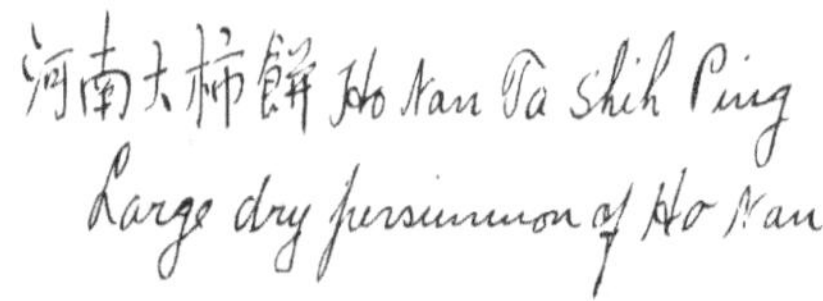

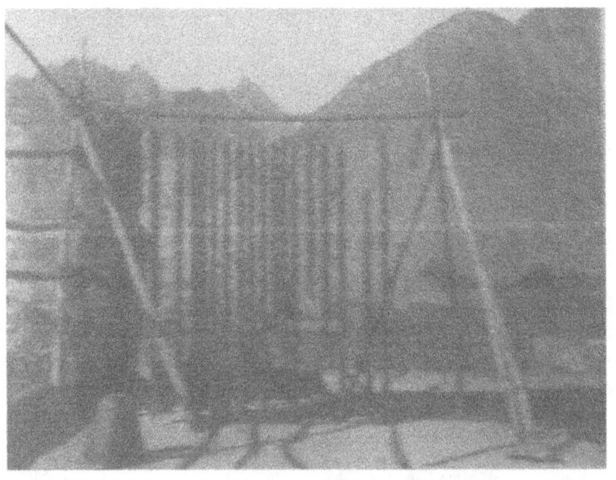

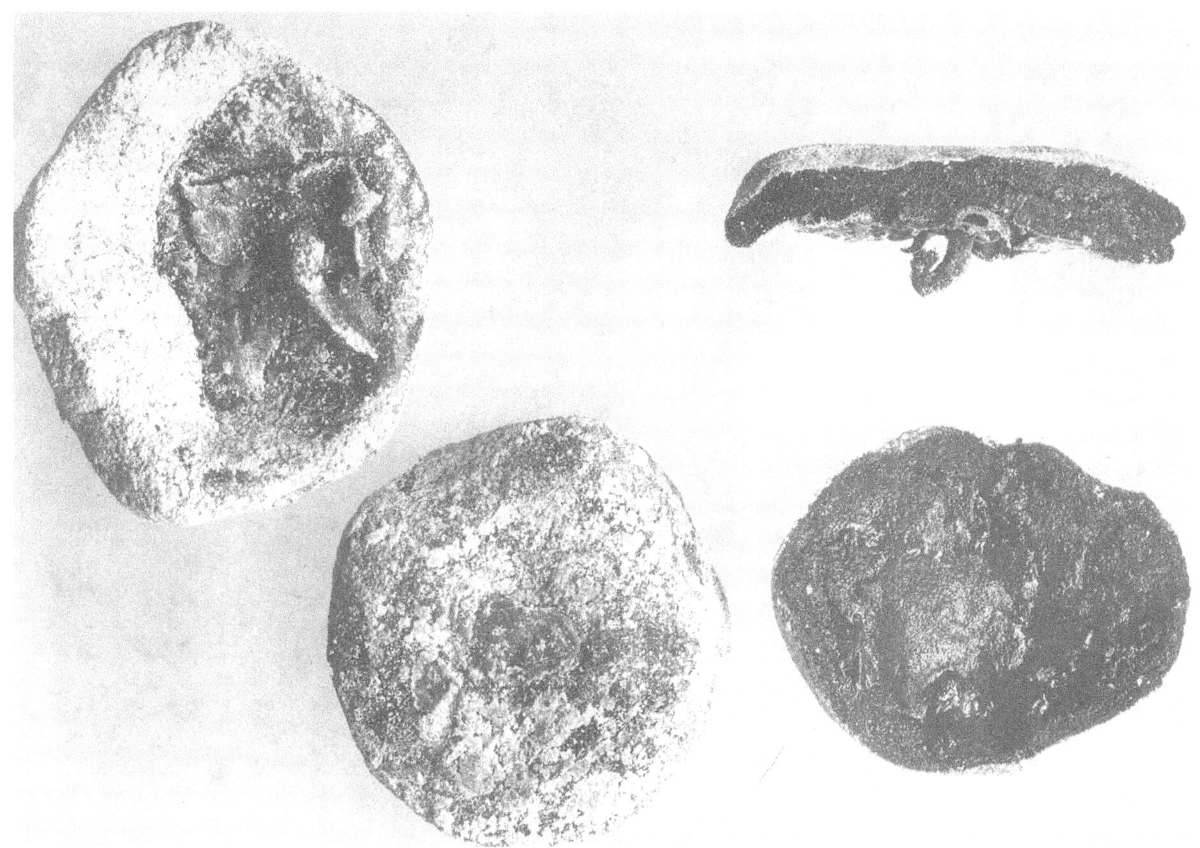

328132. *Dec. 18, 1924. Peking. A life-size picture of dried persimmon fruits from Shang Tung - Tsao Chon Fu - purchased in the Peking market. These sell for about 12 cents Mex. per caltic. (Ed.: As shown here, dried persimmon fruits are often coated with a whitish residue: sugar crystals that form naturally on the outside of the fruit as it dries. Dorsett collected a quantity of this sugar residue and shipped it, as Item #7444, to USDA scientist "Mr. Thomas" on Nov. 11, 1930.)*

河南小柿餅 Ho nan Hsiao shih Ping
small dry persimmon of Ho nan

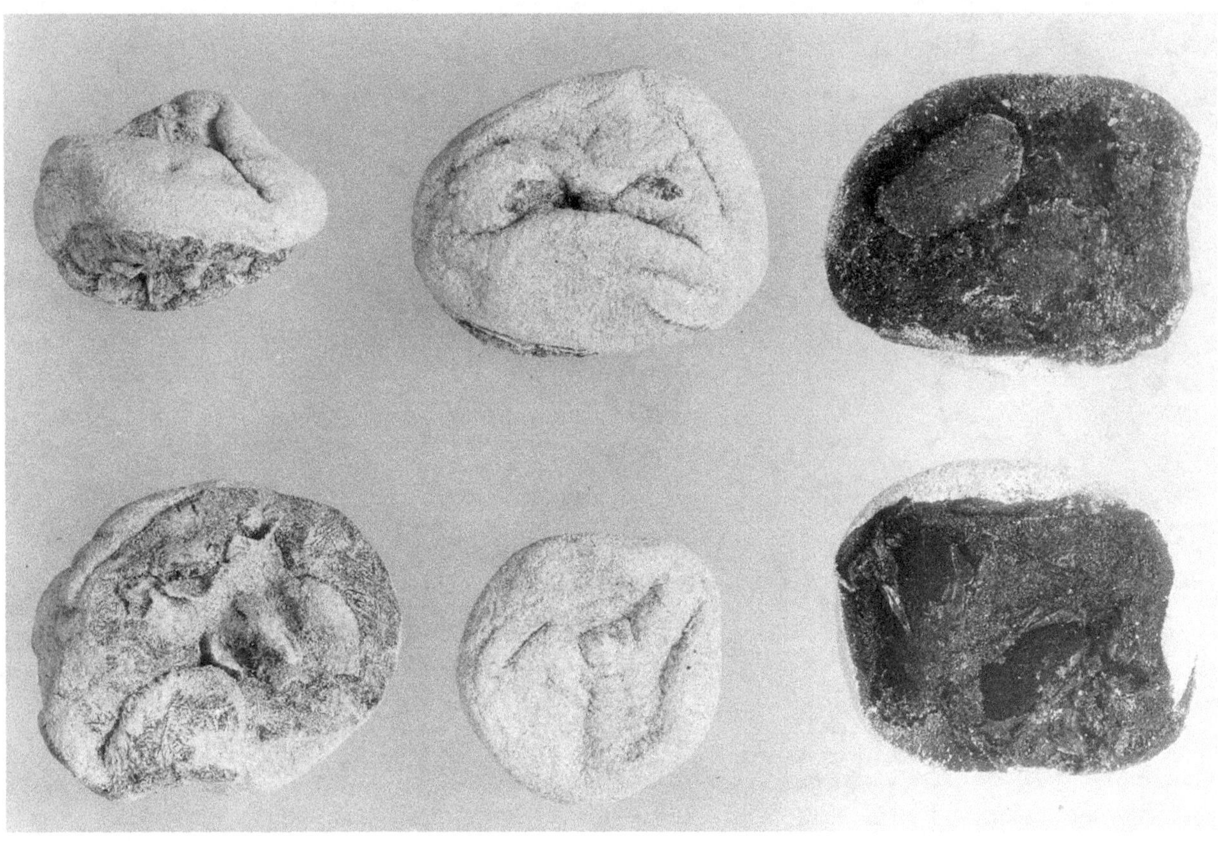

38204. *Jan. 7, 1925. A life-size picture of medium to small dried persimmons from Ho Nau. Some of these dried fruits have seeds. The fruits cost 12 cents Mex. per caltic.*

河南小柿餅 Ho Nan Hsiao shih Ping
small dry persimmon of Ho Nan

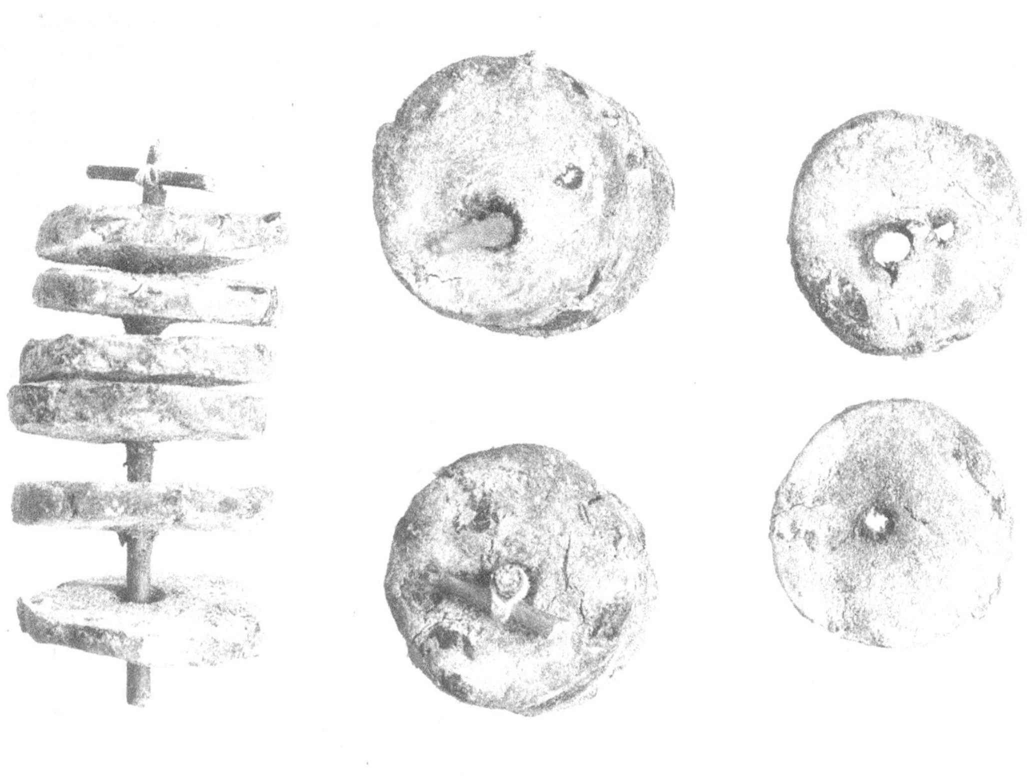

38136. *Dec. 20, 1924. A life-size picture of dried Chinese black date fruits. To us they were not attractive or appetizing.*

KILN TEMPERATURE MEASUREMENTS

We made temperature records of the air and of each of the containers in an eight-container kiln during its operation on the night of Nov. 4, 1930. The kiln was located in the outdoor compound of the Wan Shun Tien Inn in Peking, where persimmons are nightly "depuckered" throughout the season from about Sept. 20 to Nov. 20.

The fruit was put into the containers about 2 PM Nov. 4 and the kiln was first fired between 6 and 7 PM. The second firing was between 3 and 4 AM Nov. 5, and by 6 or 7 AM the persimmons were being counted out to purchasers.

The temperature of the water in the containers into which the fruit would be added registered 44C using a stem Centigrade thermometer. (This degree of heat was typically determined by "rule of thumb" by local kiln operators.) When all the fruit was immersed into this hot water, the temperature was reduced to about 20C.

The table which follows, shows both the outside air temperature and that of the water and fruit in each of the containers in the 8-container hot water processing kiln. For convenience, the containers were numbered consecutively from 1 to 8 facing the kiln, with 1-4 on the left and 5-8 on the right.

Table of Air and Kiln Container Temperature Readings–November 4-5, 1930

Outside		*Container #1*		*Container #2*		*Container #3*		*Container #4*	
Temp.	*Hour PM*	*Temp.*	*Hour PM*	*Temp.*	*Hour PM*	*Temp.*	*Hour PM*	*Temp.*	*Hour PM*
7C	7:10	19C	7:03	20C	7:05	18C	7:07	22C	7:10
4C	7:17	20C	7:39	19C	7:41	23C	7:42	24C	7:44
2C	8:00	26C	8:03	24C	8:06	24C	8:08	27C	8:11
	AM		*AM*		*AM*		*AM*		*AM*
-0C	2:58	25C	3:00	26C	3:03	26C	3:06	29C	3:08
-0C	3:45	26C	3:25	28C	3:27	28C	3:29	30C	3:30

Table of Air and Kiln Container Temperature Readings–November 4-5, 1930 (continued)

Outside		Container #5		Container #6		Container #7		Container #8	
Temp.	Hour PM	Temp.	Hour PM	Temp.	Hour PM	Temp.	Hour PM	Temp.	Hour PM
7C	7:15	17C	7:11	24C	7:12	20C	7:13	21C	7:14
4C	7:17	24C	7:45	25C	7:47	26C	7:49	26C	7:51
2C	8:00	23C	8:13	25C	8:15	27C	8:17	26C	8:20
	AM		AM		AM		AM		AM
-0C	2:58	25C	3:10	28C	3:13	31C	3:15	30C	3:16
-0C	3:45	25C	3:32	29C	3:34	34C	3:37	33C	3:39

The thermometers used were not graduated to read below 0C, and as a result (regretfully) the outside air temperatures lower than 0C, which probably occurred, are not given.

It will be noted that in no instances did the temperatures in any of the containers go very high or very low, or even vary greatly from each other. The average temperature of containers 1-4 was 24.25C, while that of 5-8 was 25.875C, a difference of only 1.625C which, under the circumstances was, we believe, quite remarkable.

This, perhaps, is the first temperature record ever made during the hot water processing of persimmons since the practice first began perhaps centuries ago, and on this account, even though not very satisfactory, is extremely interesting.

On Nov. 11, at the Wan Shun Tien Inn compound, we again conducted temperature readings in 2 containers in a 6-container kiln. In this instance, a hollow bamboo cane was centered in each of the containers into which the thermometers could be suspended for readings at intervals during the processing period.

It is believed that the following notes and temperature readings made during the course of filling containers number 1 and 4, and during the operation of the six-container kiln, may prove to be of interest. At 1:05 PM Nov. 11, the thirteen inches of water in container #1, before any fruit was filled in, registered 20C with an outside air temperature of 3C. At 1:32 PM, immediately after 860 first- and second-grade persimmons had been filled into this container, the temperature in the small bamboo cane at the center of the container registered 15C.

The temperature of the 13 inches of water in container #4 before any fruit was put in registered 34C. At 1:43 PM, immediately after 750 first-grade persimmons had been filled into this container, the temperature of the water in the bamboo tube at the center of the container registered 17C.

We feel sure the following table of hourly (or oftener) outside and kiln temperature readings throughout the period of the processing of the two containers of persimmons during the night of Nov. 11, 1930, will be of interest.

Table of Air and Kiln Container Temperature Readings (Centigrade)
November 11-12, 1930

Time	AM or PM	Outside Temperature	Container #1	Containter #2
3:00	PM	2	14	14
4:00	PM	2	15	15
5:05	PM	0	15	15
6:00	PM	-1	14	14
6:10	PM	-1	15	15
6:40	PM	-1	17	17
7:00	PM	-1	19	19
7:10	PM	-1	19	19
7:40	PM	-1	20	20
8:00	PM	-1	20	21
9:00	PM	-1	20	20
10:00	PM	-1	20	20
11:00	PM	-2	20	21
12:00	Midnight	-2	21	21
1:00	AM	-3	20	20
2:00	AM	-4	20	20
3:00	AM	-4	19	20
4:00	AM	-4	19	19
4:10	AM	-4	19	19
4:40	AM	-4	20	20
5:00	AM	-4	21	21
6:00	AM	-5	21	21
7:00	AM	-4	21	22
7:15	AM	-4	22	23
Totals		55.5	451.5	456.5
Averages		-2.3	18.31	19.02

Remarks:

(1) Started fire at 6:10 PM. Two front drafts open. If four or six containers are full, four drafts are open. Firing was light and slow. Used old reed-grass matting and burned it by small amounts.

(2) Stopped firing at 7:10 PM and closed two front drafts, but not fire box.

(3) Started firing at 4:10 AM. Opened front drafts, but kept back ones closed. Fire was light and slow. Used old reed-grass matting and burned it by small handfuls.

(4) Stopped firing at 4:55 AM. Closed upper drafts but not firebox.

(5) Started selling fruit at 7:15 AM.

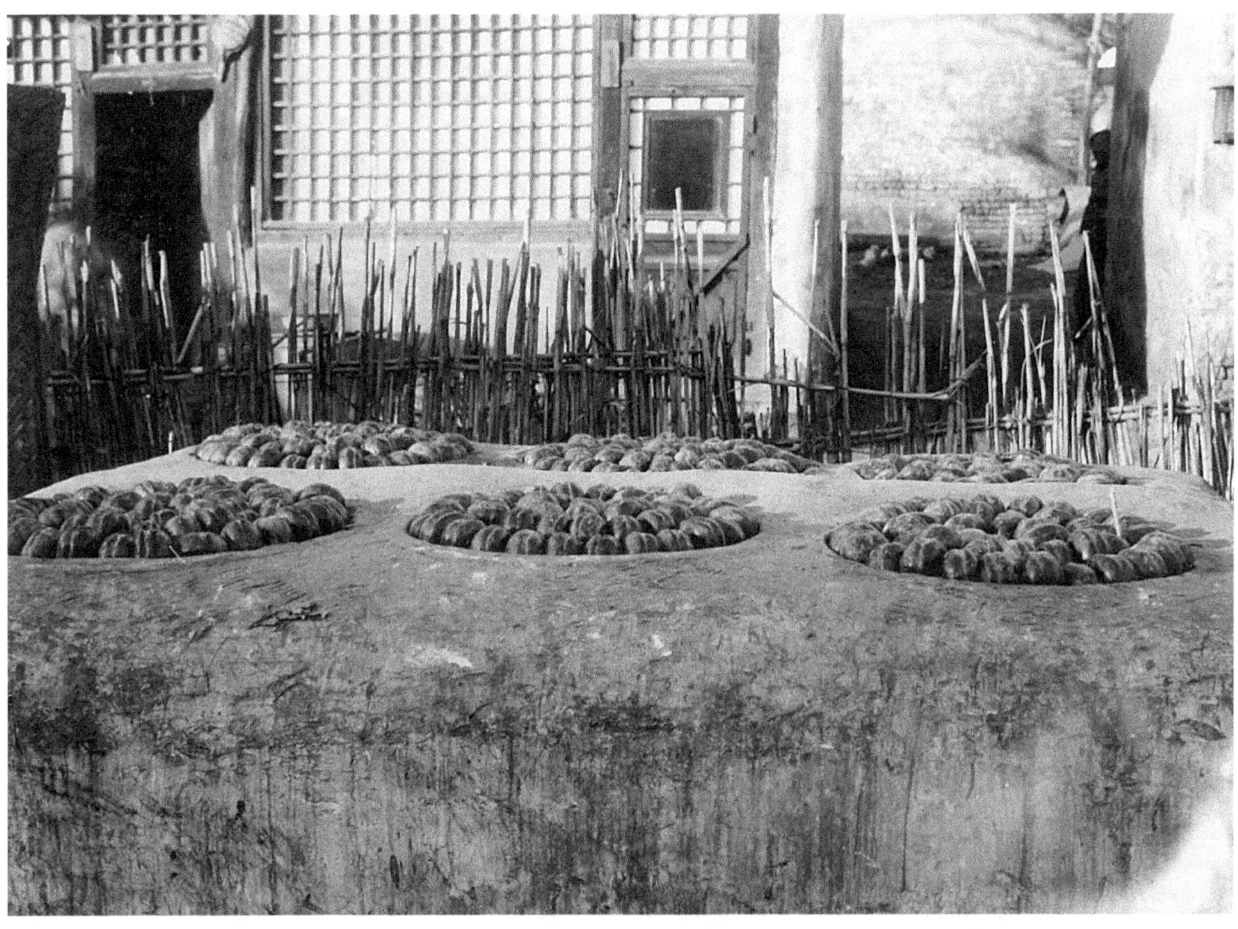

46162. *Nov. 4, 1930. A nearby view showing only the top and a little of the side of the main kiln with the six containers. Note the regularity with which the fruit at the top is placed. Also note the U.S. government stem Centigrade thermometer in the nearby container at the right.*

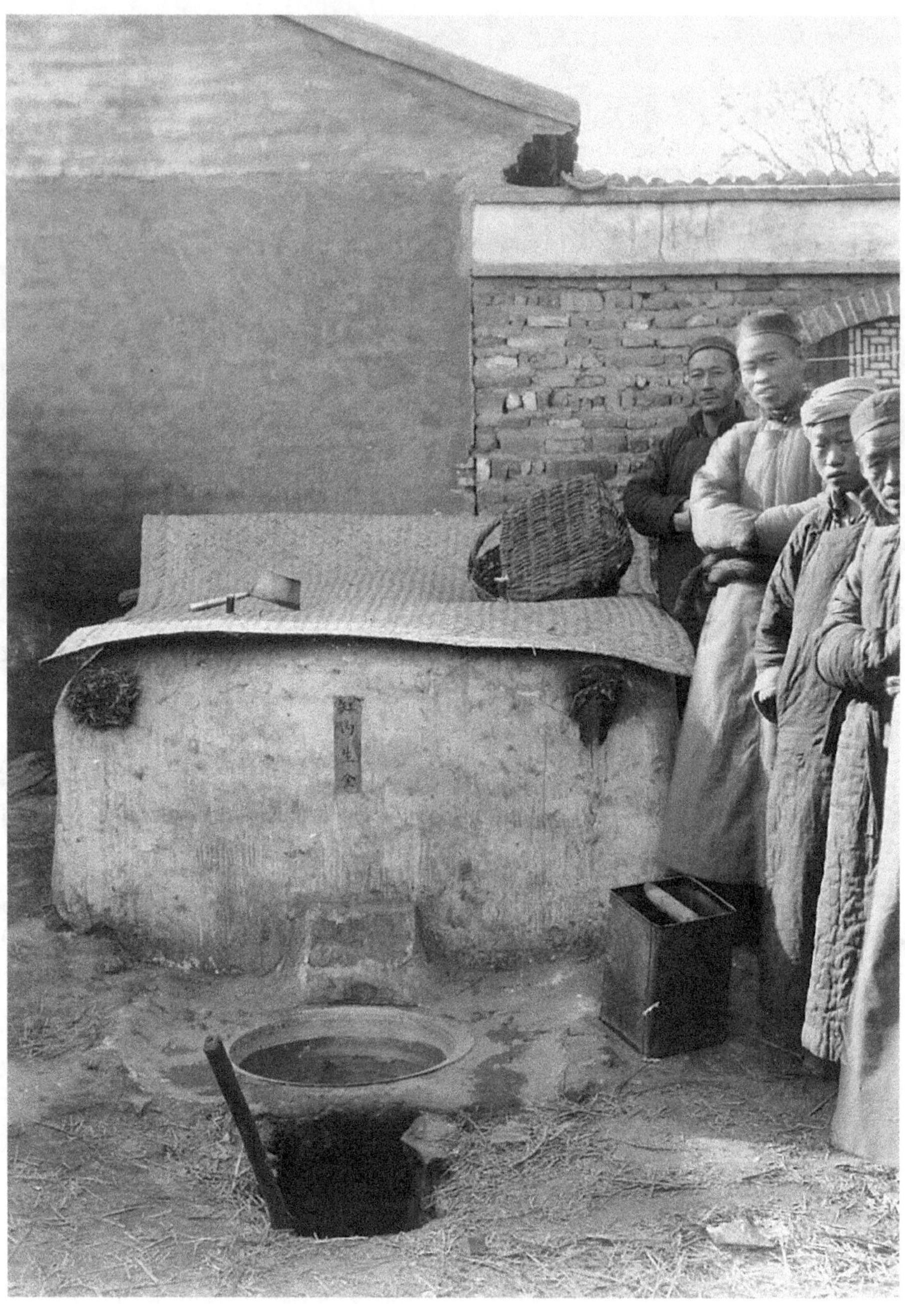

***46215.** Nov. 11, 1930. Peiping. A nearby front view of a 6-container kiln used in the hot water processing of persimmons to render them non-astringent. The covering of woven reed-grass matting covering the kiln is for the protection of the fruit from outside freezing temperature during the period of processing. Two pieces of a small bamboo cane protrude through the matting, one near the dipper at the left, the other near the basket to the right; each rests on the bottom and at the center of the two front containers. In each is suspended a commercial Centigrade thermometer. In each case, the thermometer bulb is about 20" below the surface and at the center of the container. This arrangement allowed us to make hourly and oftener temperature readings in each of the containers without uncovering or in any way disturbing the fruit. (On Nov. 4-5, we were unable to make the last reading early in the morning because the kiln tenders would not let us raise the covering to take the reading, due to below freezing temperature outside. The present arrangement was made to overcome this problem.)*

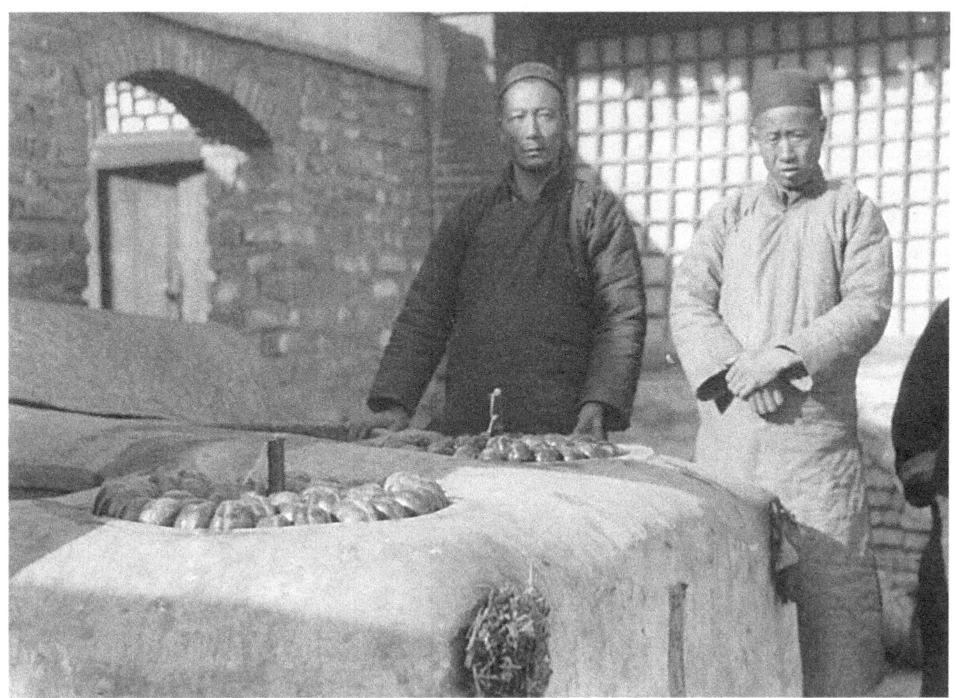

***46211.** Peiping. Two Chinese persimmon dealers at the side of the hot water treating kiln. The two filled containers are the ones we took temperature readings of from 1PM Nov. 11 to 7:15 AM Nov. 12, 1930.*

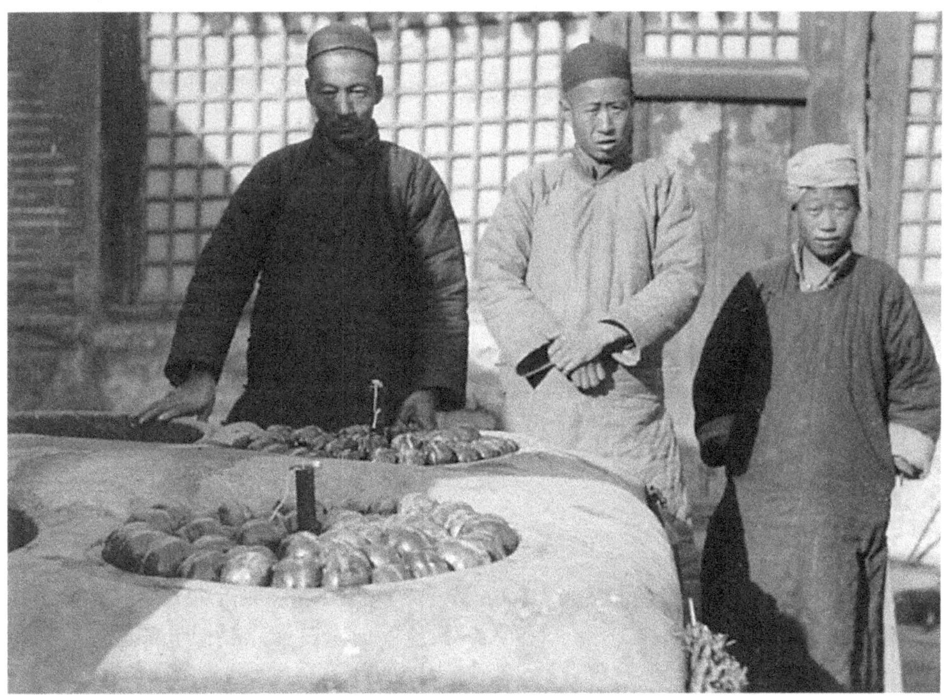

***46212.** Peiping. Another nearby view of the two filled containers in the kiln. The thermometers hang in the bamboo canes so that the mercury bulb is at about the center of the container.*

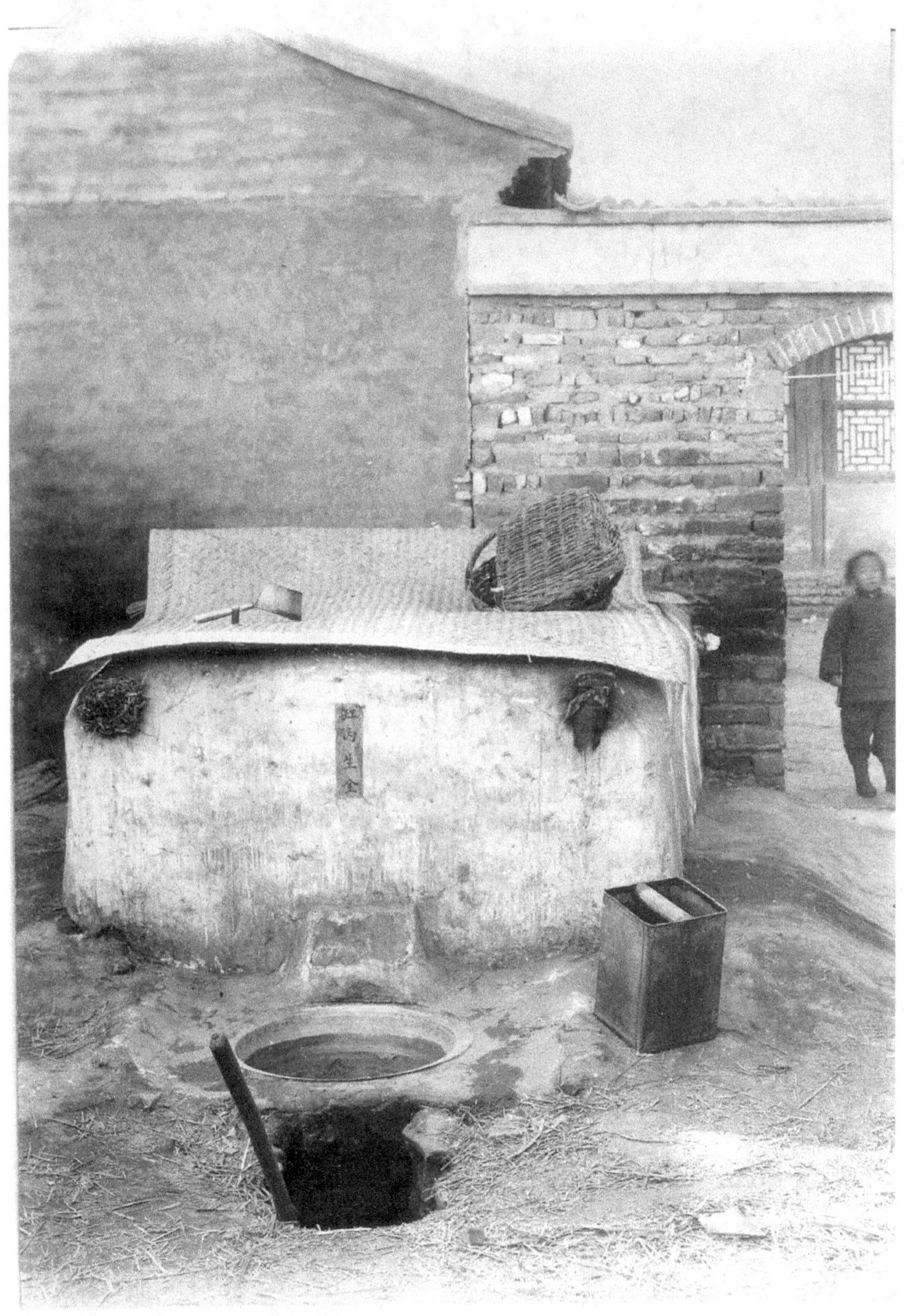

46213. *Peiping. View from in front, showing the fire opening, hot water vessel, and front view of the kiln used in the treatment of persimmons with hot water. We made temperature readings in the two front containers from 1 PM , Nov. 11, to 7:15 AM, Nov. 12, 1930.*

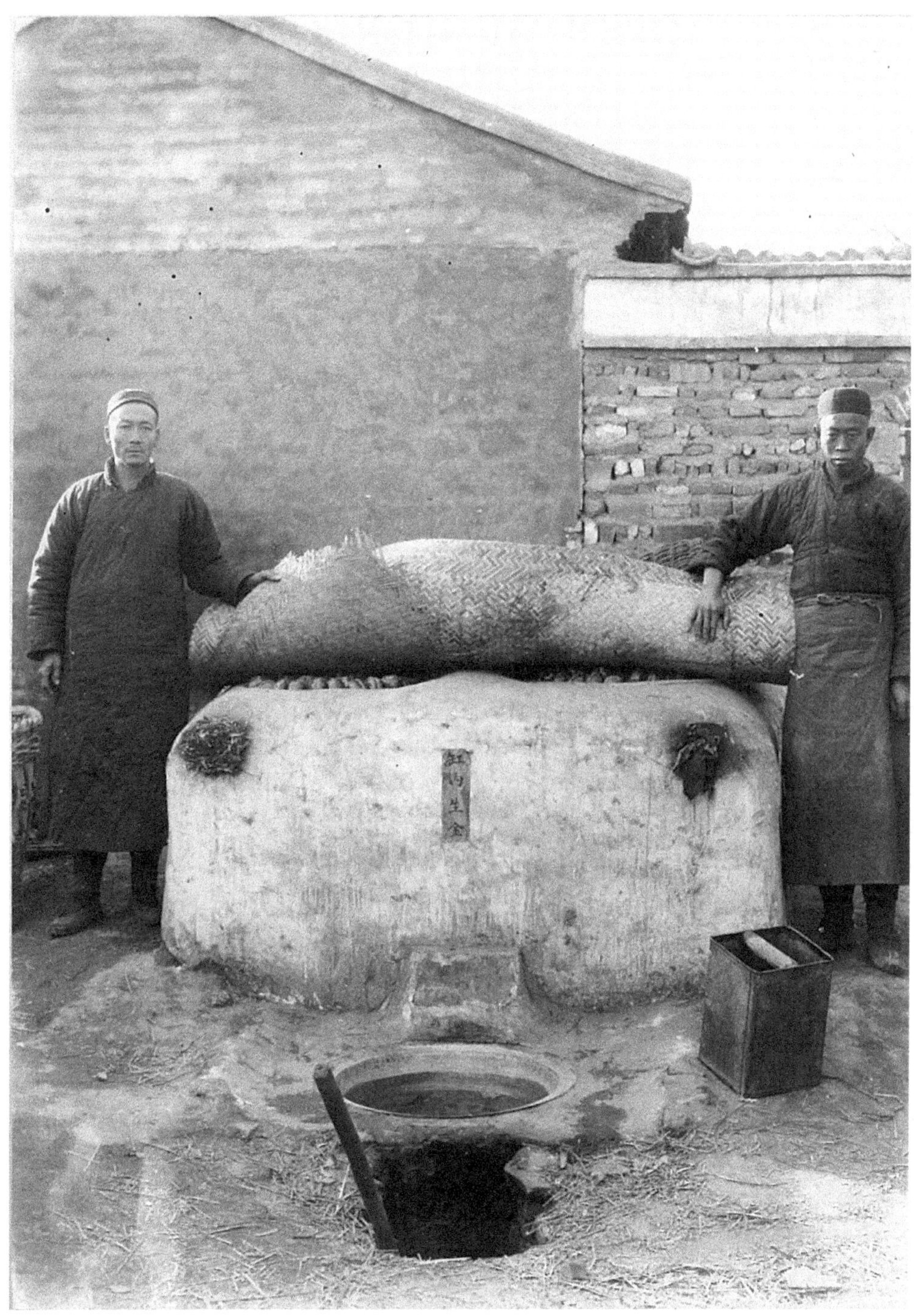

46214. ***Peiping.*** *Nearby front view of the 6-container kiln in which we took temperature records from 1 PM, Nov. 11, to 7:15 AM, Nov. 12, 1930. On each side of the kiln stand two Chinese men who assist in operating the kiln, holding back the reed-grass matting cover to expose a portion of the fruit in the two containers used in getting temperature records.*

OPEN-AIR STORAGE

The open-air storage of persimmons in the vicinity of Peking is a unique and interesting practice and, so far as is known, is peculiar to northeastern China. By this method the fruit in good condition and excellent quality may be had throughout the season from October until the middle or last of March. Meyer records the following observations on the winter storage of persimmons:

"By careful handling and by keeping the persimmons at a low temperature they can be preserved for several months. To keep them through the winter, the Chinese pile them in heaps, let them freeze thoroughly, and keep them frozen until they are needed. When wanted they are simply put into a vessel with cold water, to be thawed slowly, and they are then as good as when freshly picked. They can also be eaten when slightly frozen like sherbet, and occasionally are quite acceptable in that condition."

It is difficult to realize that practically the entire winter's supply of persimmons grown in the vicinity of Peking, amounting to many millions of fruits, is stored in beds, on the ground in the open, along terraced river banks, in the orchards along the streams, in village compounds, and on river bottoms of sand and gravel, without protection of any kind other than a bed of kaoliang stems (a variety of sorghum) beneath and a covering of a single thickness of reed-grass matting which, after the fruit is frozen, is supplemented with a covering of dry mountain grass or other available litter to a depth of about 2 feet.

The storage grounds are, as a rule, located in places not only advantageous for the handling of fruit from the orchards where it is grown, but also for the transportation of the frozen fruit by donkey or camel trains to the markets during the winter. The storage grounds are sometimes owned or leased by a fruit grower with extensive orchards or by one or more men who own or lease the storage grounds and purchase the fruit from the nearby growers and look after its storage and marketing. Sometimes the growers pool their interests and harvest, store, and market the fruit cooperatively. Each storage ground is provided with a watchman who has a hut nearby and who, with his dog and a long-handled spear, makes his rounds at regular intervals, to see that all is well and that none of the fruit is being carried away by robbers.

The storage beds are simple affairs, usually about 12 feet in width and of any desired length. The bed is prepared by digging four trenches, which, with the dirt taken from them and piled on the sides, are about 12 inches in depth and about the same in width. A bed of kaoliang stems 3 to 4 inches in thickness is laid across the ridges, and upon this the fruit is placed by hand, in regular layers, generally six persimmons deep, sometimes fewer, but never more. The five bottom layers are placed with the stems of the fruits down, while the top layer is placed with the stems up. In some sections, especially in village compounds, timbers or logs are laid on the ground and take the place of the earth ridges, and the bed of kaoliang stems is rolled down over them. After the beds are filled with persimmons, kaoliang stems or other available litter is put about the ends and sides of the beds to protect the fruits from injury. They are then covered with a single thickness of reed-grass matting, which in some instances is tied down with a small grass rope, while in others it is weighed down with small stones to prevent its being carried away by the wind. After the persimmons are frozen, this covering is supplemented by from 18 to 24 inches of loose, dry grass or other litter.

Men at the storage grounds explained that the trenches and spaces under the persimmon beds were for drainage in case of rain or snow. However, it is probable that their greatest importance is to allow a circulation of air, which in the fall, assists in reducing the temperature of the fruit in the beds, and in the winter insures a more even freezing than otherwise would be possible.

In one locality, near the village of Panpitien, above Toli, the writers saw persimmons bedded down in a mixture of dry grass and leaves and covered with reed-grass matting supported over the beds on a low A-shaped frame made of kaoliang stalks. This was on March 8, 1925. The owner of the small storage yard was reluctant to uncover any portion of the beds, claiming that on account of the lateness of the season, the fruit, when exposed to the air, would have a tendency to turn dark, thus reducing its market value.

An approximate idea of the importance of the persimmon industry in the vicinity of Peking and the extent to which open-air cold storage of the fruit is practiced may be gained from the fact that in a walk of a day and a half up the small valley of Clearwater River, above Toli, about 50 miles northwest of Peking, storage beds were seen which were estimated to contain from 7,000,000 to 8,000,000 persimmons, and it was said that more than 10,000,000, or slightly more or less than 2500 tons, were in storage in that one small valley.

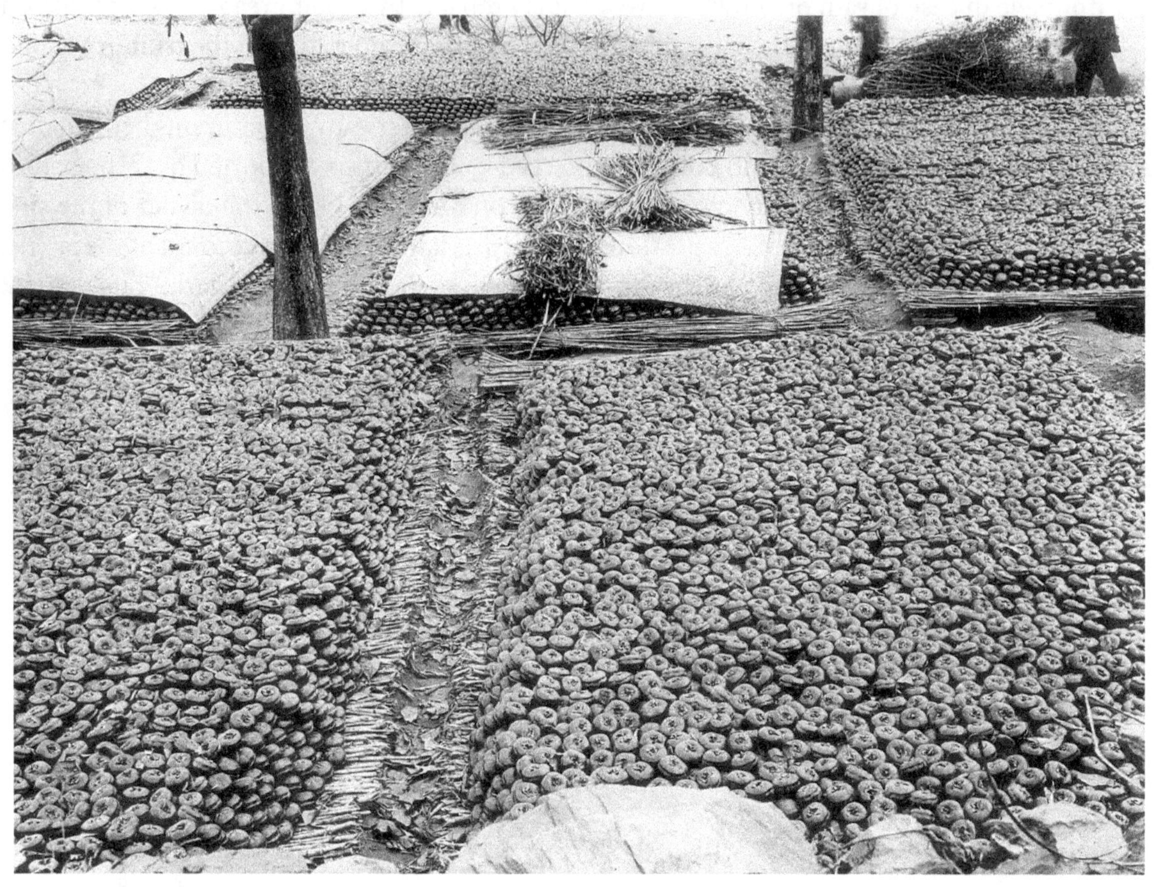

29844. *Nov. 6, 1924. Hei Lung Kuan. A close-up view of covered and uncovered beds of persimmons on the storage ground.*

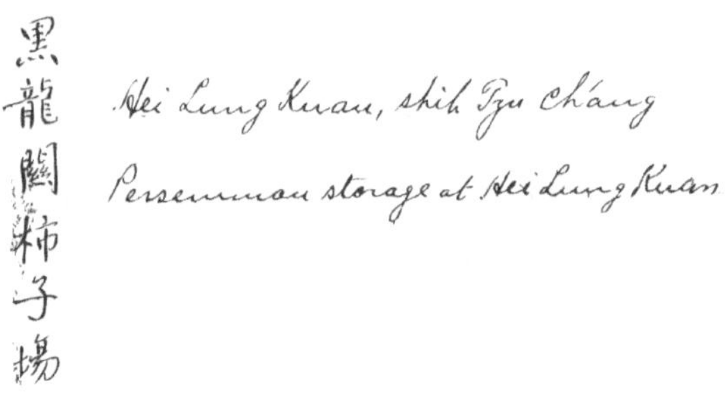

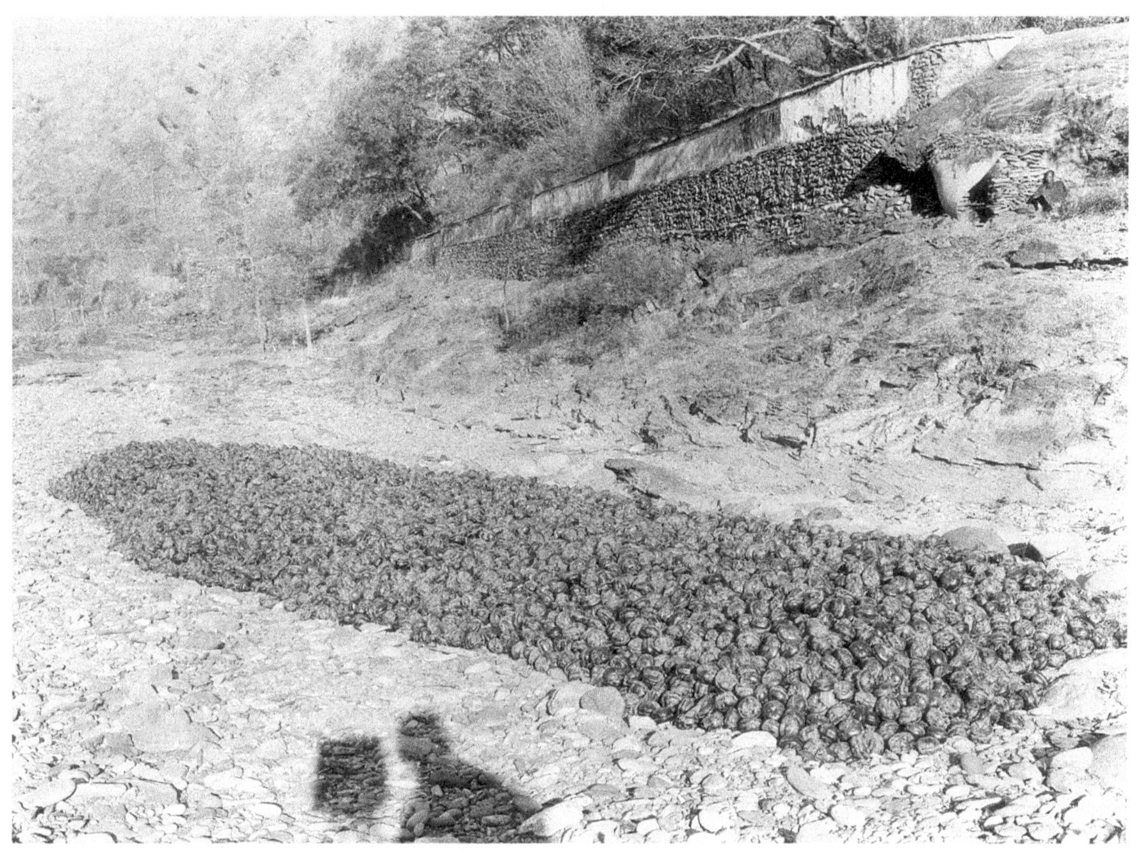

29841. *Nov. 6, 1924. Hei Lung Kuan. Persimmons piled on the rocky river bottomland.*

黑龍關 village Hei Lung Kuan
柿子, Shih Tzu, Persimmons

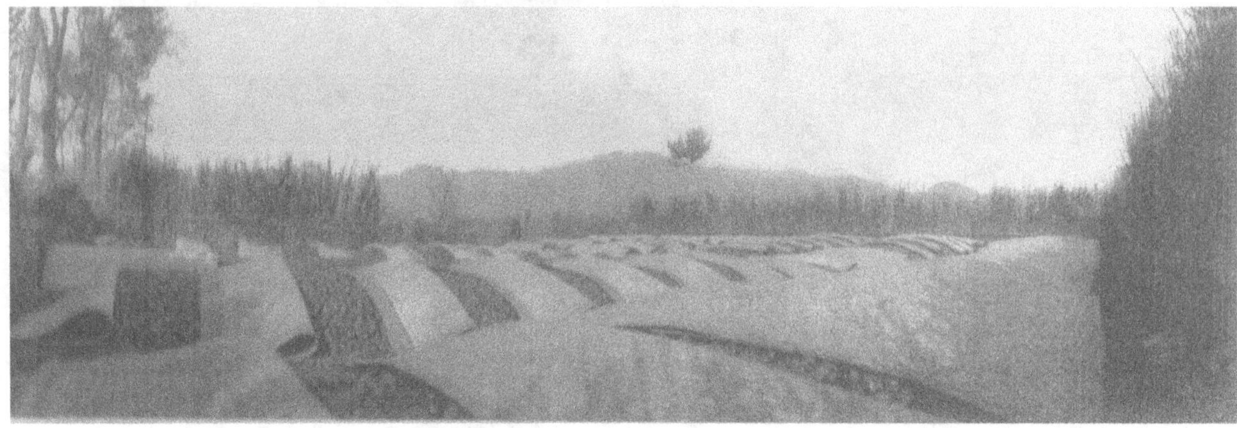

46197. *Hsiang Tang village. A panoramic view of a portion of the first persimmon storage yard visited at the village, some 25 miles to the north of Peiping.*

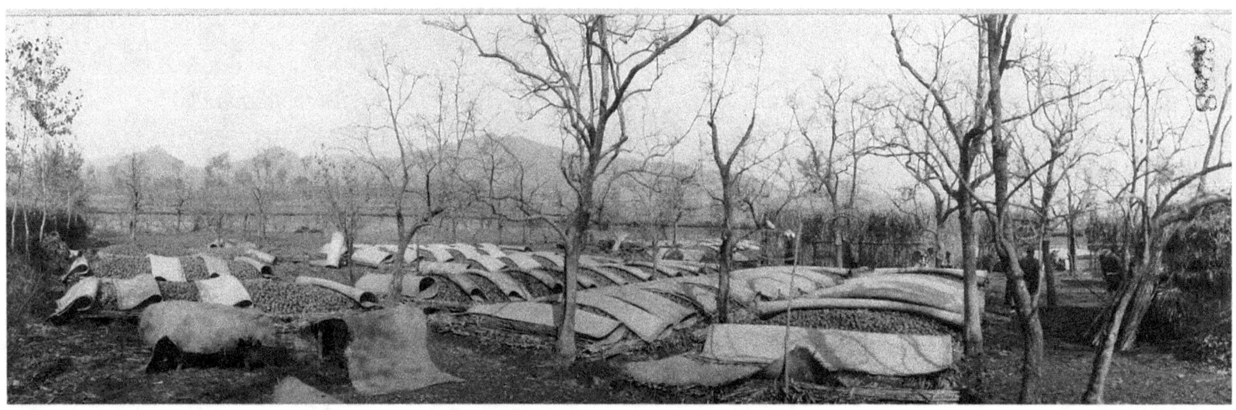

46188. *Hsiang Tang village. A panoramic view showing a good portion of the open-air persimmon storage yard at the village, some 25 miles to the north of Peiping.*

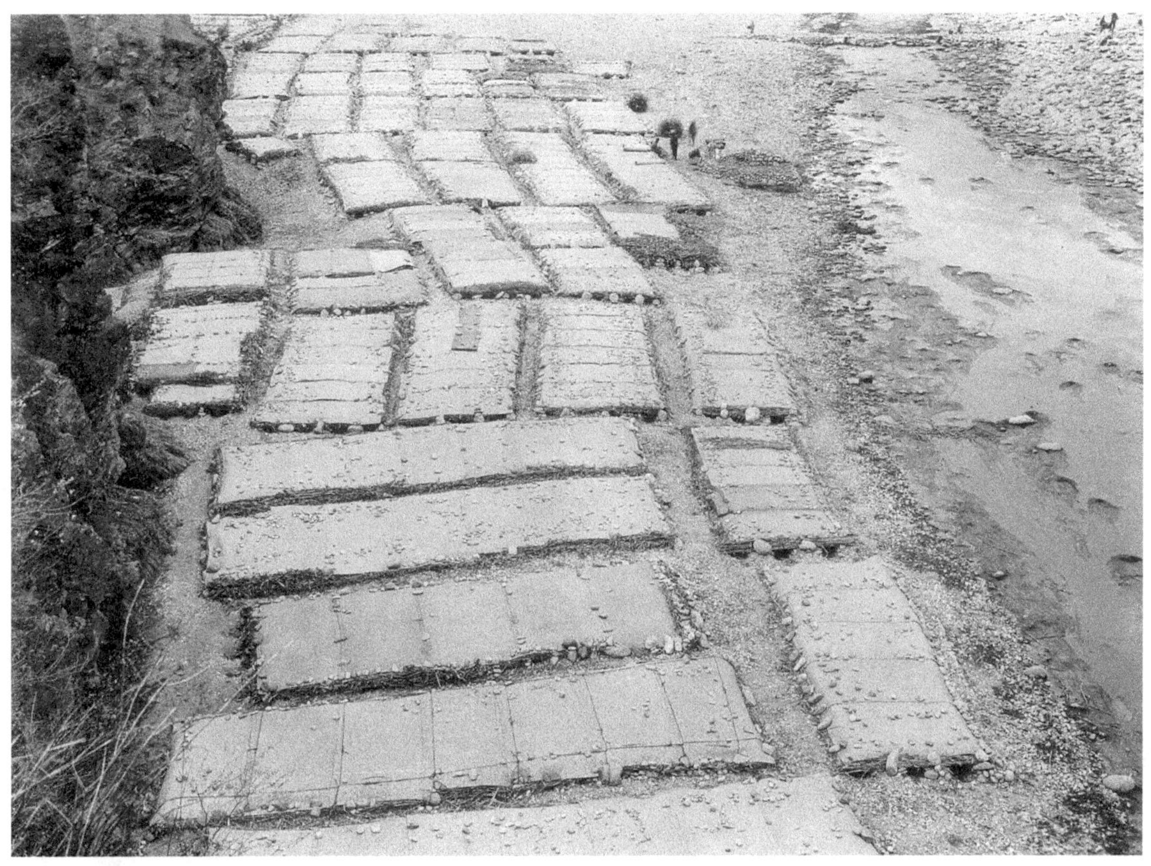

29846. *Nov. 6, 1924. Fo Tzu Chuang. Upwards of 2 million persimmons stored on the north side of a river bluff on the gravelly Clearwater River bottomland.*

佛子庄柿子場

Fo Tzu Chuang shih Tzu cháng

Persimmon storage at Fo Tzu Chuang

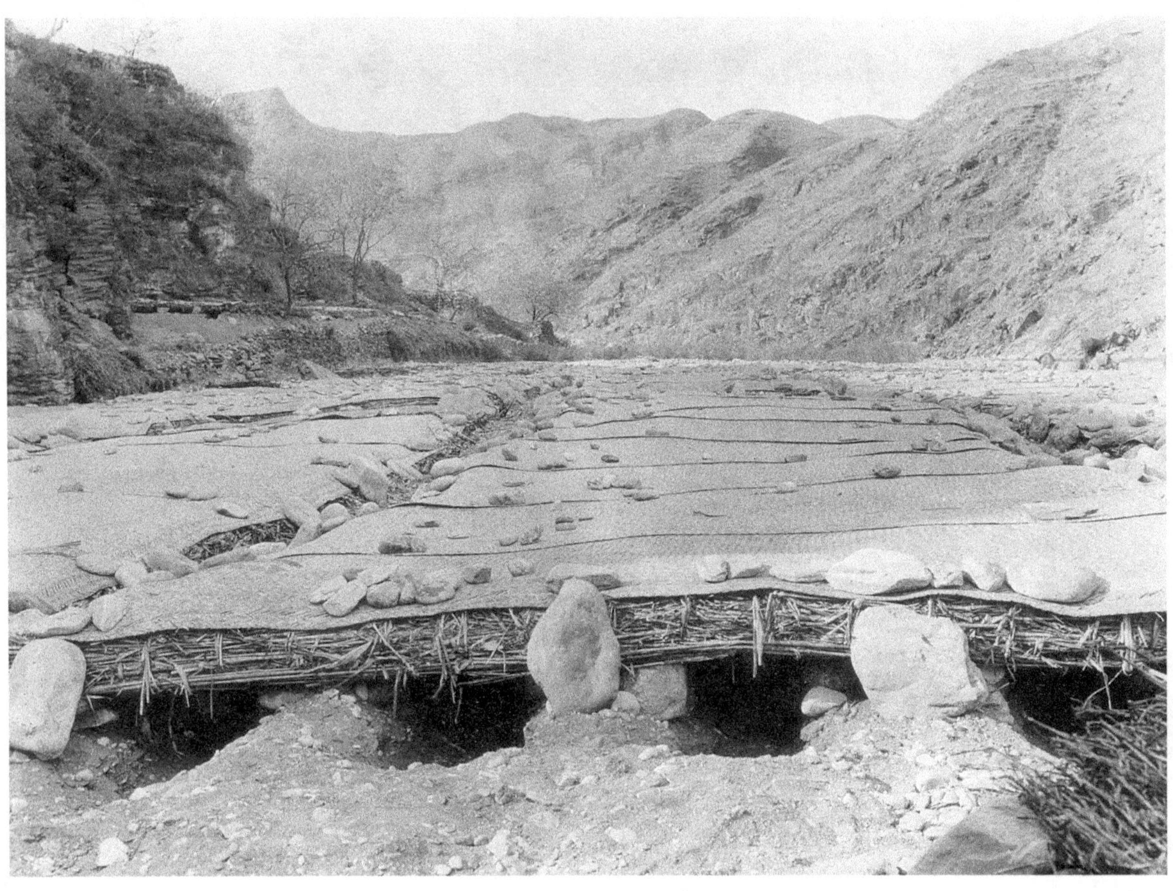

29848. *Nov. 6, 1924. Fo Tzu Chuang. Looking over beds of stored persimmons and at the end of one of the beds on the river bottomland showing drainage and air trenches.*

佛子庄柿子場

Fo Tzu Chuang shih Tzu cháng

Persimmon storage at Fo Tzu Chuang

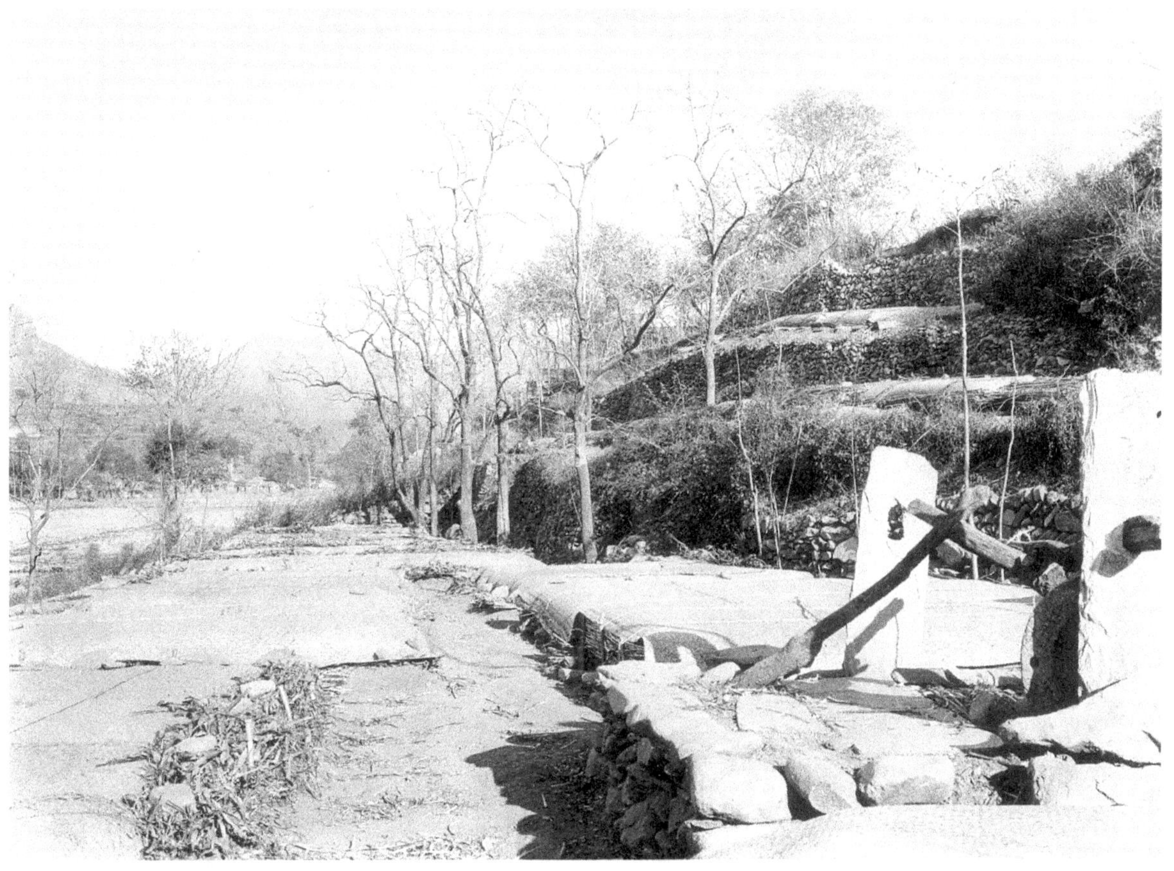

***29824.** Nov. 5, 1924. Ho Pei village. Open-air winter storage beds of persimmon fruits on a terraced bank of the Clearwater River near the village, about 60 miles north of Peking. The grass mat coverings are in some instances tied down with small handmade grass ropes and in others weighted down with small stones. This is to prevent their being dislodged by the wind. Later in the season, after the fruit is frozen, an additional covering of about 2 feet of loose dry grass or other litter is added to guard against thawing of the fruit due to temperature variations throughout the storage season (November to March).*

河北柿子場

Ho Pei, shih Tzu Chang

Persimmon storage at Ho Pei

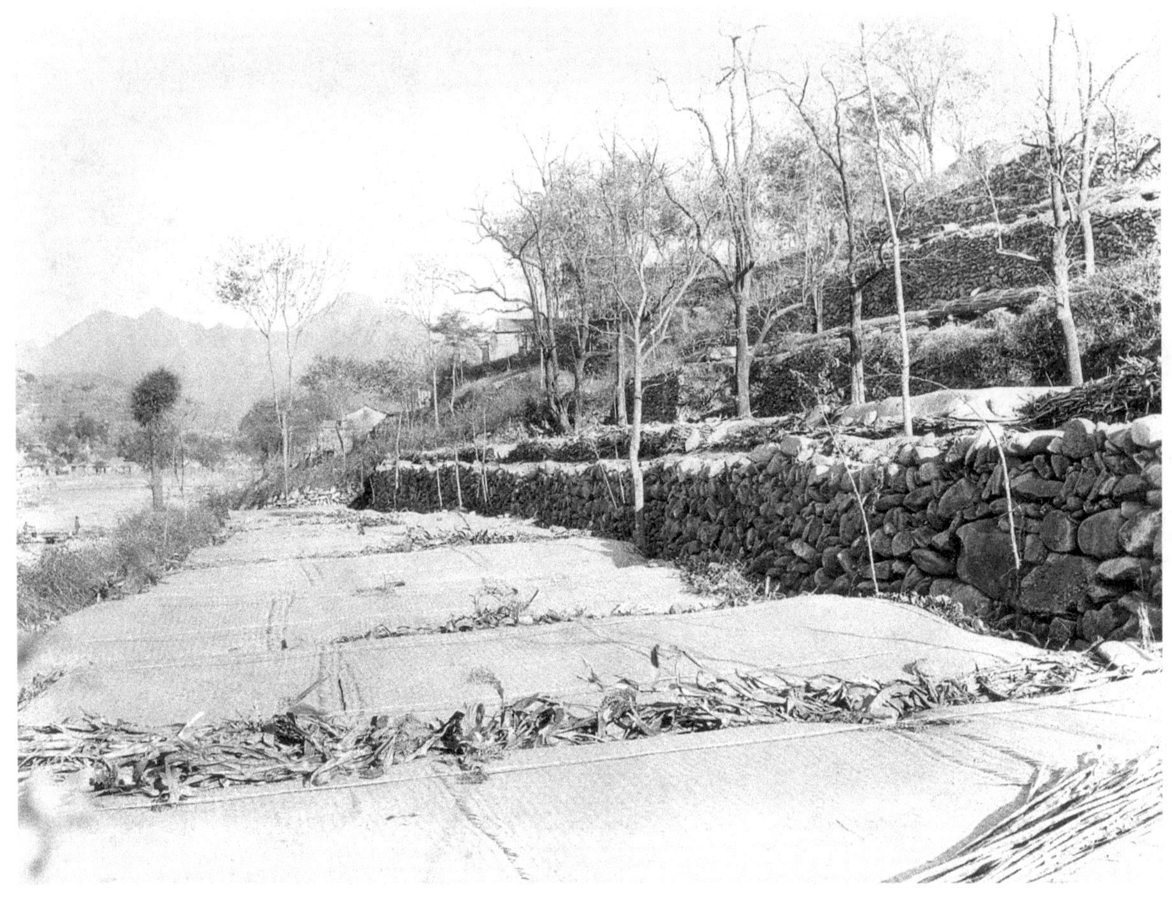

29826. *Nov. 5, 1924. Ho Pei village. Portion of persimmon storage bed on river bank terraces on Clearwater River near Ho Pei.*

河北柿子場
Ho Pei, shih Tzu Cháng
Persimmon storage, at Ho. Pei.

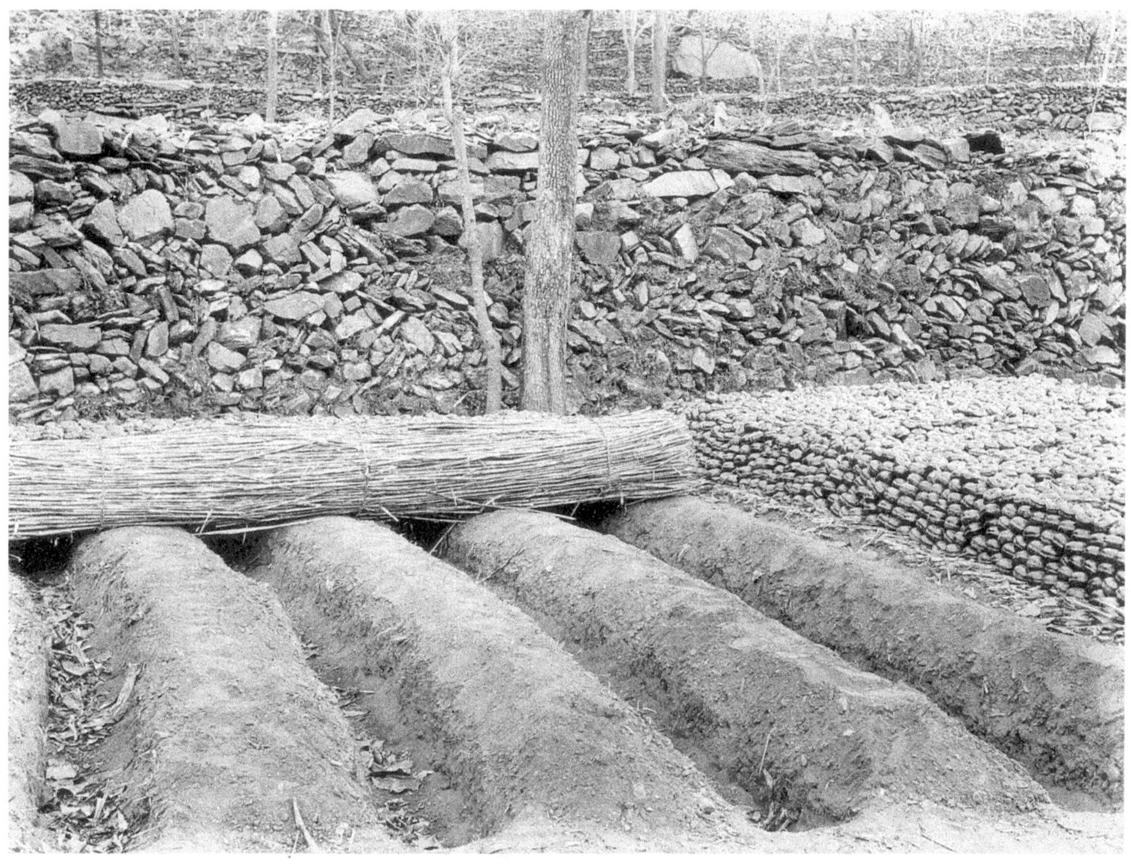

***29829.** Nov. 5, 1924. Hei Lung Kuan. Trenches over which kaoliang (sorghum) stalks are placed to make the bed for persimmons. The trenches serve two purposes: drainage and cold air conductor.*

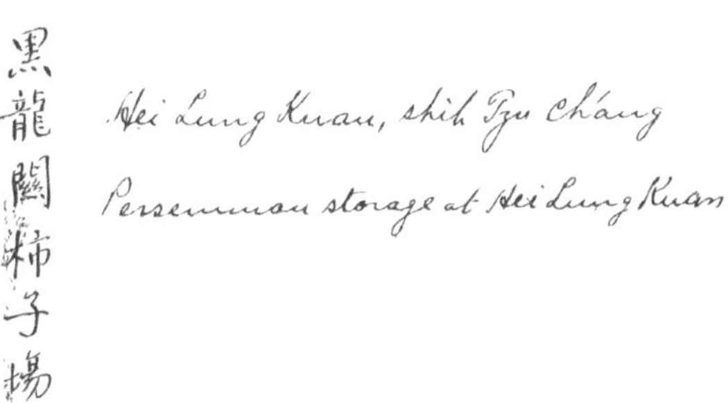

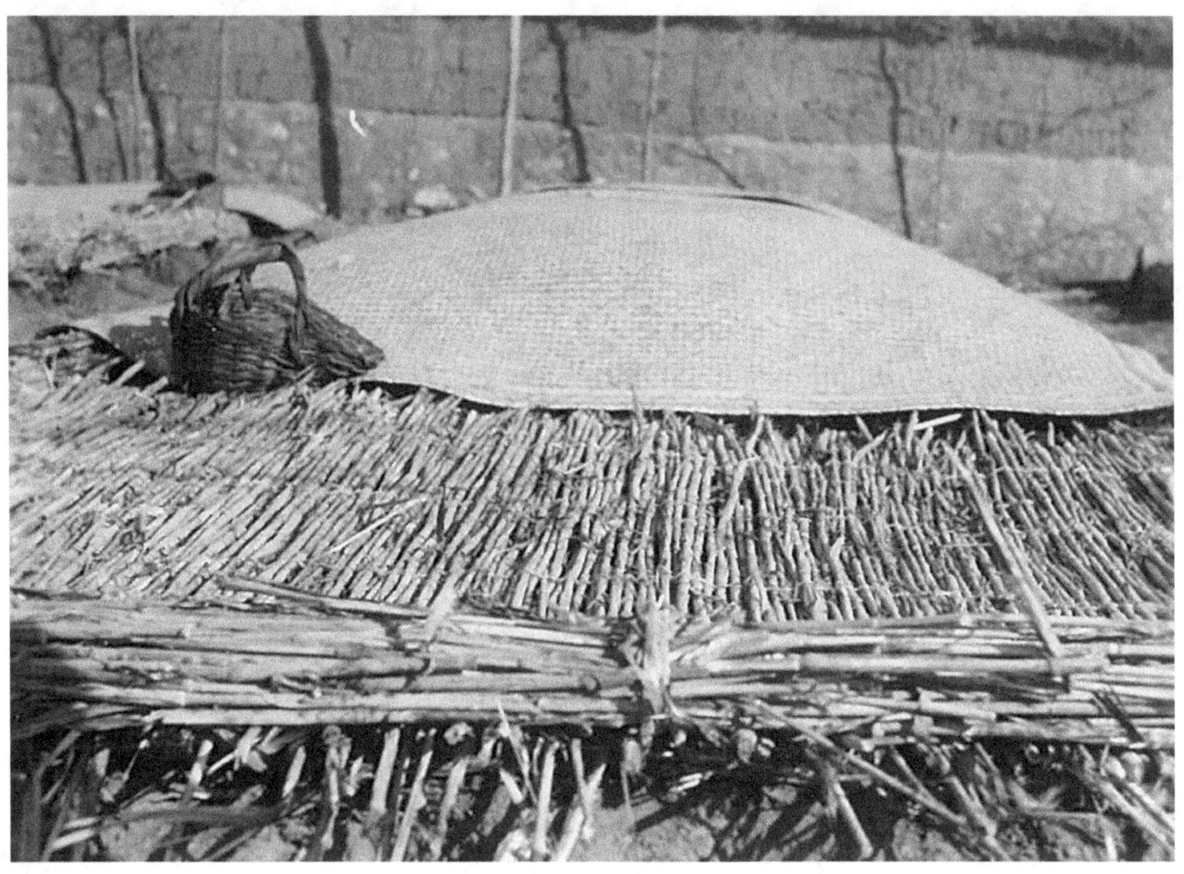

46235. *Hsiang Tang village. Bed mat and covered beds in Mr. Chi's persimmon storage yard. In the foreground is the bed or mat of kaoliang stems on which the persimmons are piled. Further back is a filled bed covered with a mat.*

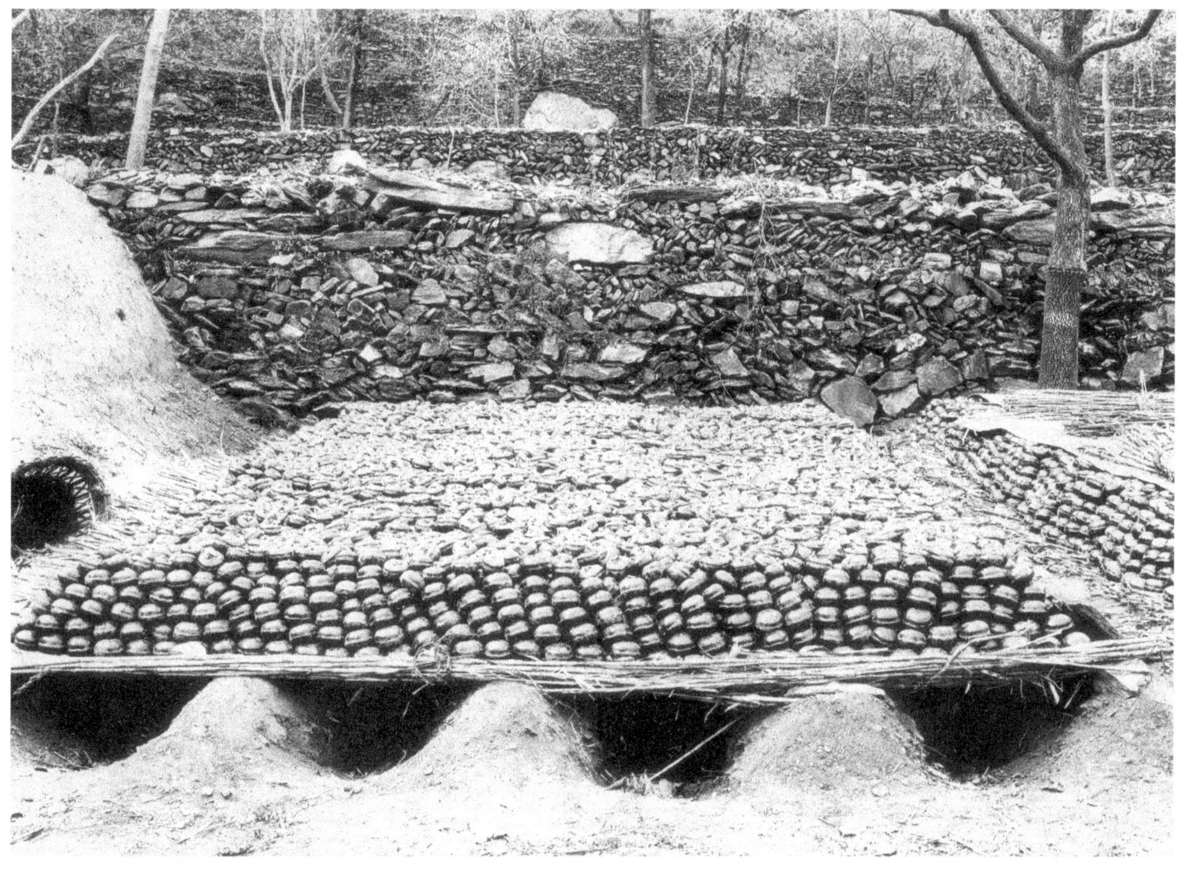

29842. *Nov. 6, 1924. Hei Lung Kuan. A close-up view of the end of an uncovered bed of persimmons showing trenches under the bed.*

黑龍關柿子塲
Hei Lung Kuan shih Tzu ch'ang
Persimmon storage at Hei Lung Kuan

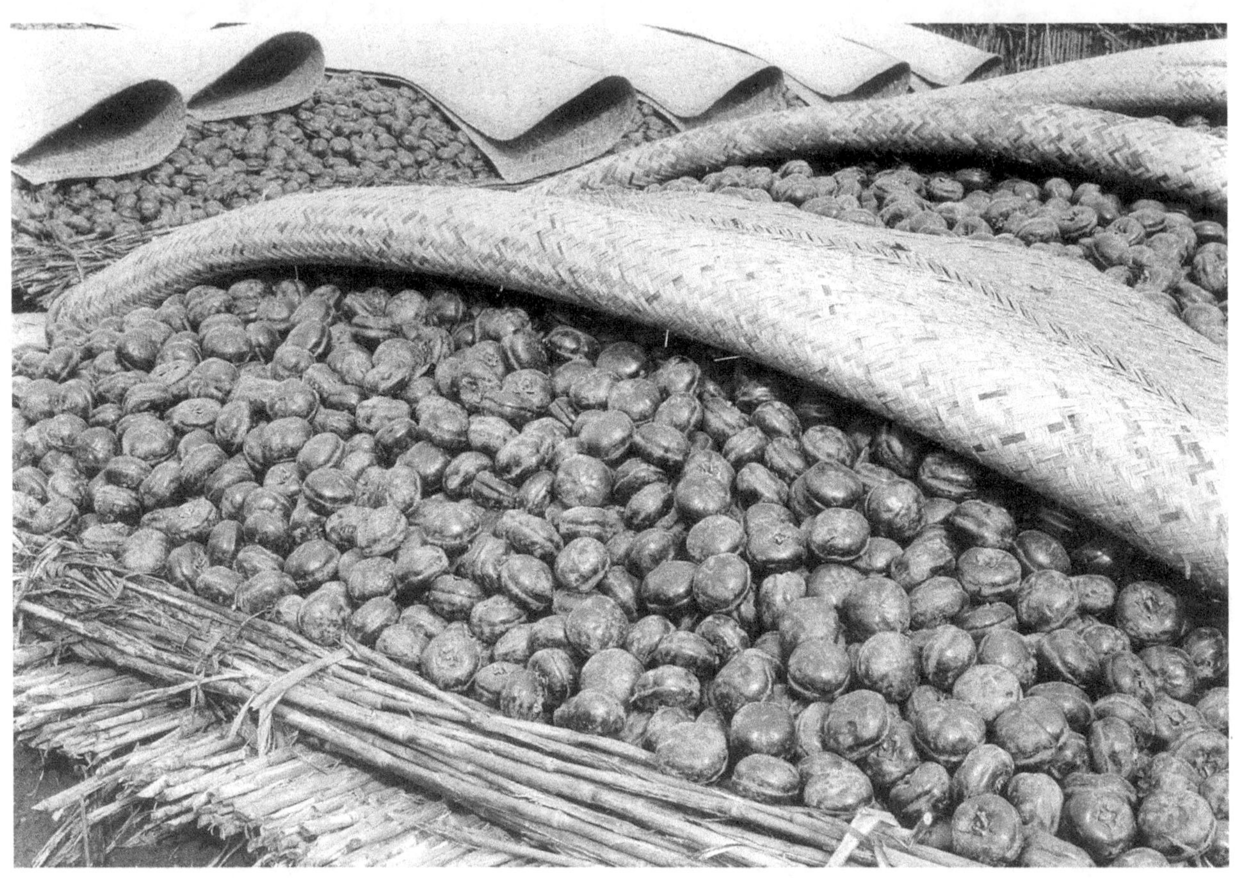

46180. *Hsiang Tang village, a few miles northwest of Tang Shan. A fairly nearby view of the greater part of the end of one of the numerous beds in this storage yard where about 1,000,000 persimmons are being stored.*

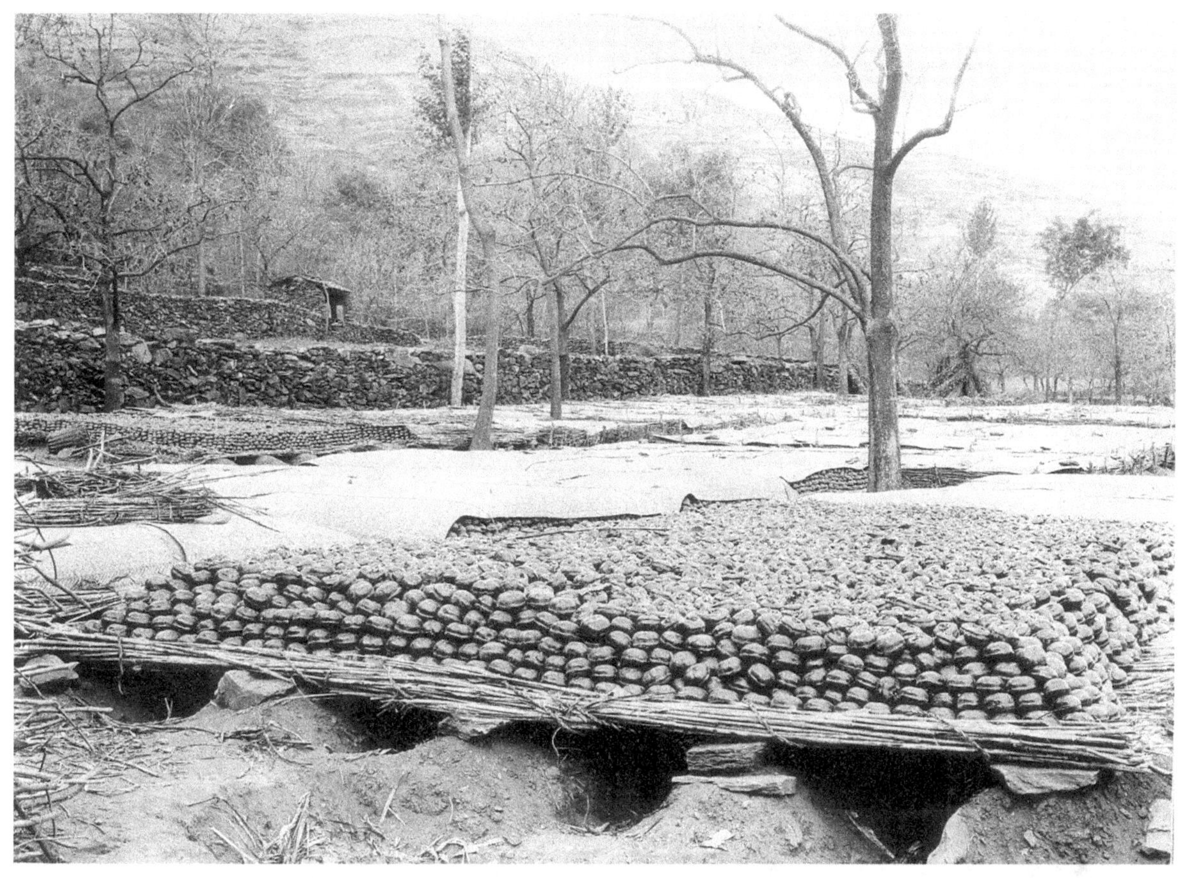

***29845.** Nov. 6, 1924. Hei Lung Kuan. View of the end of one of the large persimmon storage beds showing trenches, kaoliang bed, and layers of persimmons.*

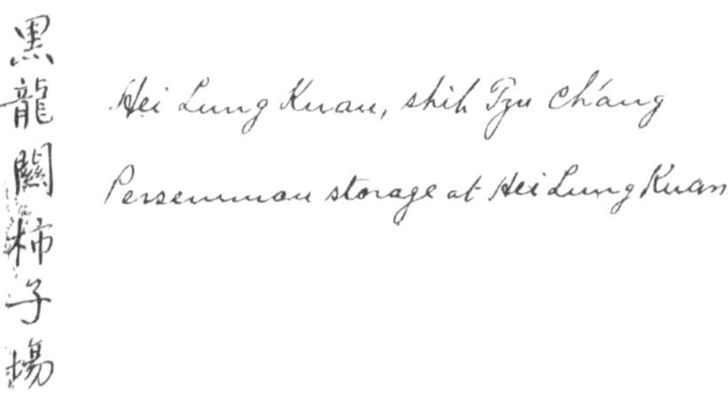

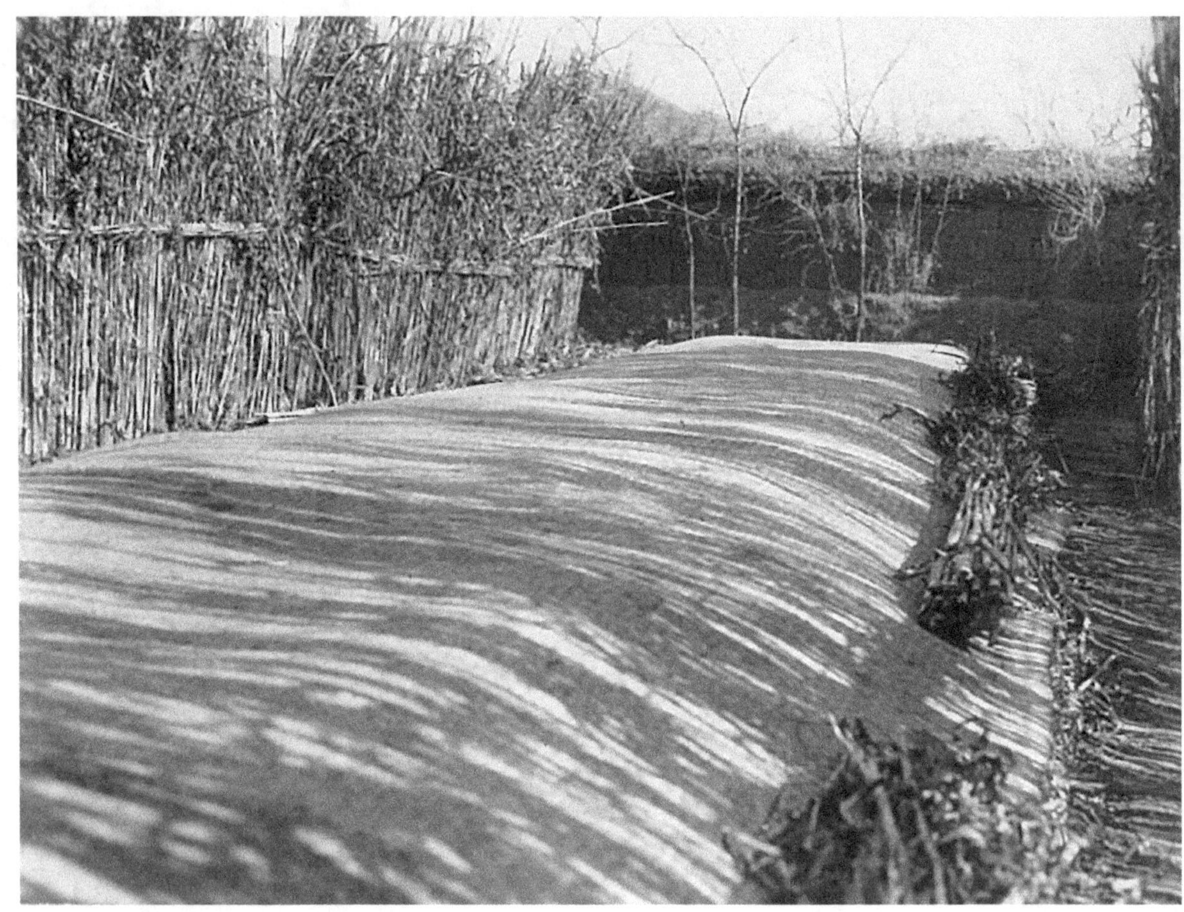

46233. *Hsiang Tang village. A bed of fruit covered in the storage yard of Mr. Chi. The temporary kaoliang stalk fences are to cast shading on the persimmon beds to keep them cool.*

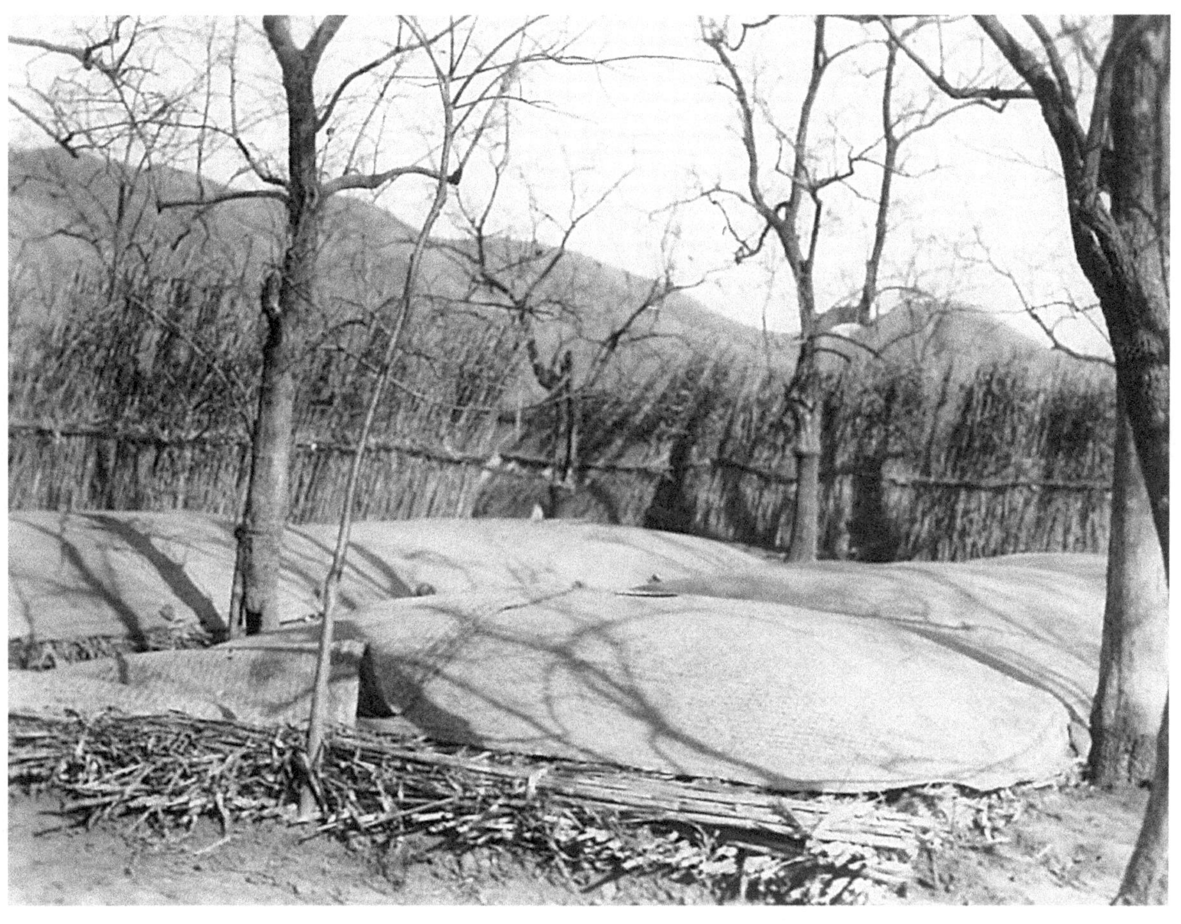

***46234.** Hsiang Tang village. Persimmon storage beds in Mr. Chi's storage yard. Fenced beds are covered with reed-grass mats. These beds are located among persimmon trees which cast some shade on the beds.*

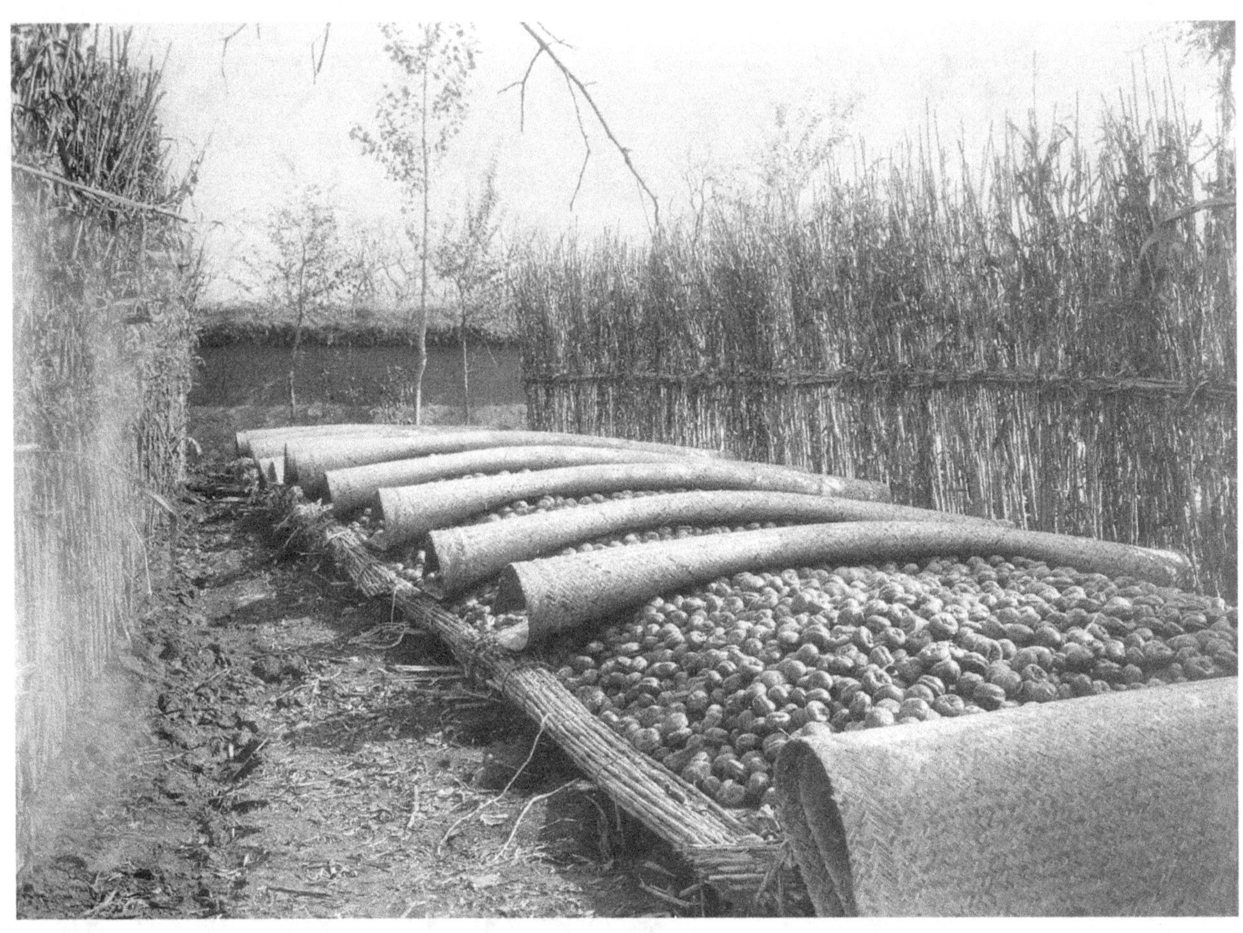

46192. *Hsiang Tang village. View of one of a number of similar storage beds in Mr. Chi's open-air storage yard. The koaliang fences to the sides of the beds are for winter shade to help carry the beds at an even temperature.*

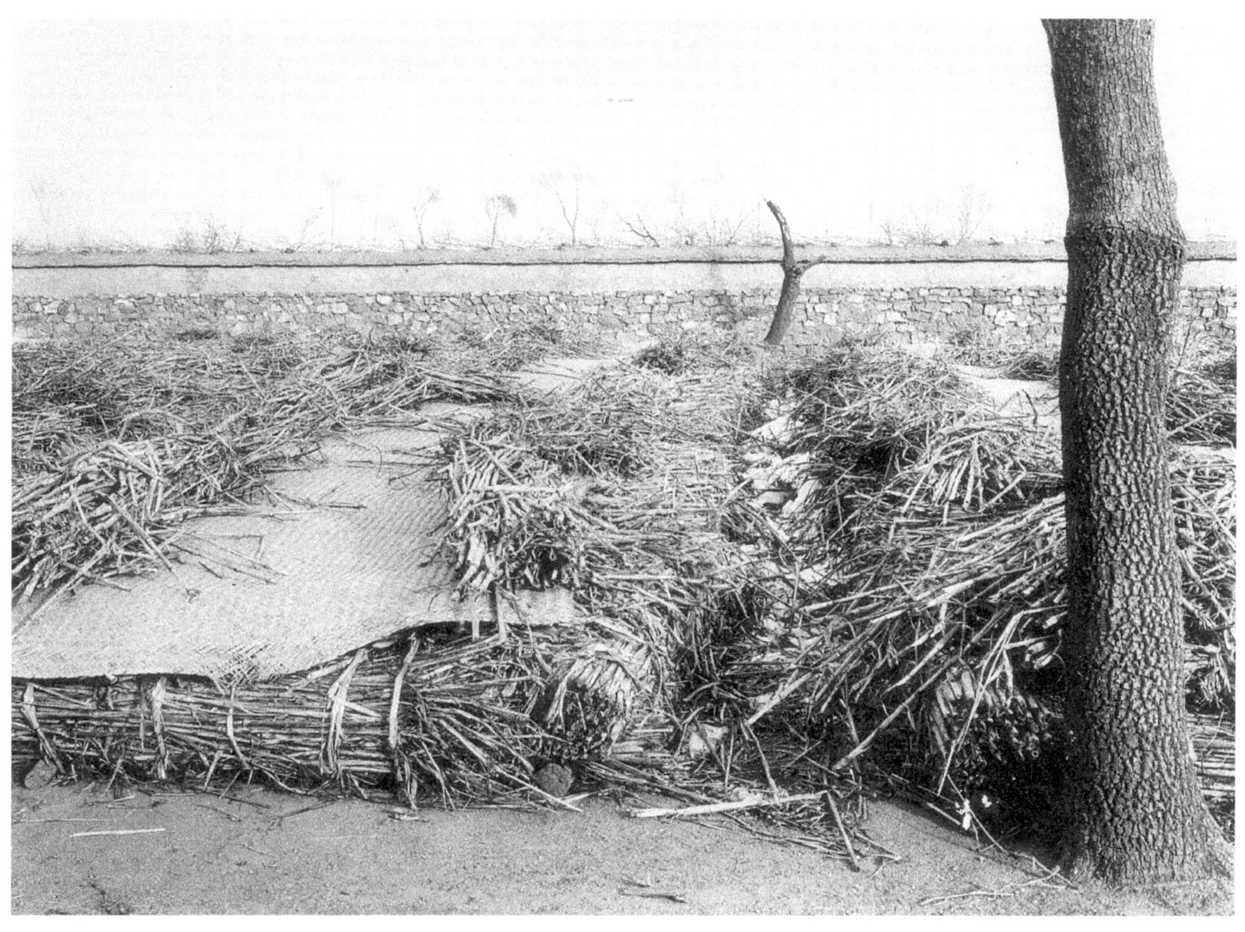

***38045.** Nov. 28, 1924. Tai Ling Yuan. Looking over and between beds of stored persimmons. The white between the beds is snow.*

太陵園 village, Tái Ling Yuan
柿子場 Shih Tzu Chang
Persimmon storage

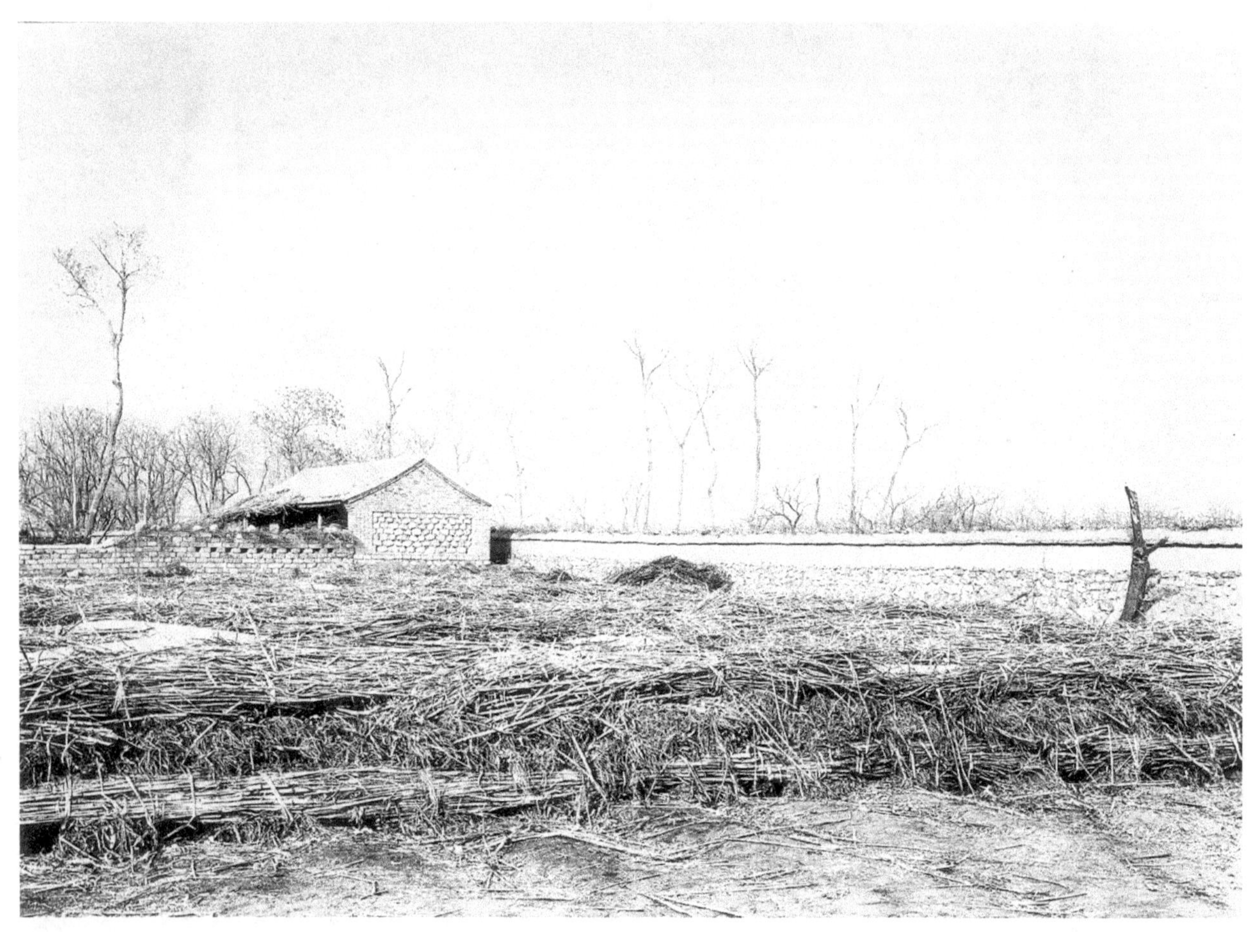

38042. *Nov. 28, 1924. Tai Ling Yuan. A portion of the winter persimmon storage ground where an estimated 200,000 to 300,000 persimmons are bedded down for the winter.*

太陵園 village, Tai Ling Yuan
柿子場 Shih Tzu Chang
Persimmon storage

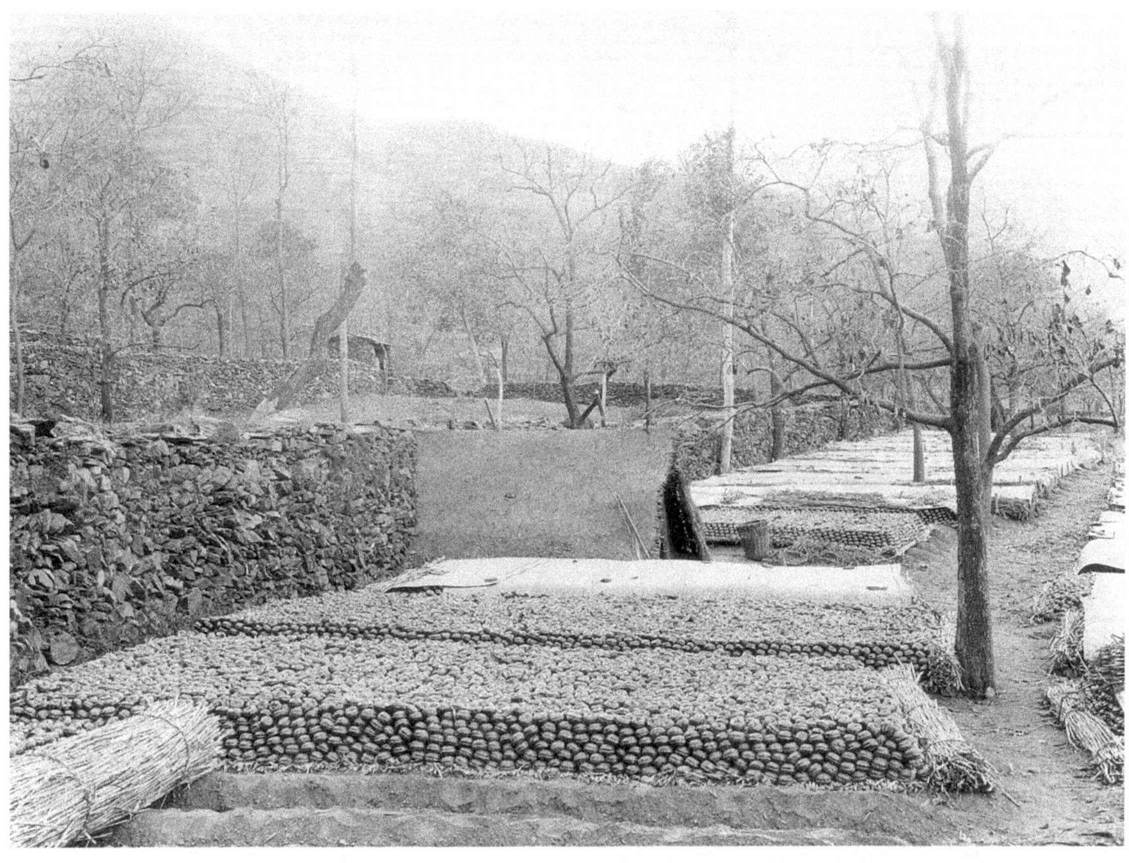

29827. *Nov. 5, 1924. Hei Lung Kuan. A long line of persimmon storage beds at the base of a storm wall terrace. Some of the beds are still uncovered.*

黑龍關柿子場
Hei Lung Kuan shih Tzu ch'ang
Persimmon storage at Hei Lung Kuan

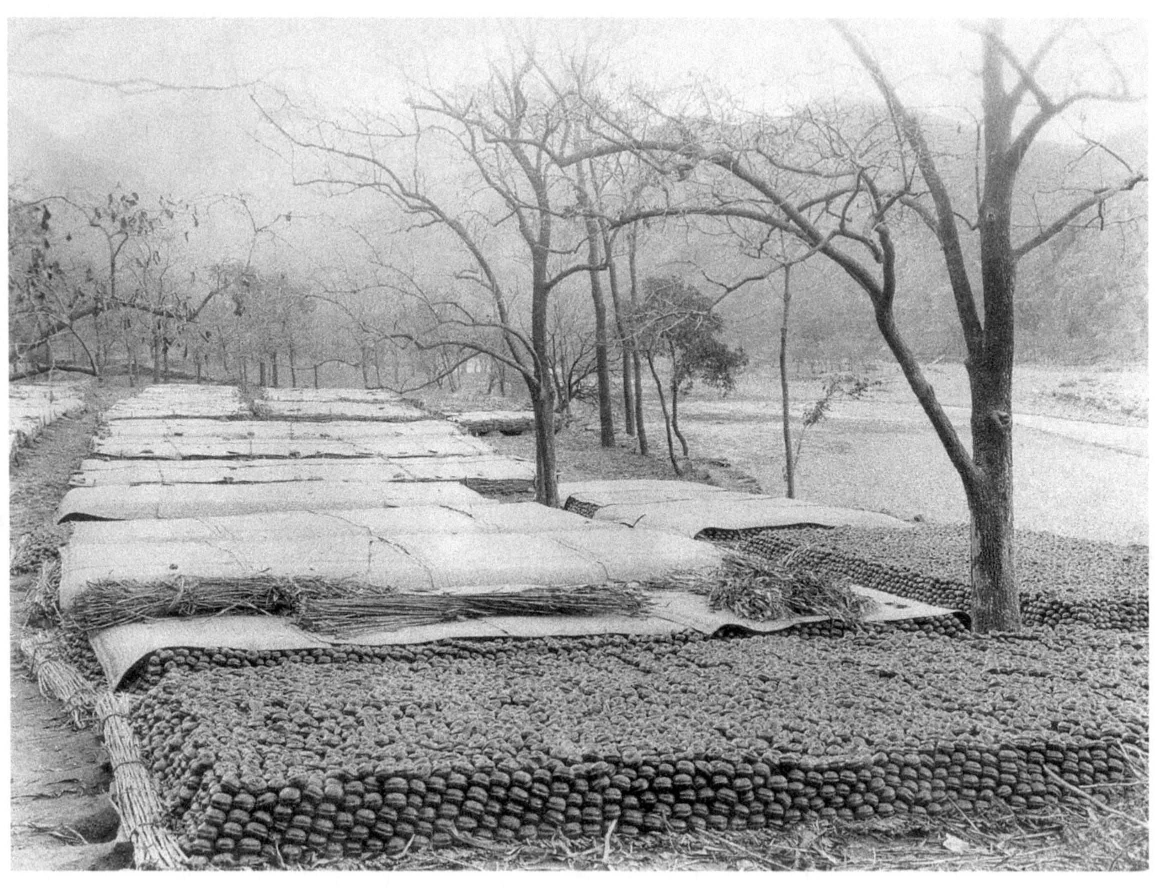

29828. *Nov 5, 1924. Hei Lung Kuan. Quite a number of persimmon storage beds, containing 1 to 1 ½ million fruits.*

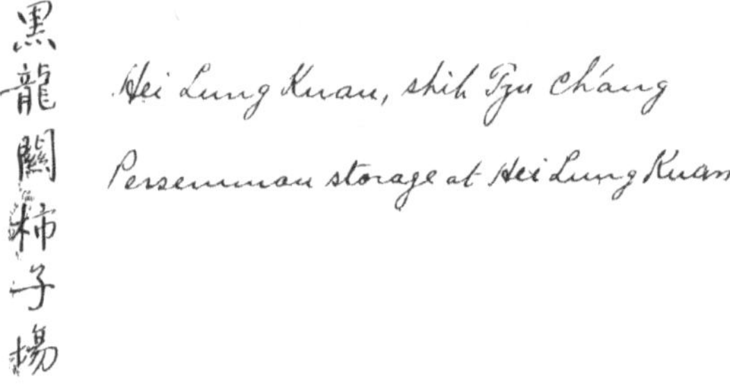

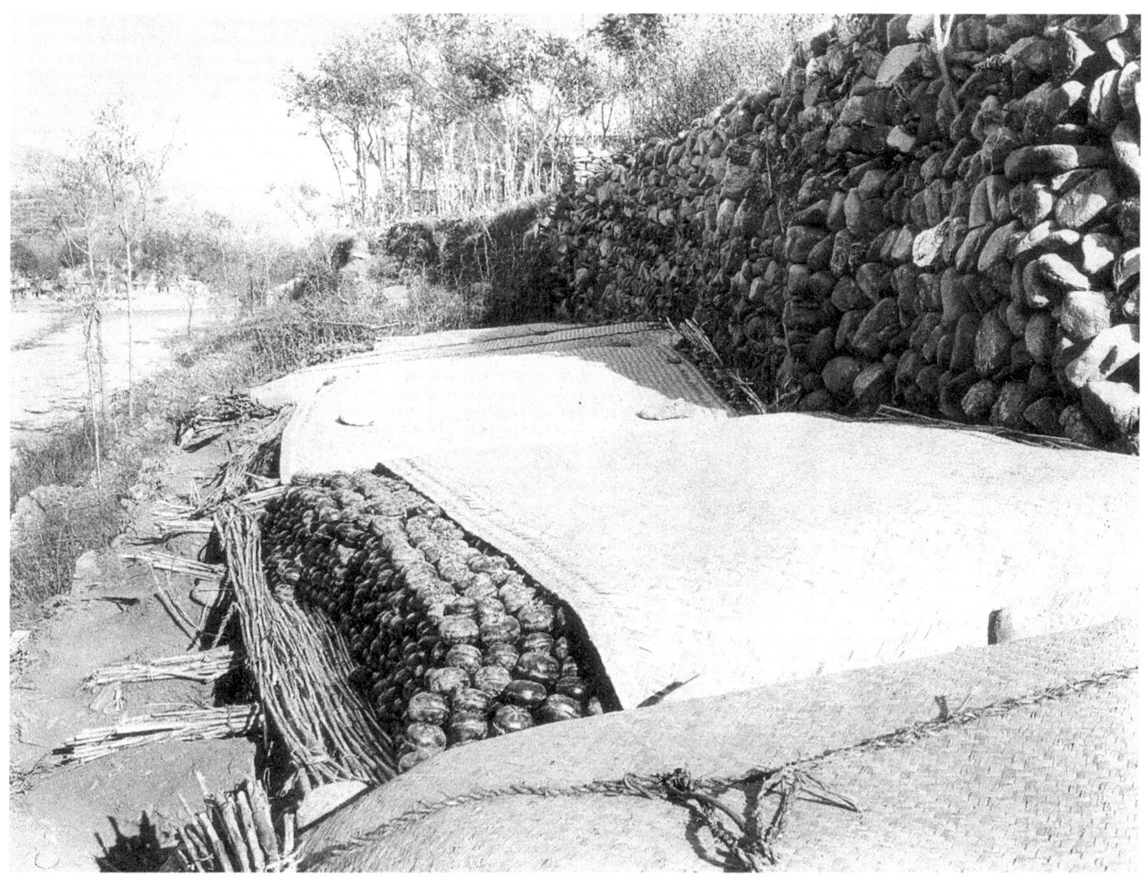

29825. *Nov. 5, 1924. Ho Pei village. A close-up view of a few of many storage beds of persimmons near Ho Pei on the bank of the Clearwater River.*

河北柿子塲
Ho Pei, shih Tzu Cháng
Persemmon storage, at Ho Pei

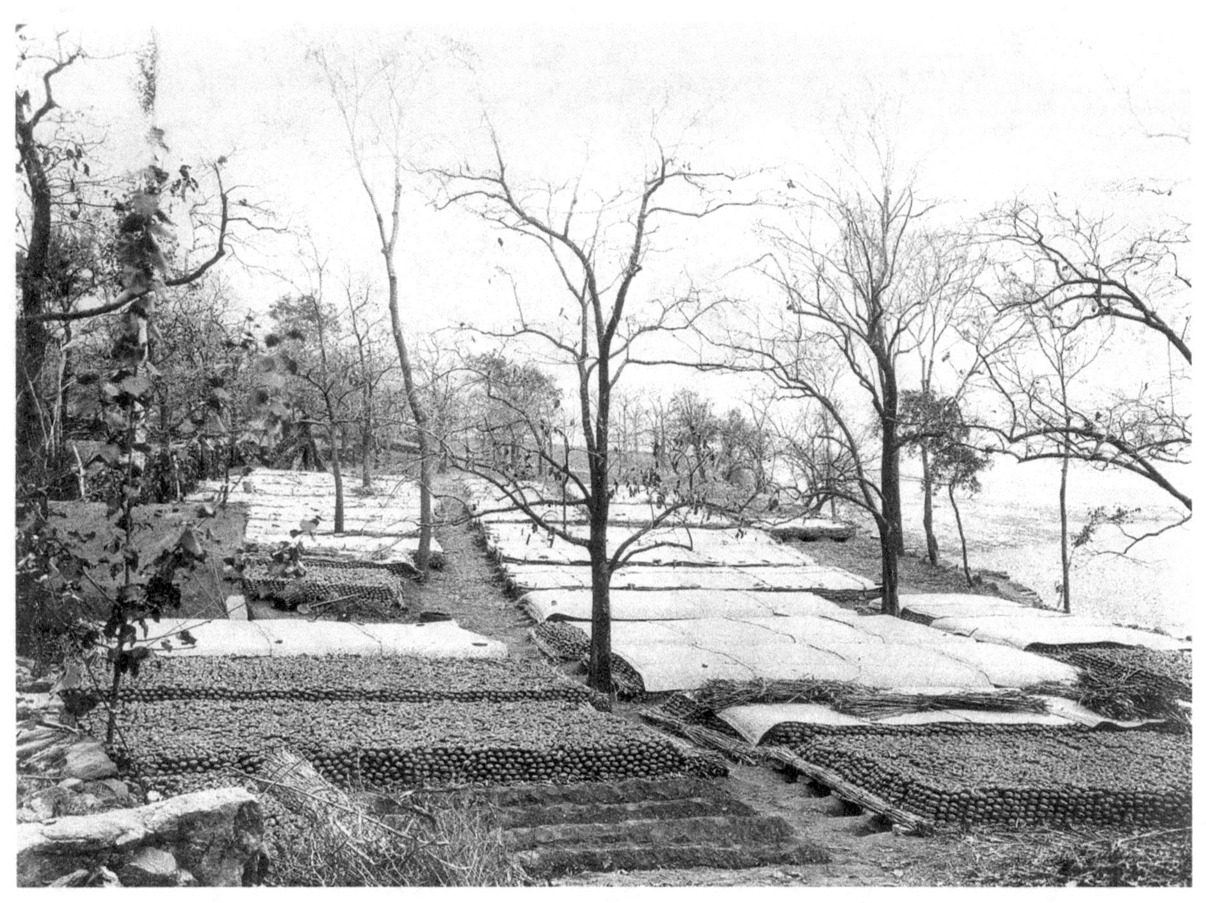

29843. *Nov. 6, 1924. Hei Lung Kuan. A general picture of persimmon storage beds.*

黑龍關柿子場

Hei Lung Kuan, persemmon storage
Hei Lung Kuan, shih Tzu Cháng

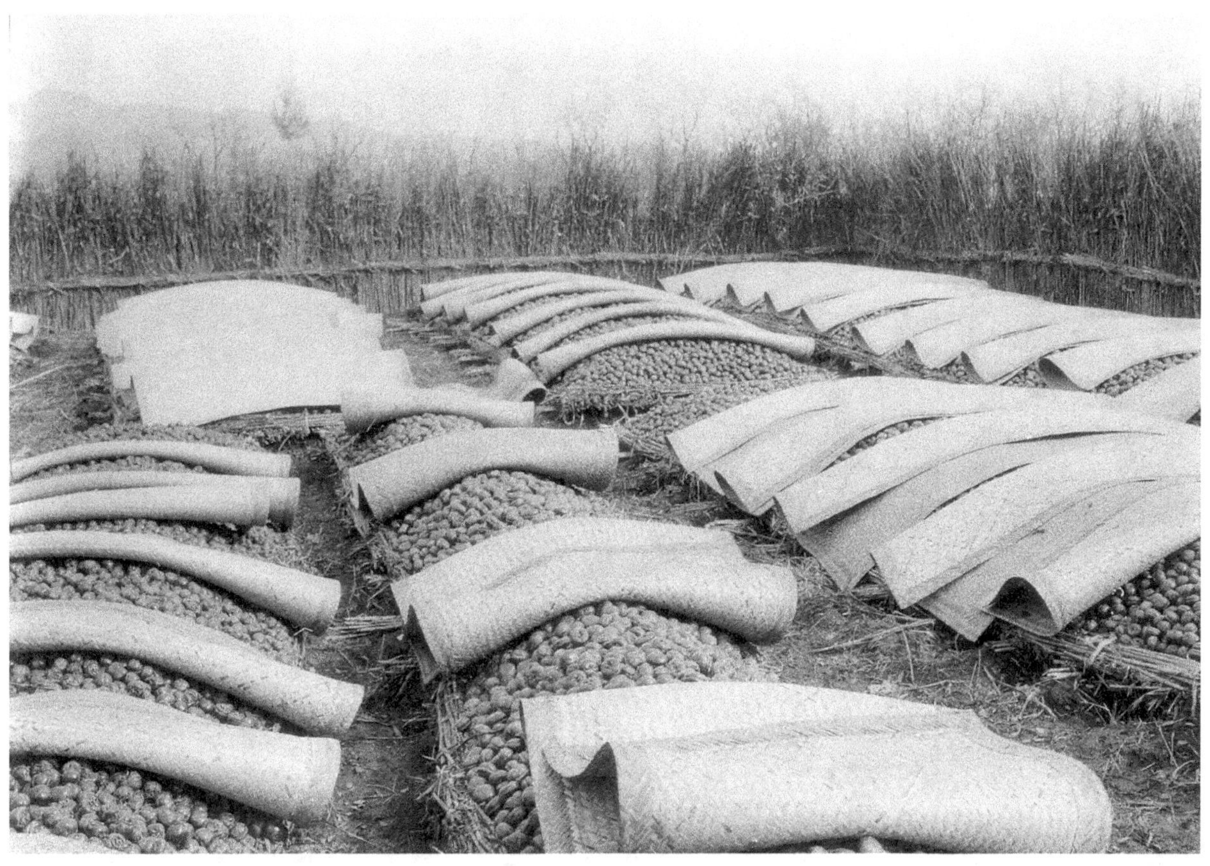

46176. *Hsiang Tang village, a few miles to the northeast of Tang Shan. View from the top of the west rock fence between this storage yard and that of the yard adjoining on the west. This view shows a portion of the filled beds with folded reed-grass mats across them for use in case of rain or for night covering.*

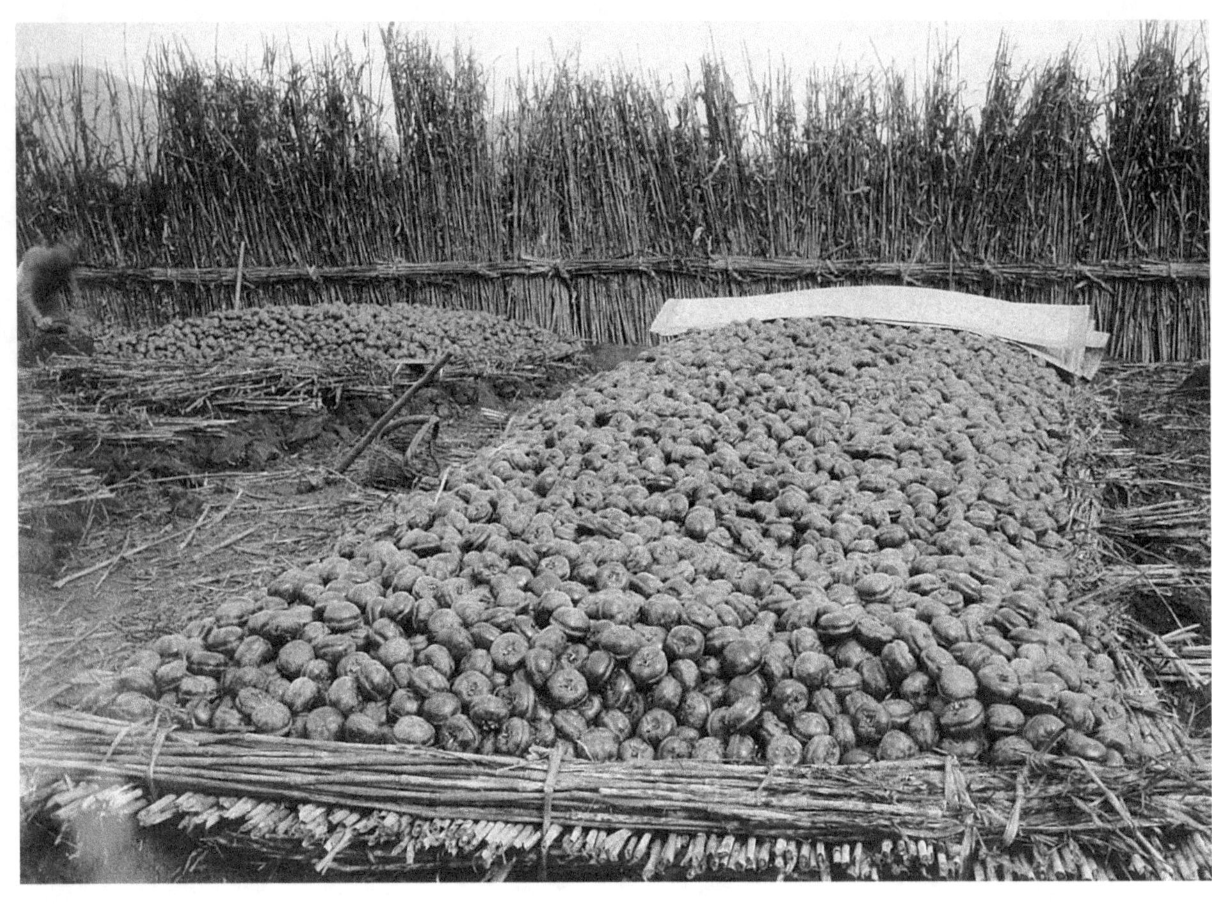

46179. *Hsiang Tang village, 4-6 miles to the northwest of Tang Shan. Looking at the end and over the top of one of the filled beds of persimmons and, to the left, one in the process of being filled.*

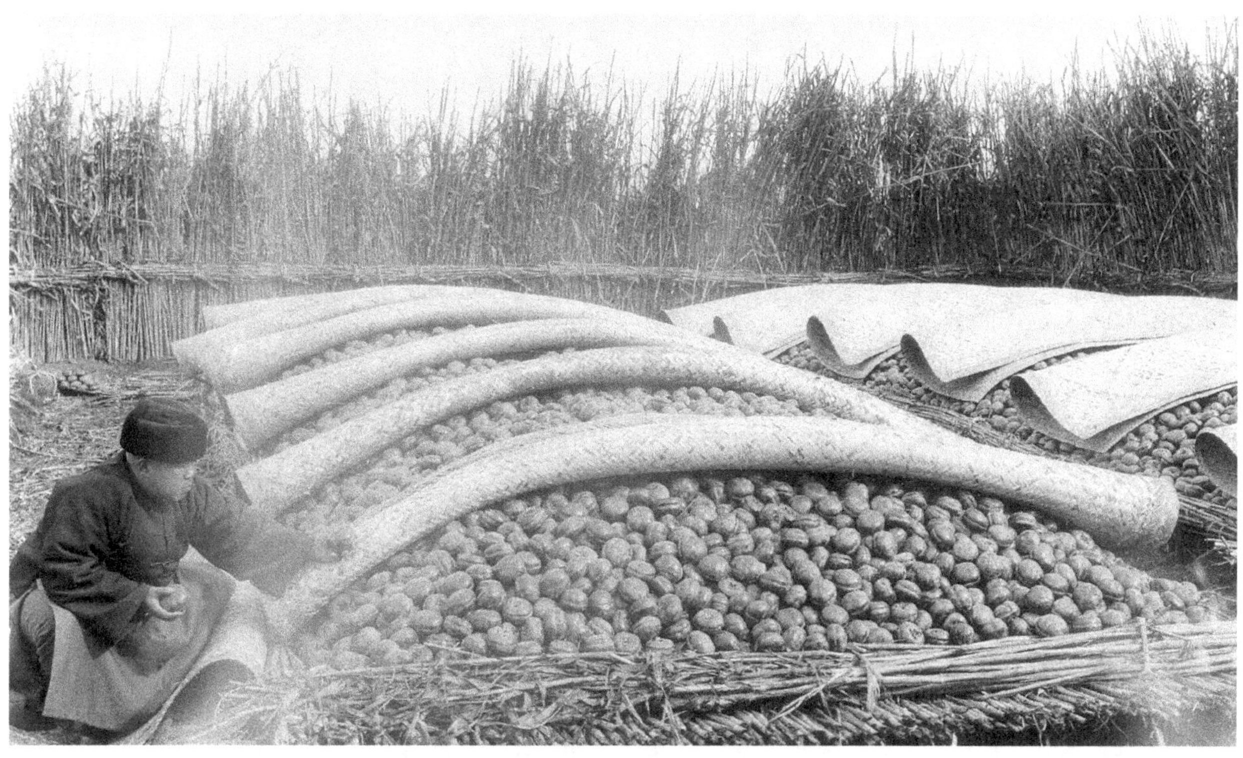

46178. *In the village of Hsiang Tang, a few miles to the northwest of Tang Shan, in the foothills of the Western Hills. A fairly nearby view of the end of one of the eight-foot (8-10 foot) wide persimmon storage beds, showing how the fruit is piled in the beds. In the Toli district, the fruit is piled in regular layers, normally six fruit deep. This piling is quite different.*

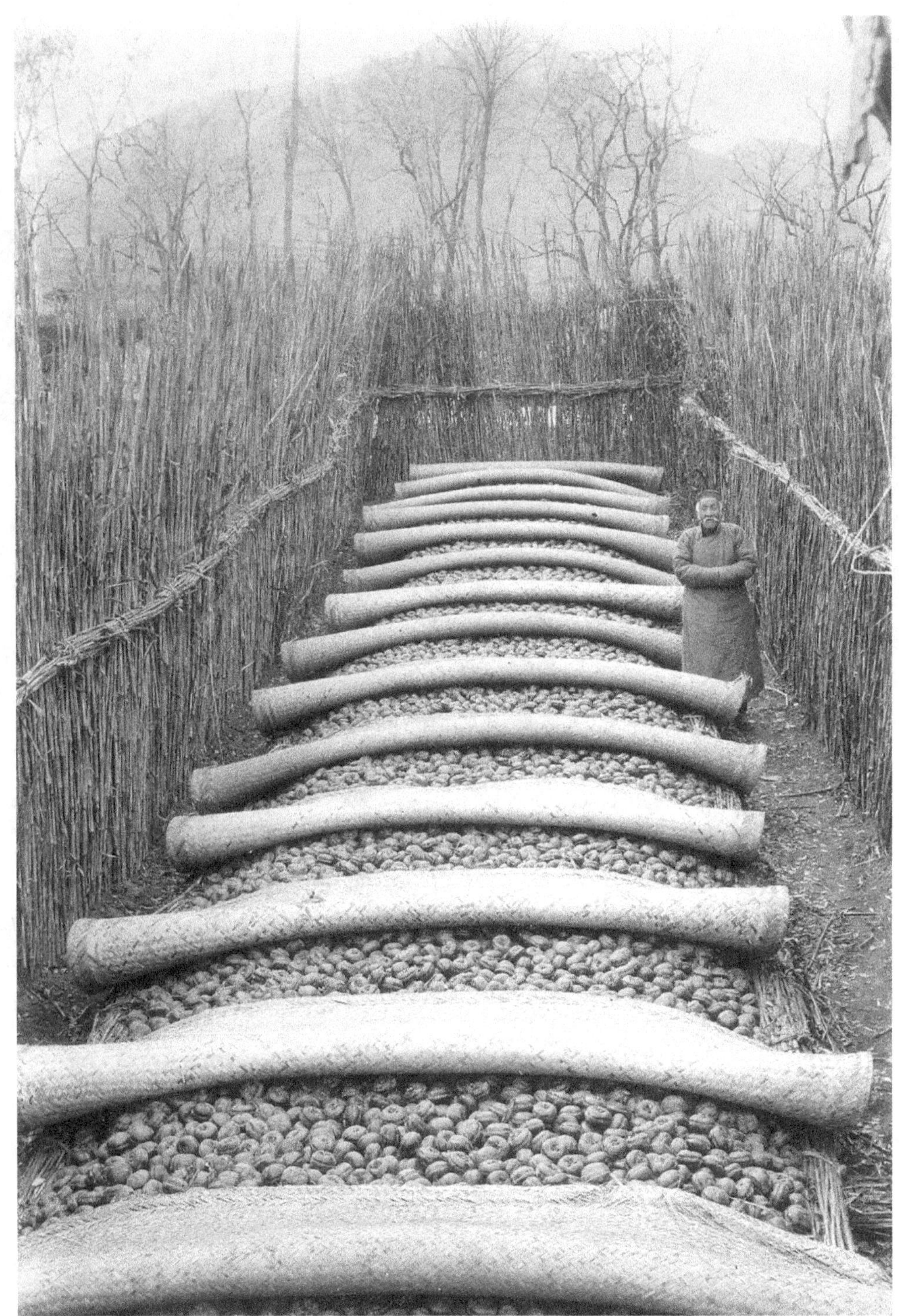

46228. *Nov. 13, 1930. Hsiang Tang. An open-air winter storage bed of persimmons reported to contain 60,000 fruits, each ranging from 3 to 4 inches in diameter. The fruit is covered at night with a single layer of reed-grass matting. This bed, and a number of others like it, are surrounded by a windbreak fence made of kaoliang (a species of sorghum) stems. The owner of this open-air winter cold storage operation is Mr. Li, located at the right and about halfway the distance of the length of the bed.*

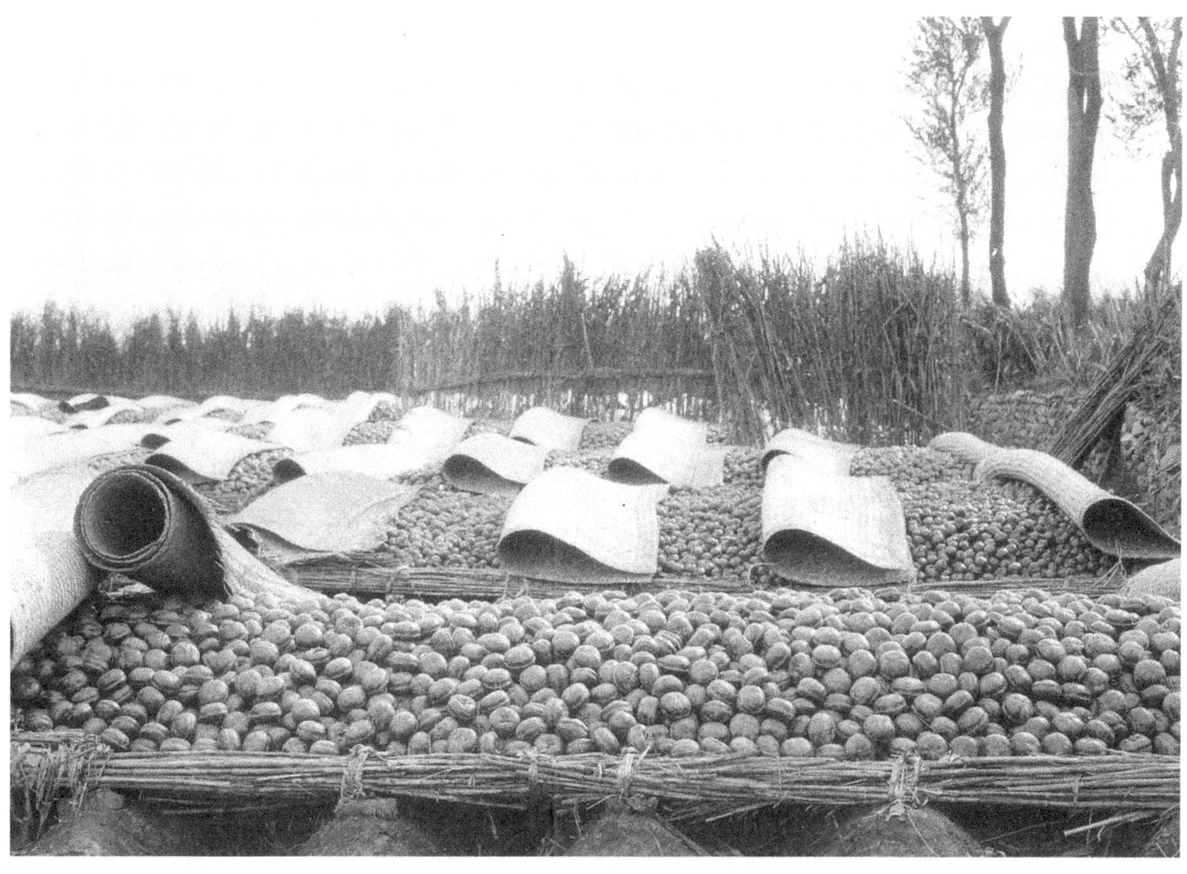

***46177.** Hsiang Tang village a few miles northwest of Tang Shan. A view of a portion of one of the filled persimmon beds near the north side of the yard, and also across the filled beds. Portion of kaoliang stalk fences seen at the right will eventually extend along the south side of each eight foot bed for its length, to shade the beds after the fruit is frozen.*

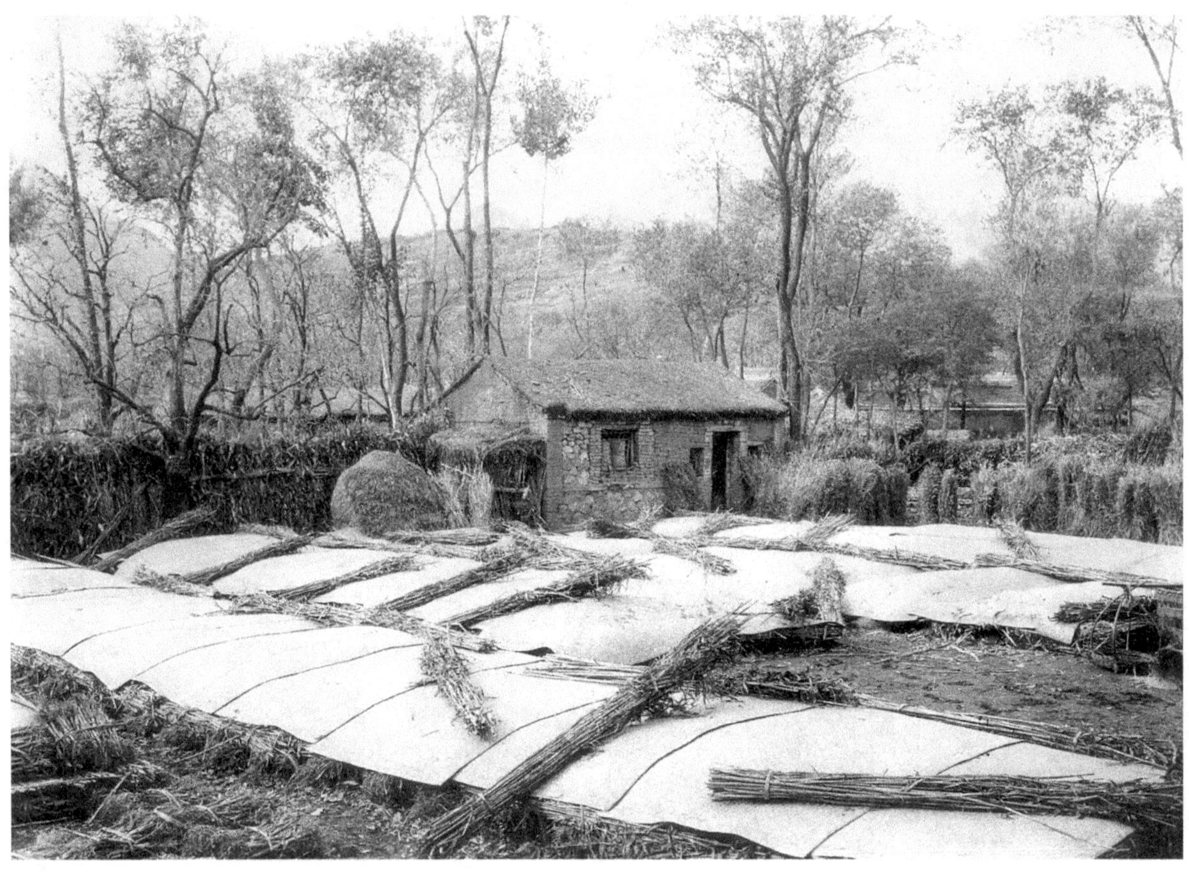

***46182.** Hsiang Tang village, a few miles to the northwest of Tang Shan, in the foothills of the Western Hills. This view looks over a somewhat smaller persimmon storage yard where the filled beds are covered with reed-grass matting and weighted with bundles of koaliang stalks to prevent the matting from blowing off.*

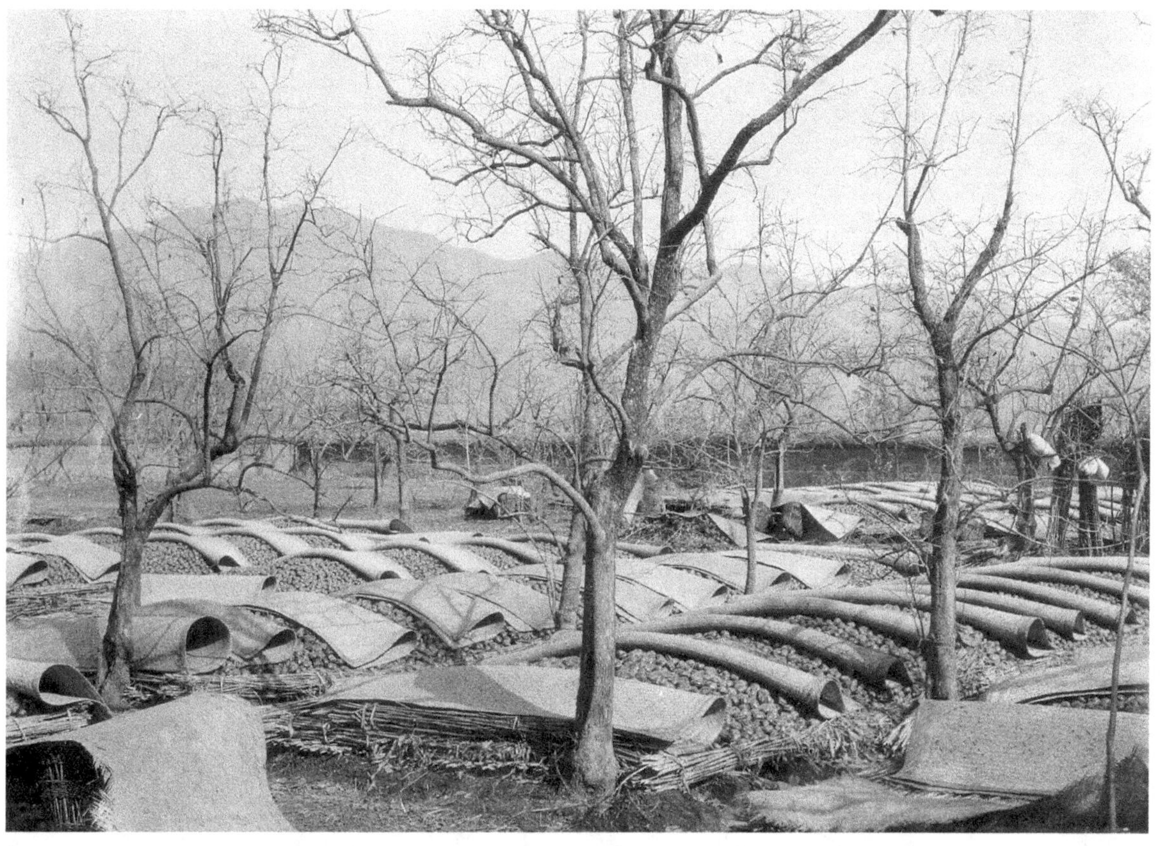

46189. *Hsiang Tang village. View of a good portion of the many storage beds in the storage yard of Mr. Chu Li Chi. Note that the beds are laid in an orchard of persimmon trees.*

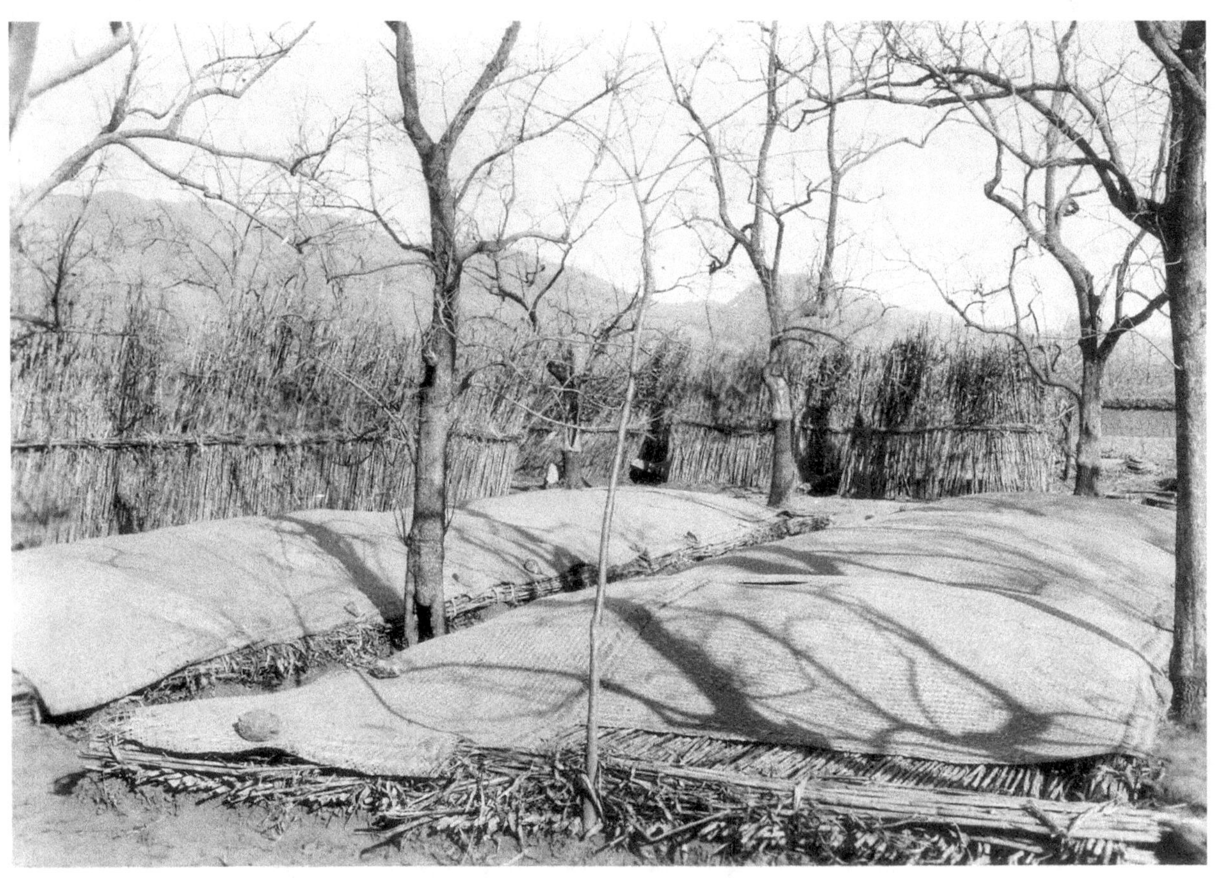

46232. *Hsiang Tang village. Covered beds of persimmons in the open air storage yard of Mr. Chi.*

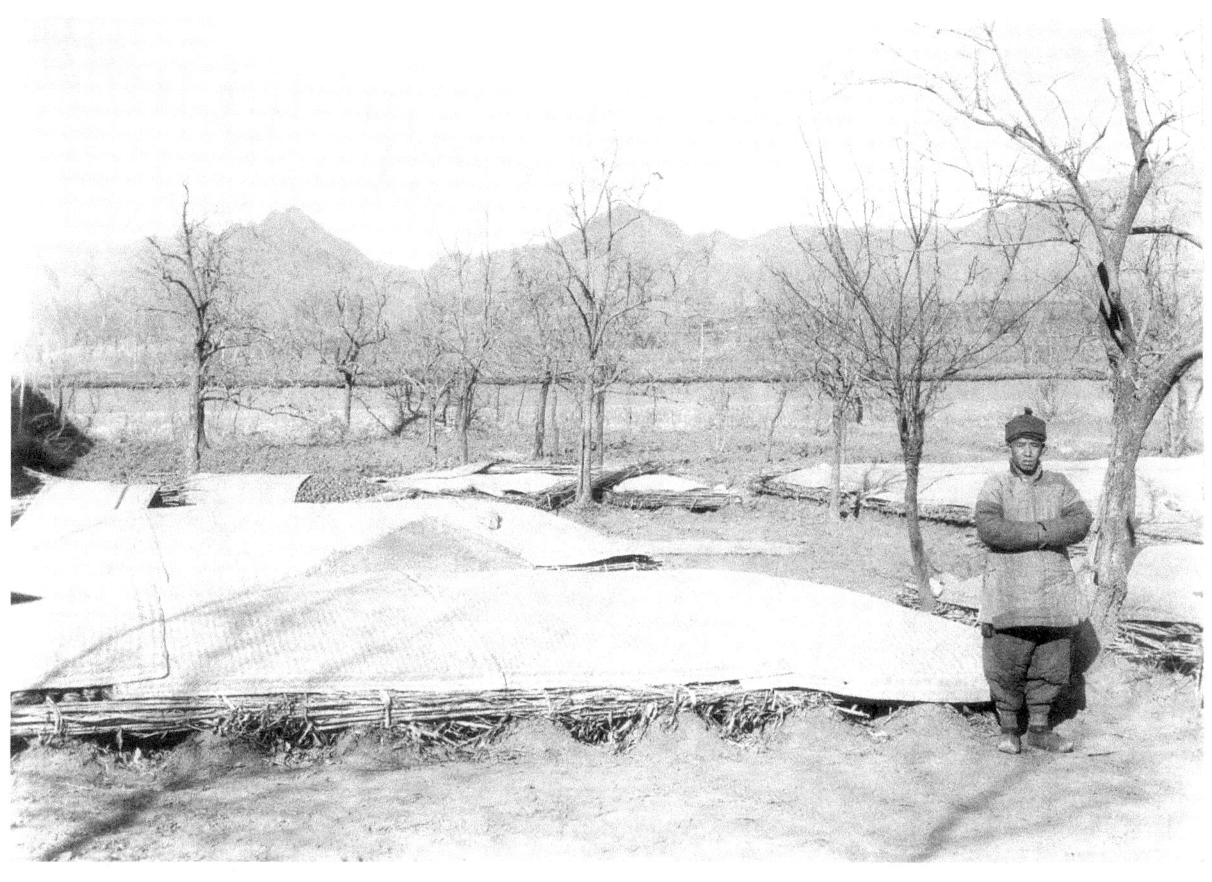

46231. *Hsiang Tang village. Storage yard of Mr. Chi. The beds were all covered on this sunny day because a strong north wind was blowing.*

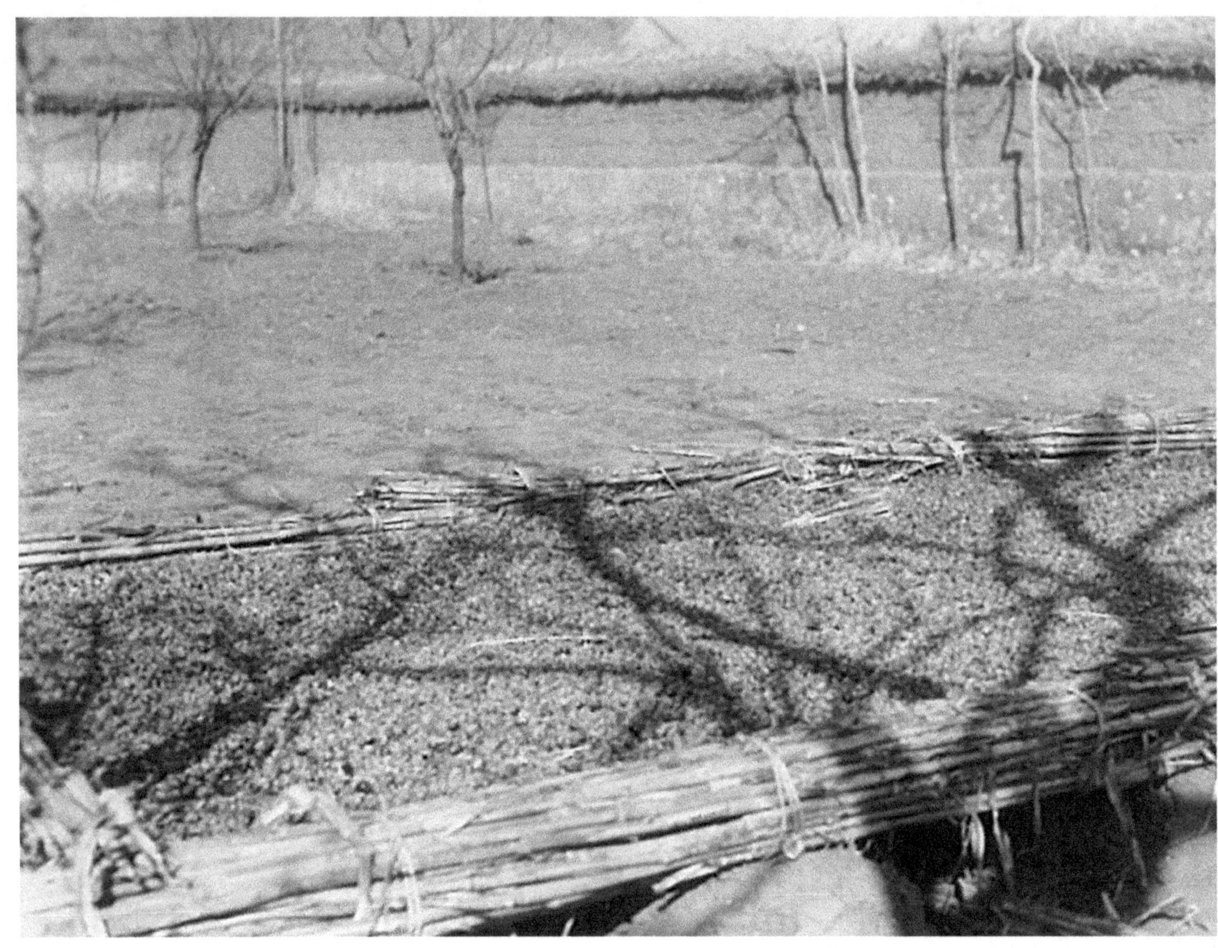

46237. *Hsiang Tang village. Chinese black date or wild persimmon (Diospyros lotus) in the storage yard of Mr. Chi. View shows a portion of a bed in which fruit of this wild persimmon are laying uncovered.*

BED TEMPERATURE MEASUREMENTS

On Nov. 6, 1930, we unpacked the Foxboro 8-day 12-inch dial-registering 3-bulb 3-pan recording thermometer #A60711, which was purchased in Washington, D.C. This was brought for the specific purpose of securing continuous temperature records of the ambient air and open-air storage beds of persimmons throughout the winter season.

We bored three 3/4" holes in one end of one of our fiber trunks near the bottom about three inches on centers, then, by means of 3 stove bolts, clamped the clock dial to the bottom of the trunk and riveted the ends of the bolts on the inside to guard against their being removed.

In our room at the Inn, we then set the trunk on end, just as we would install it at the side of a persimmon bed. By placing the bulbs between two of the coils of a steam radiator, we found, when facing the clock, the bulb attached to the short cable and intended for registering the temperature of the air, is attached to the purple pen arm. The next one to the left of center with a long bulb cable is attached to the center pen which has a red arm, and the third also having a long bulb cable is attached to the pen which has a green arm. These latter two bulbs are intended for insertion into the persimmon storage bed.

We then brought the apparatus to the village of Hsiang Tang to seek permission from Mr. Chi to install it at one of his beds. Mr. Chi, after seeing the thermometer and learning what we wanted to do, said that he had no objection. He advised, however, that as it was something new, and as the yard is near the village, there would be many of the village people come to see the apparatus, and that would result in more or less trouble and inconvenience. He also stated that he would have to put a man to watch and see that the thermometer was not meddled with, and that there would be more or less expense as a result of these conditions. We told him that we would be willing to pay him $6.00 Mex. per month for the use of one of his beds to install the thermometer. He took a few moments to think over the proposition and then told us to go ahead.

We installed the trunk next to one of his beds by attaching it to a stake by means of a screw. The air bulb was attached to the stake at the back of the trunk out of the sun's rays. The bulb on the center cable was placed across the bed 6-8 feet into the center of the bed and about 1/3 down, positioned over a ridge and next to a trench under the bed. The 3rd bulb was placed in among the fruits also, about 6 feet from the 2nd, and above the second layer of fruit from the bottom.

If we are successful in getting the persimmon open-air storage bed temperature records for this season, they will be, more than likely, the first records of this kind obtained since the practice of open air winter storage of persimmons was first undertaken.

On Nov. 21, we arrived at the Mr. Chi's persimmon bed to check on the air and persimmon storage bed temperature recording thermometer at about 11:30 AM. We regret to report that the red ink pen which is connected with the bulb in the upper portion of the fruit in the bed was only marking the chart occasionally. The green and purple ink pens, however, were registering continuously. It is fortunate that it is the pen of one of the bed thermometers which was not working, in place of the purple ink pen bulb which registers the outside air temperature. After changing the chart we set it so that the red ink pen started on the 11:30 AM line of the new chart. At about 1:45 PM we inspected the clock again and to our disgust found that the red ink pen was not recording. We made a few adjustments which appeared to bring the needle in contact with the paper with sufficient pressure to register.

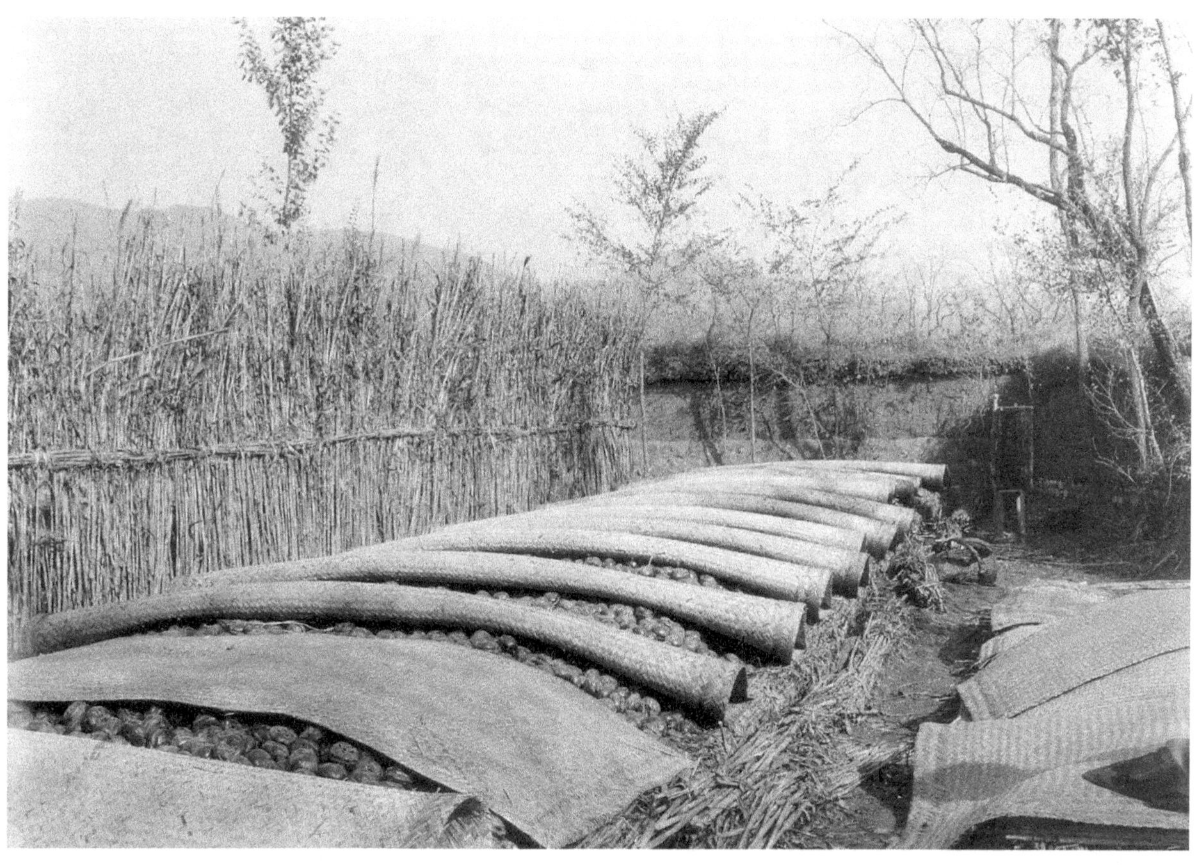

46193. *Hsiang Tang village. A view of a portion of the open-air persimmon storage beds at Mr. Chi's storage yard at the village, some 25 miles to the north of Peiping, in which we have installed the self-registering thermometer. It is in the trunk at the far end to the right. A koaliang fence is to be erected along the north side of this bed, the side on which the trunk stands.*

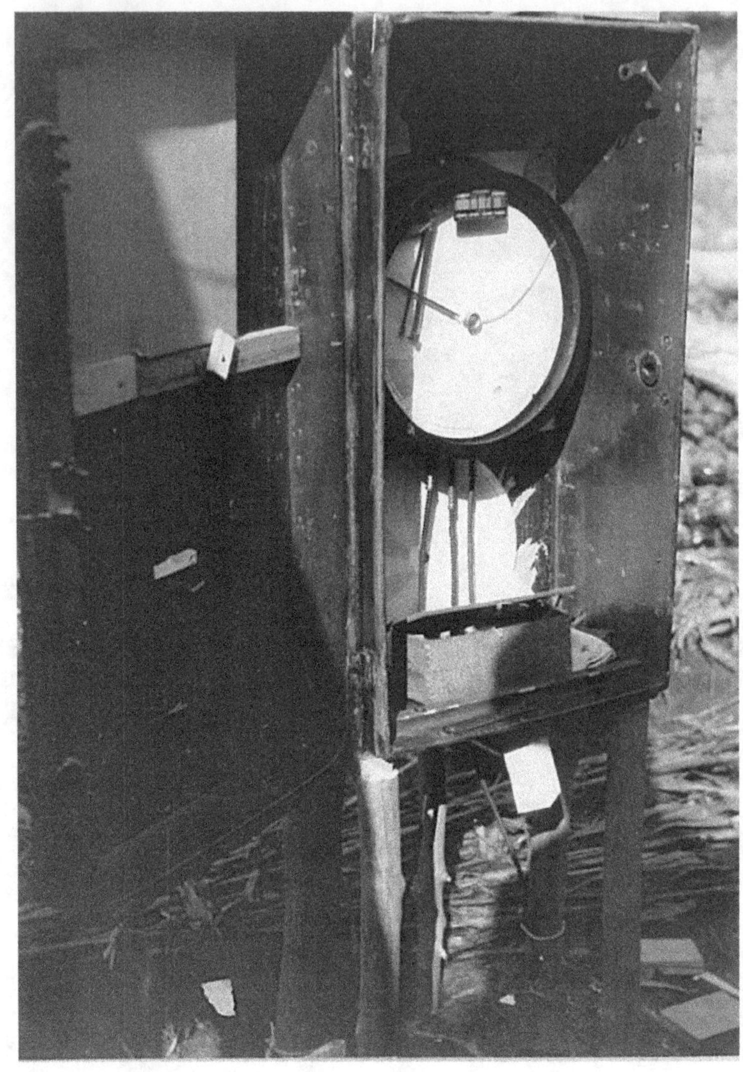

46195. *Hsiang Tang village. View of trunk set up by persimmon storage bed with apparatus to record temperatures.*

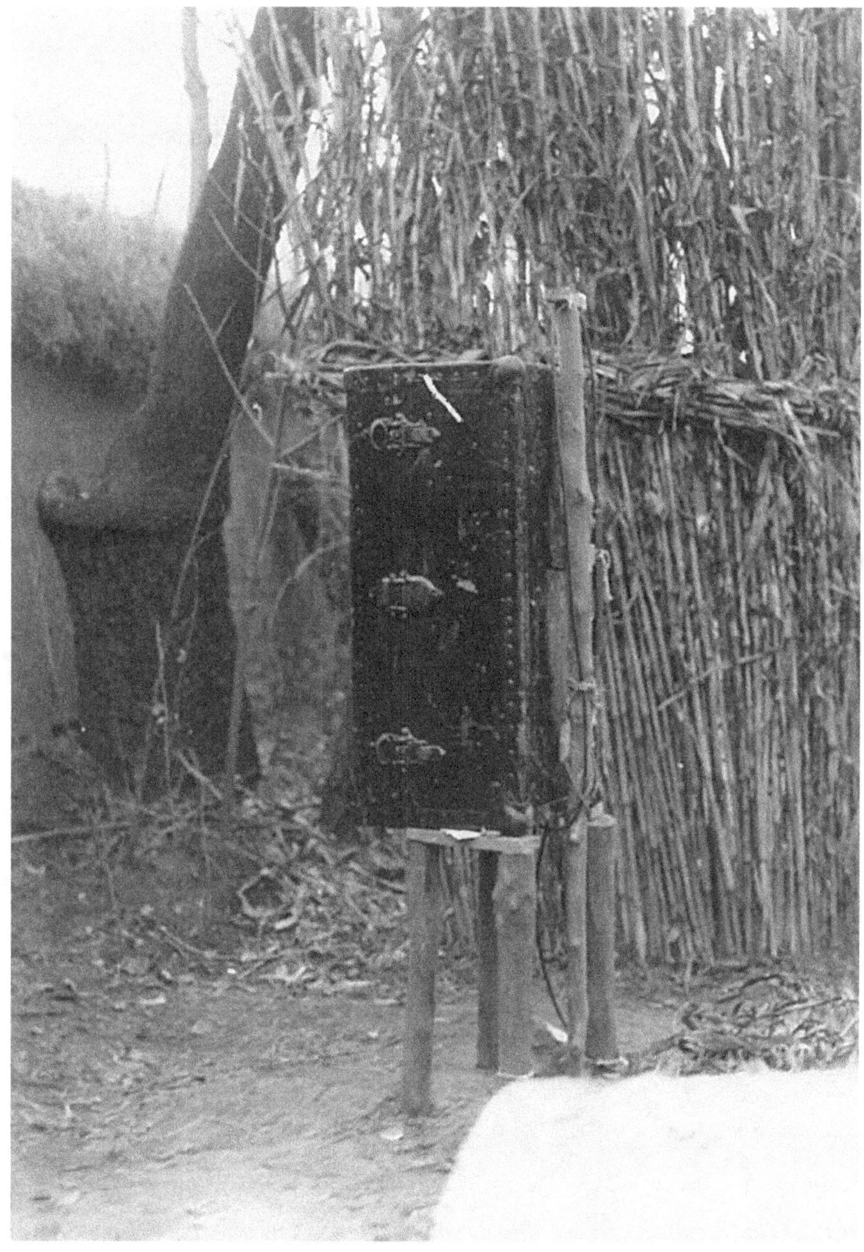

46221. *Hsaing Tang village. A close-up view showing the front of the trunk in which is installed the recording clock thermometer. The bed of fruit in which the two thermometers rest is about 18" to the right.*

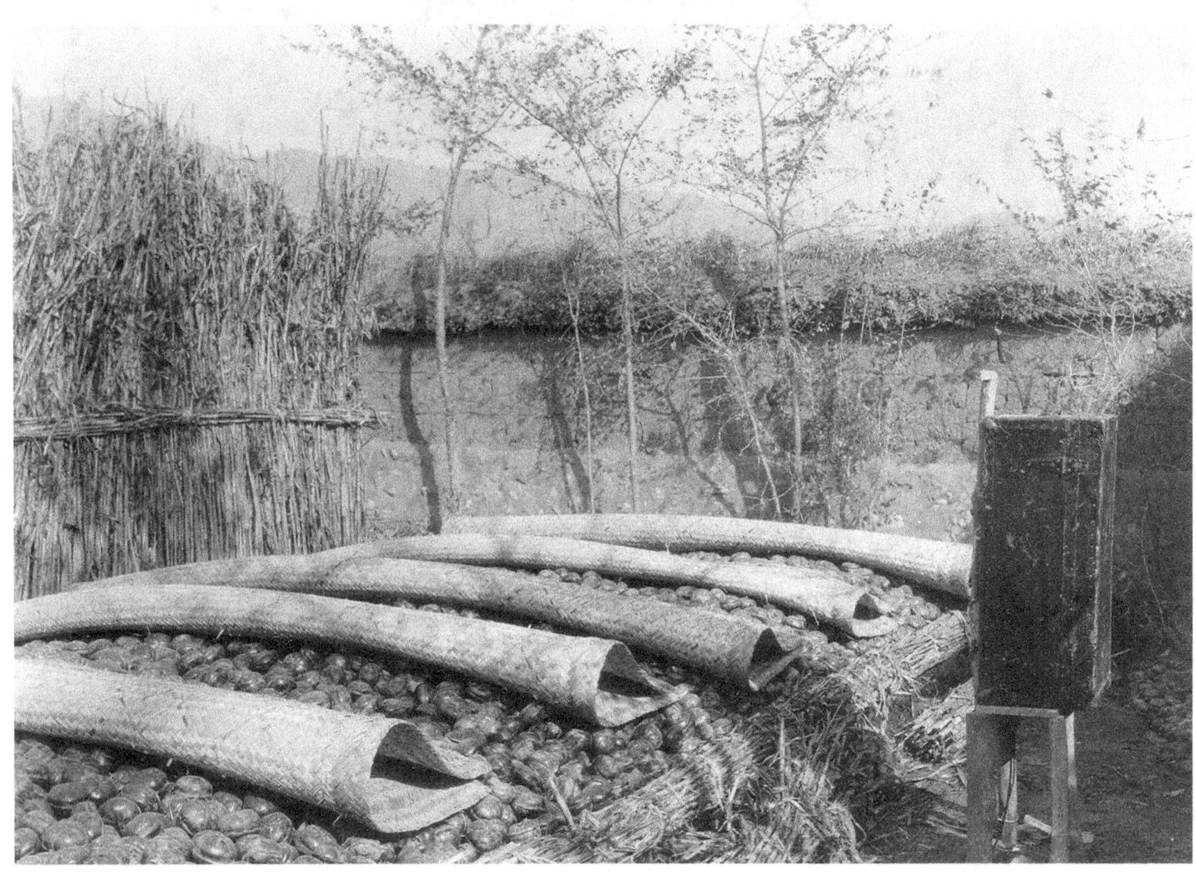

46194. *Hsiang Tang village. A fairly nearby view of the trunk containing the recording thermometer and a portion of the persimmon bed where two of the three bulbs repose. The third bulb for recording the temperature of the air is fastened to the pole at the back of the trunk.*

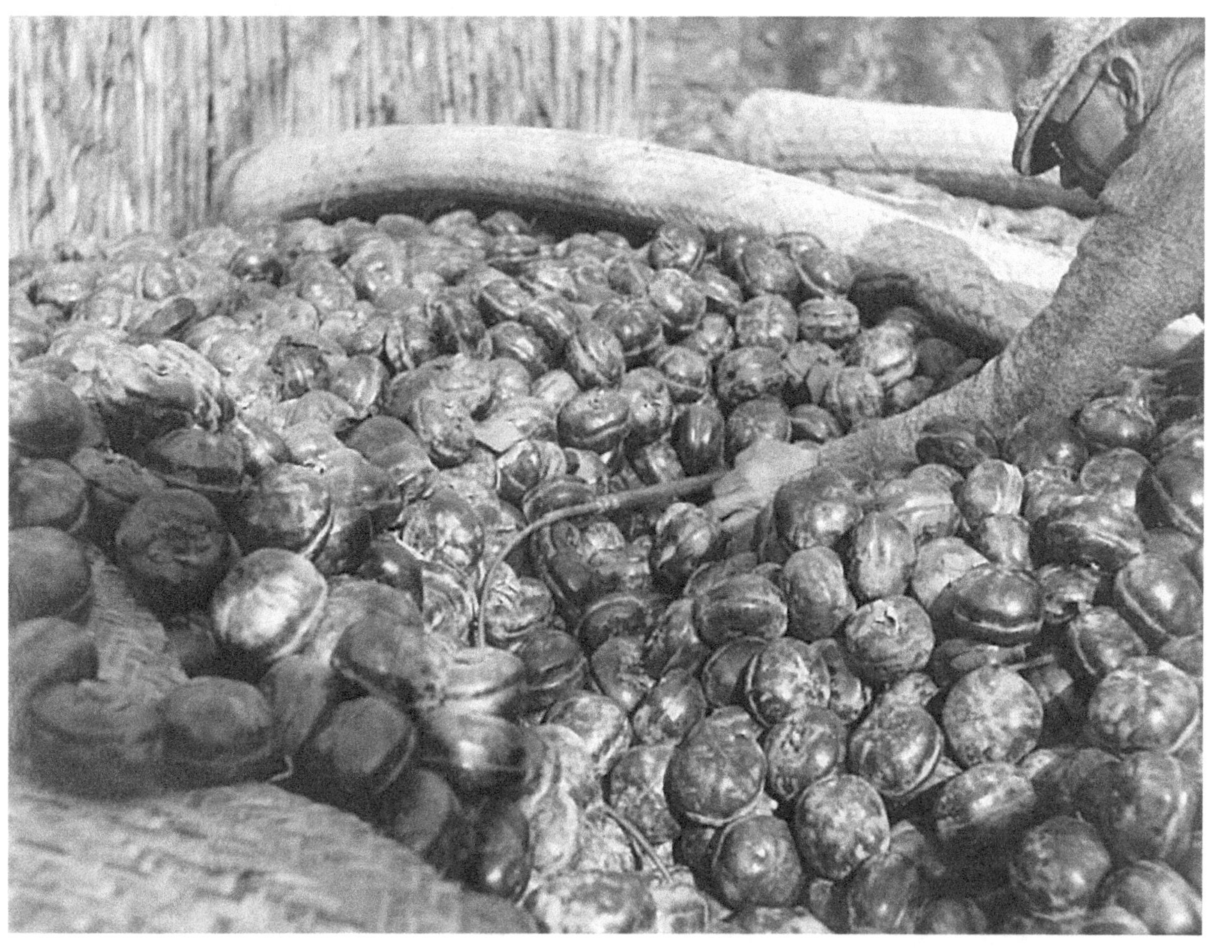

***46196.** Hsiang Tang village. Laying the cable and the bulb of one of the recording thermometers in a bed of persimmons in the storage yard of Mr. Chu Li Chi.*

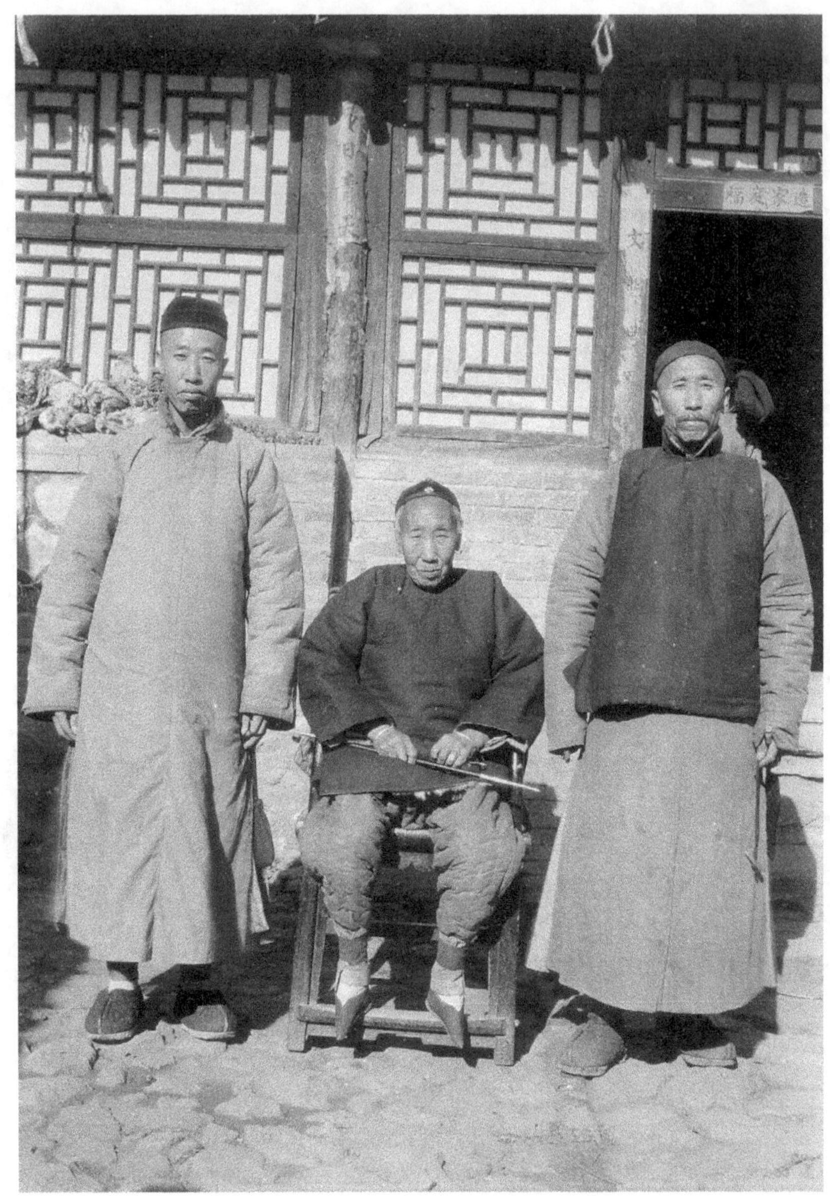

46230. *Hsiang Tang village. Home of Mr. Chu Li Chi (right) and his second brother (left) with their 80-year-old mother between them. We have our recording thermometer in the persimmon storage yard of Mr. Chi. He has 800,000 to 1,000,000 persimmons bedded down in the open.*

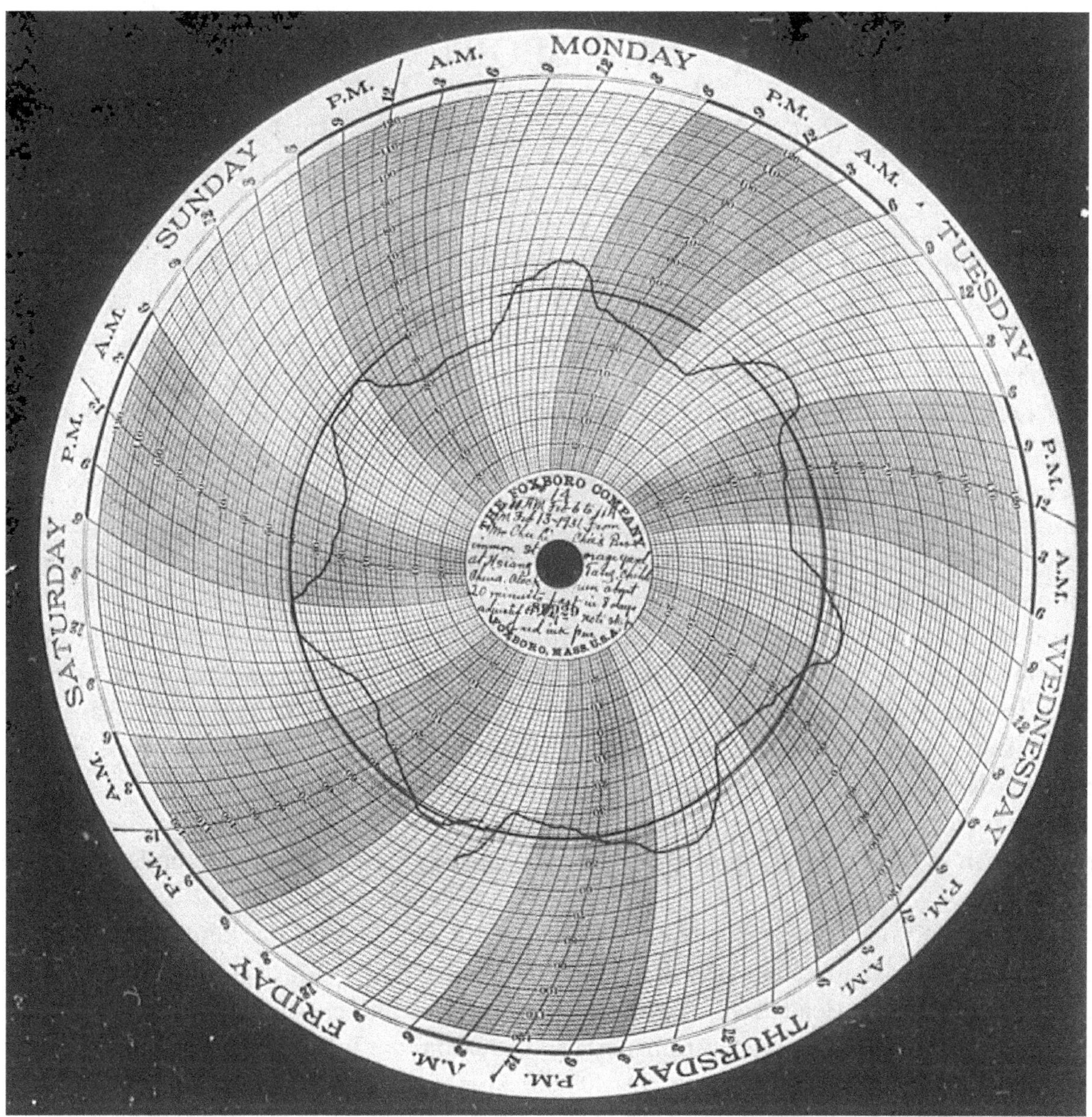

46479. *[Ed.: Temperature record disc with Dorsett's remarks stating "10 AM Feb. 6 to 11 AM Feb. 13, 1931 from Mr. Chu Li Chi's persimmon storage yard at Hsaing Tang, Chihli, China. Clock ran about 20 minutes fast in 8 days, adjusted today. Note skip of red ink pen." The disk was made by the Foxboro Company, Foxboro, Mass., U.S.A. This was a continuous record of day and night temperatures at and in a persimmon storage bed. If the figures in the disc are accurate, each day of this week in February the outdoor air temperature rose to about 50F and each night fell to about 25F, but the temperature in the bed remained constant, around 40F. Evidently, Dorsett continued to have difficulty with the red ink pen throughout the winter.]*

TRANSPORT

The transportation of farm products, fruits and vegetables, as well as practically all other commodities handled in Peiping and vicinity, is effected primarily by the following means: limited rail, quite extensive water transportation, and - almost if not quite unlimited - camel, cart, donkey, and human transportation.

Water transportation of persimmons in the vicinity of Peiping is hardly worth considering, because the persimmon-growing areas in this region are in the foothills section to the west, northwest, and north of the city, and quite distant from navigable waterways.

Rail transportation, however, reaches to Toli on the west and Hankou to the north, both of which are in fairly close proximity to extensive persimmon-growing districts, and it does some business in persimmon transportation.

Primarily the fruit is transported to the city in the fall, and to the open-air winter storage beds at harvest time, by donkeys, and to some extent by camel trains, and from nearby districts, where possible, by carts. Throughout the winter season (middle of November to March 1-15), the fruit is transported from the nearby winter storage yards by means of men, donkeys, and carts (where accessible), and from the outlying districts by camel, and to some extent, donkey trains.

Within the city, persimmons for street fruit stands and street retail trade are for the most part carried by men in two baskets suspended, one at each end of a shoulder pole, and on large-wheeled wheelbarrows.

Quite frequently one donkey man handles two donkeys. For a haul of this kind the men are paid $2.50 Mex. per 1000 persimmons of the large size (Tamopan) and $1.25 Mex. per 1000 for the Lantern (a small-fruited variety), a load of which is reckoned as double in number that of the Tamopan variety. Using the above figures, the estimated transportation rate from the Toli district, which requires three days for the round trip, and based on a load of 400 persimmons, is as follows: one donkey man caring for two donkeys would earn gross for the 3-day trip $2.00 Mex. or about 66 cents per day, out of which he must feed and keep himself and his two donkeys. It does not seem to an American that this would be a living wage even if it were in gold, let alone a currency with an exchange rate of which (Feb. 28, 1931) is $467.836. At this rate, the trio would earn .14 cents American gold per day.

The camel, sometimes known as the "desert freighter", is commonly used for the transportation of persimmons, especially the more distant trips. Camel panniers (baskets) are, as will be observed, oblong in shape. Their inside dimensions are about 15" across, 34" long, and 18" deep. The capacity of each is normally 400 large fruits. Therefore, 800 persimmons of the large variety and about double that number for the small-fruited variety, are reckoned as an average camel load.

The tariff charges for the camel transportation from districts 1 ½ day's journey from Peiping, requiring three days for the round trip, is $3.40 Mex. per 1,000. A camel man with his 4-camel caravan transports 3,200 persimmons and receives for his time and trouble $10.88 Mex., an average daily wage for himself and 4 camels of $3.63 Mex. At the rate of exchange (Feb. 28, 1931) of $467.836, this amounts to $0.775 American gold per day. With this amount, the camel man has to maintain himself, and feed and care for 4 camels. He has also to save for the purchase of panniers, saddle pads, and rope as may be needed from time to time. This amount must also pay interest on his investment, as well as provide funds for the purchase of another camel in the event that one should die or for any reason become disabled. The foregoing is a feat only to be accomplished by a plucky Chinese camel man.

Where accessible, 3-mule carts are quite commonly used for the carrying of persimmons from the orchards to Peiping in the early season, Sept. 15 to Nov. 15, and after the latter date from the open-air winter storage beds. These are ordinarily 2-wheeled Chinese carts which are in universal use throughout northern China. Cart transportation of persimmons is primarily confined to districts within a day's journey, or a little more, from the city.

For persimmon hauling, the carts are fitted with an improvised body (sides and ends) of reed-grass matting which is normally 3 to 4' in height, and held in position by the fruit on the inside, and supported on the outside by the open side framework of the cart supplemented by rope and small sticks 3-4' in length.

The number of large (Tamopan) persimmons in an average 3-mule cartload of fruit is 4,000. An average price paid for their transportation from the orchard, or later in the season from the open-air winter storage beds, is $2.00 Mex. per 1,000. Based on these figures, the cart man with his cart and 3 mules receives $8.00 Mex. gross for their 2-day round trip. He therefore earns the munificent sum of $4.00 Mex. per day, which at the rate of exchange (Feb. 28, 1931) of $467.836, amounts to $0.85 cents American gold.

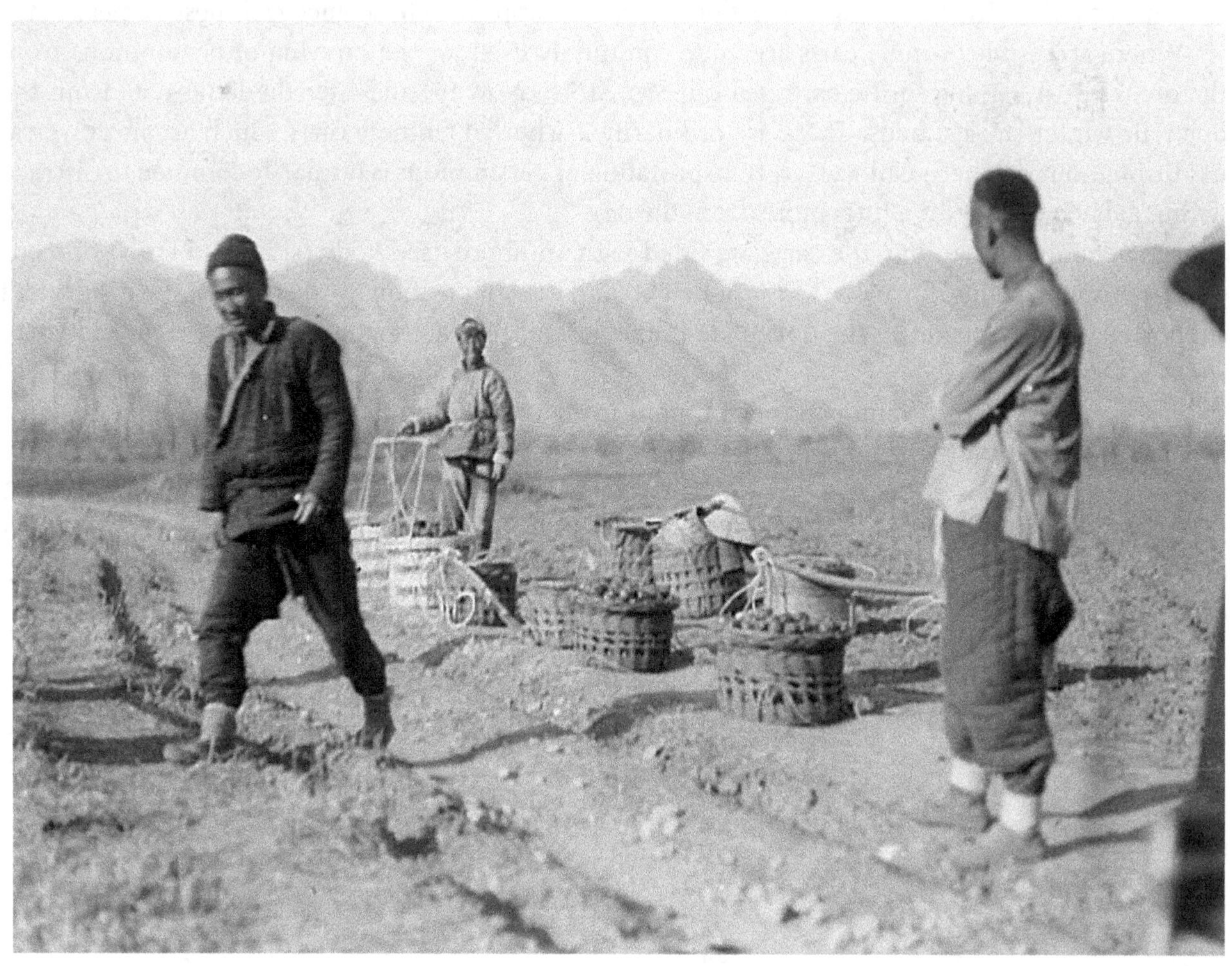

***46384.** Dec. 5,1930. Chinese persimmon hawkers each with 2 baskets of fruit on the road to Peiping. They are only a mile or so from the open-air winter storage beds in the village of Hsiang Tang, at the edge of the foothills to the extreme left in the background. These men have a tramp of some 25 miles into Peiping, and have stopped here to rest. A man-load of persimmons on a hike of this kind is from 200-300 fruit, depending on the size of the fruit. In this instance they have about 300, for they are carrying Lantern persimmons, a small fruited variety.*

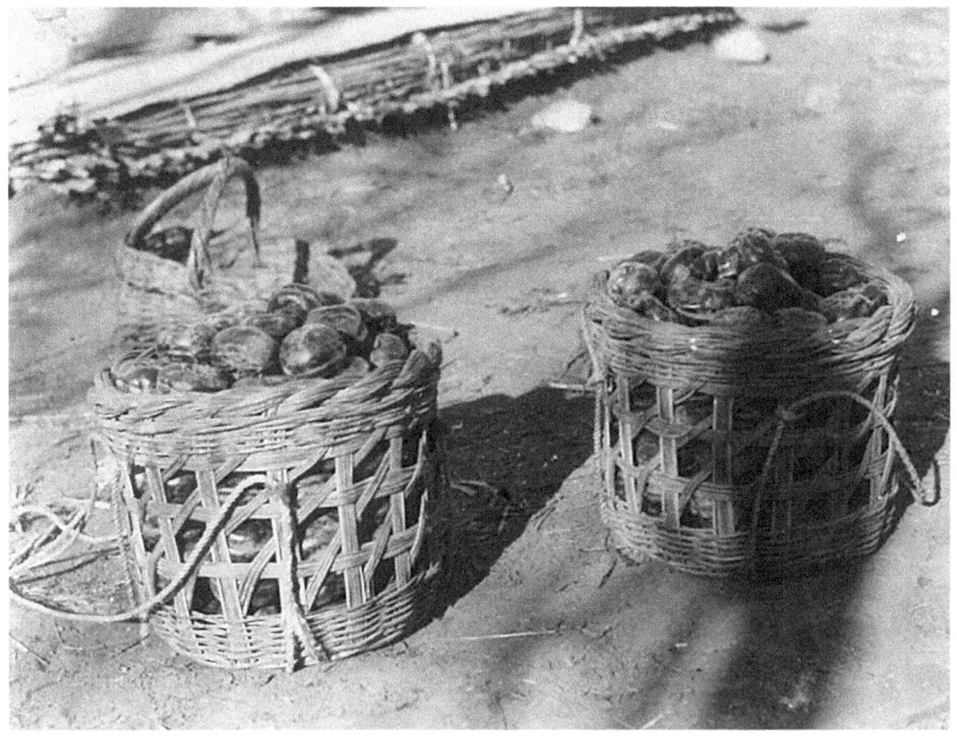

46455. *Hsiang Tang. A nearby view of two baskets of persimmons. This is the large or Tamopan variety of which about 100 fruits fill a basket of this size. The weight of the 2 baskets is approximately 120 pounds, a pretty good weight for a man to tote 25 miles to market.*

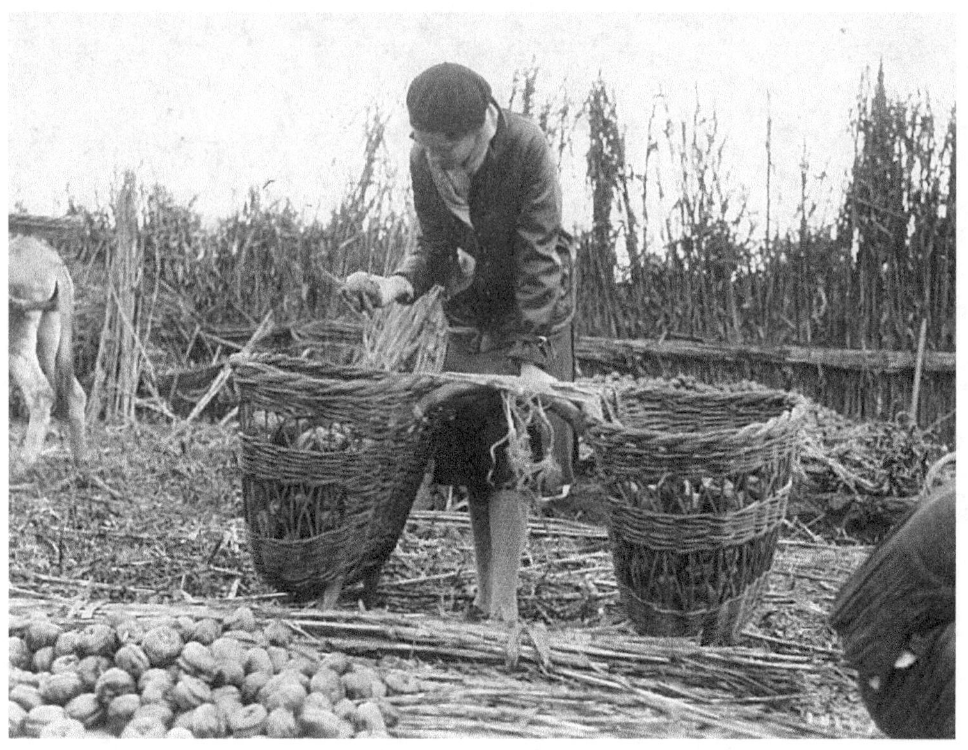

46173. *Hsiang Tang village. Daughter-in-law Ruth B. Dorsett examining fruit of the large Tamopan persimmons brought to the storage yard on donkeys. These baskets each measure (inside) 14 ½ " across, 21" deep. A donkey load is 450 fruit in each basket of the Lantern variety and 225 fruit of the Tamopan.*

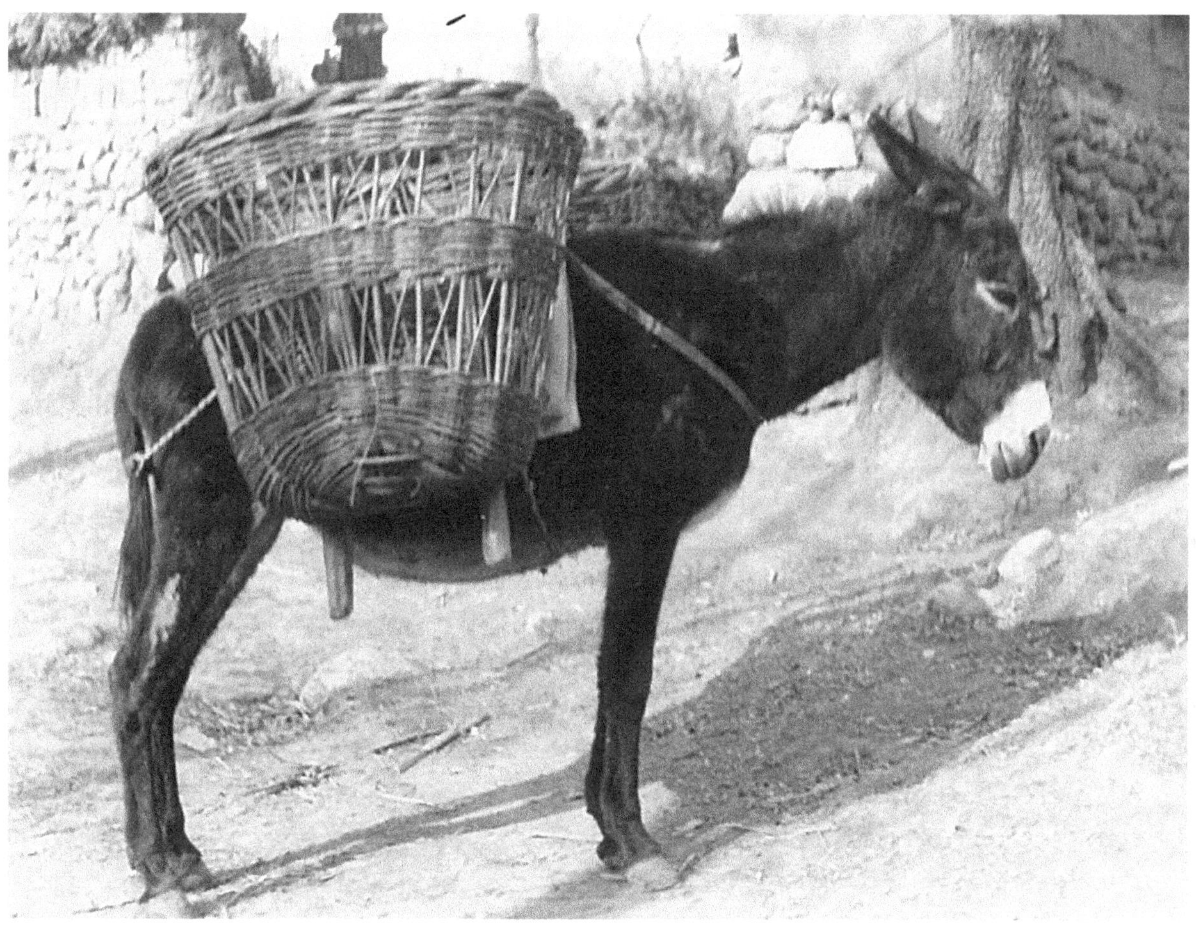

***46219.** Nov. 14, 1930. The donkey, a native member of, perhaps, the greatest carrying force in North China, and probably in the Empire, standing at the entrance to the persimmon storage yard of Mr. Chu Li Chi. This fellow does not appear to be very enthusiastic about being loaded for a tramp of 25 miles into Peiping.*

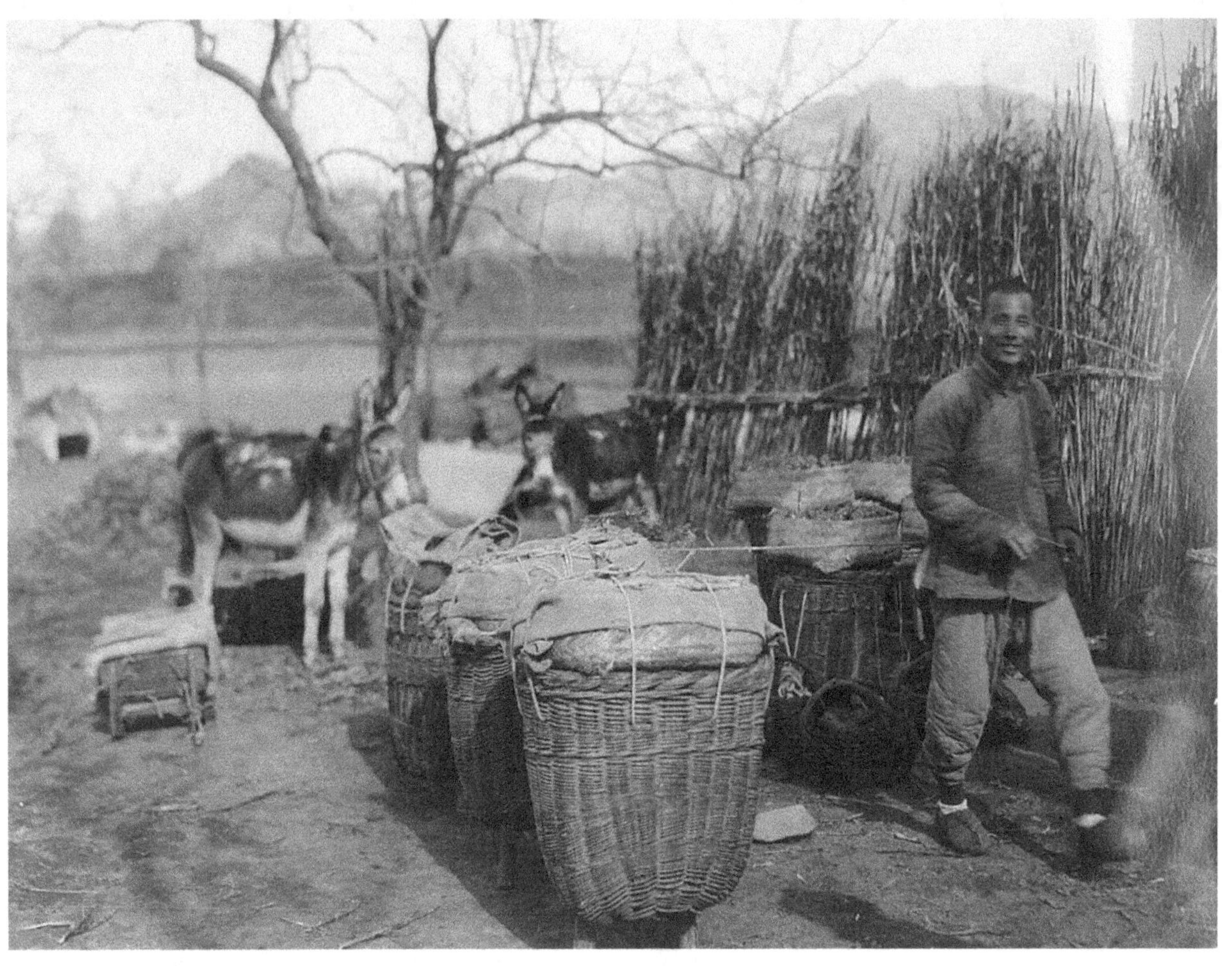

46223. *Nov. 14, 1930. Hsiang Tang. A fairly nearby view of two donkeys viewing, perhaps with some degree of apprehension and disgust, their augmented load of persimmons which will soon be on their backs. In the foreground are the connected baskets called "Lung tuos", filled with fruit. The trip of some 25 miles to Peiping with such a load probably makes the donkeys wish they were at their journey's end before starting. The donkey is a sure-footed and efficient little beast of burden. The donkey man probably thought he was out of camera range, judging from his smile of satisfaction.*

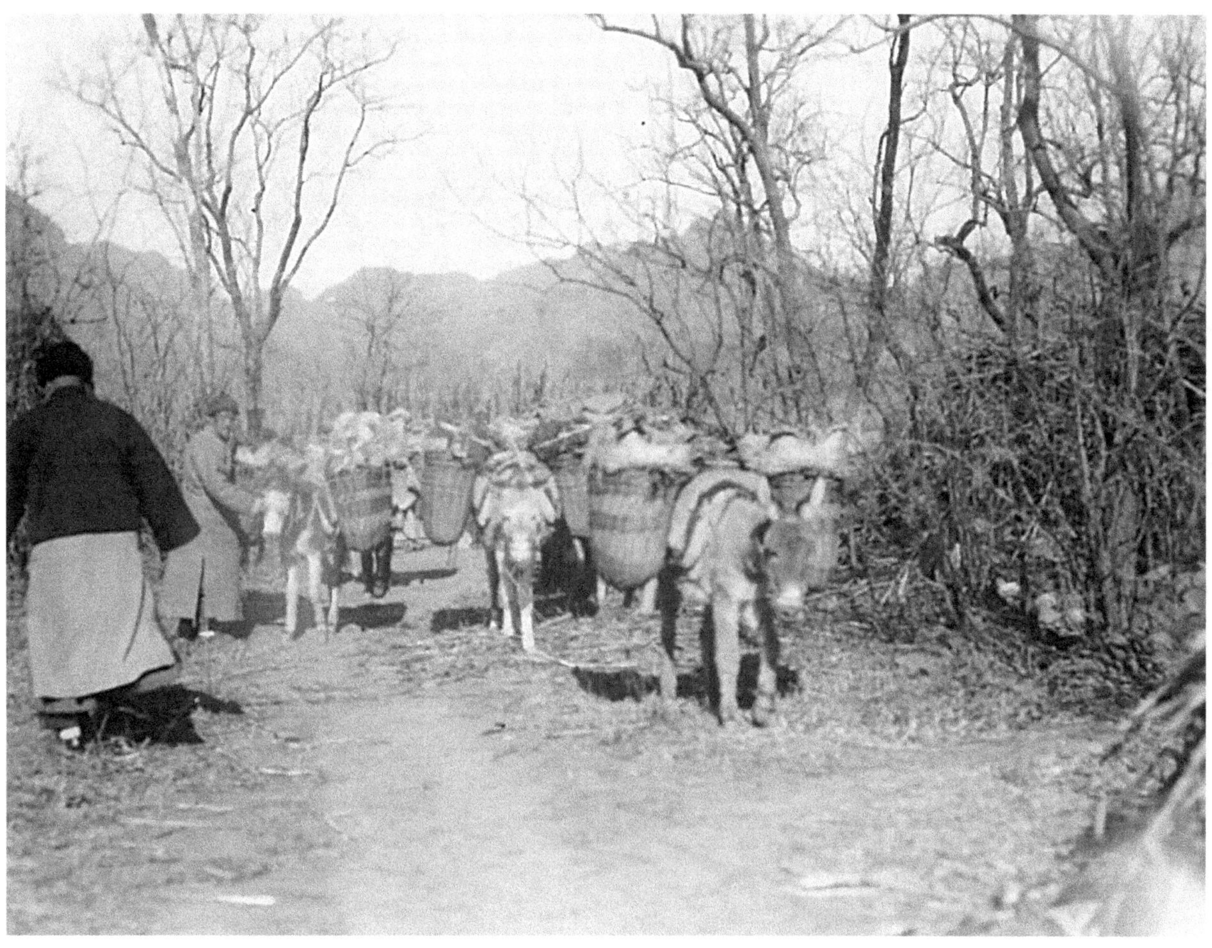

46240. *Dec. 3, 1930. A donkey train of half a dozen or more animals leaving the persimmon storage yard of Mr. Chu Li Chi, in the village of Hsiang Tang. The donkeys are headed for Peiping, some 25 miles distant, and each has on its back 600 persimmons, considerably more than 300 pounds.*

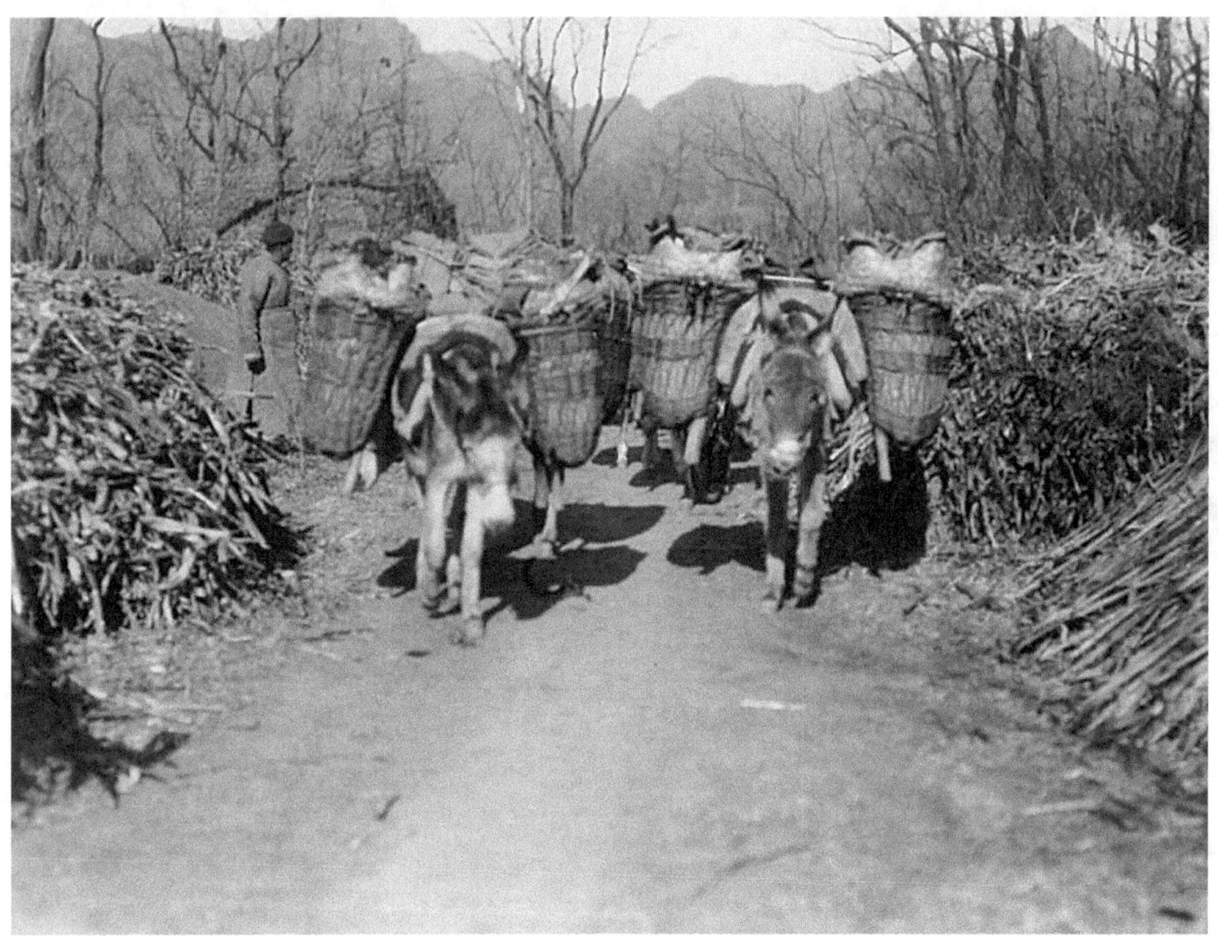

46239. *Dec. 3, 1930. Hsiang Tang. View of a donkey train leaving the storage yard of Mr. Chi. A little later they were out on the road in single file headed for the metropolis.*

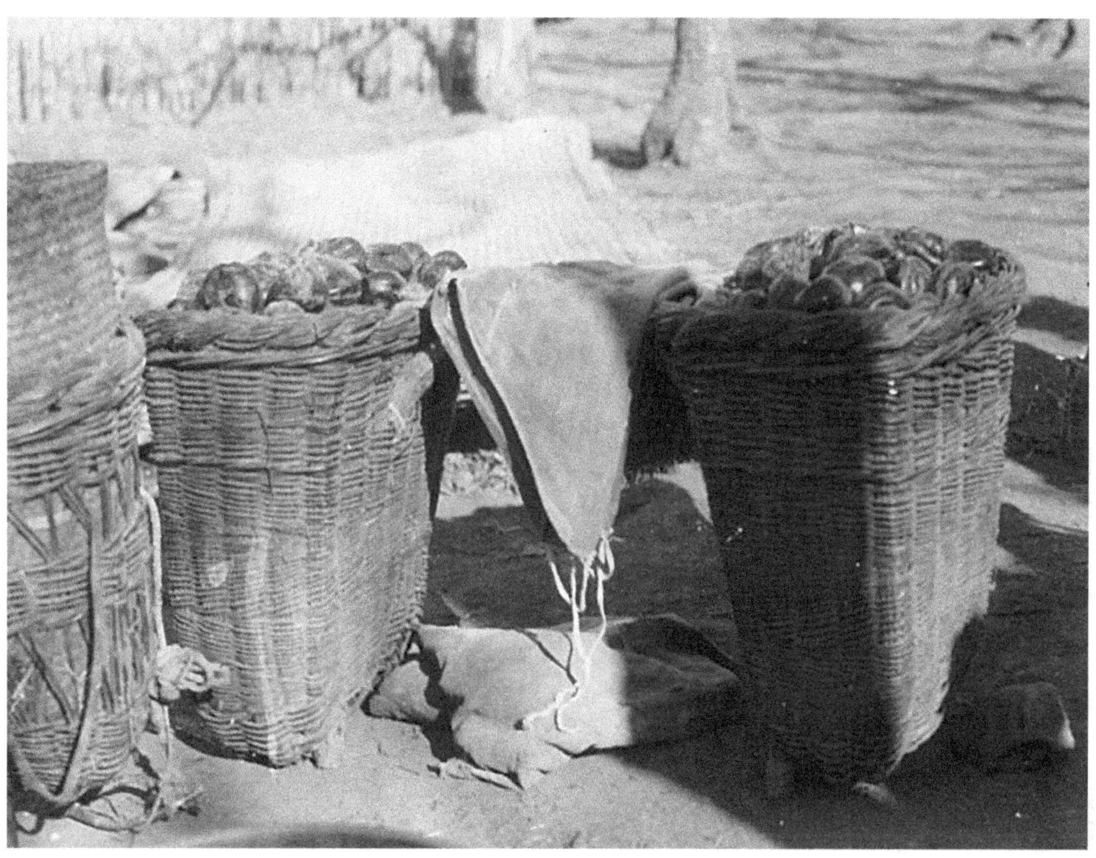

46454. *Jan. 23, 1931. Hsiang Tang. A nearby view of donkey panniers. Filled in this way, each basket holds from 200-250 persimmons, depending on the size of the fruit. Baskets filled in this way are reckoned as a normal donkey load, but not uncommonly such a load is augmented by two additional light baskets on top, each holding about 100 persimmons.*

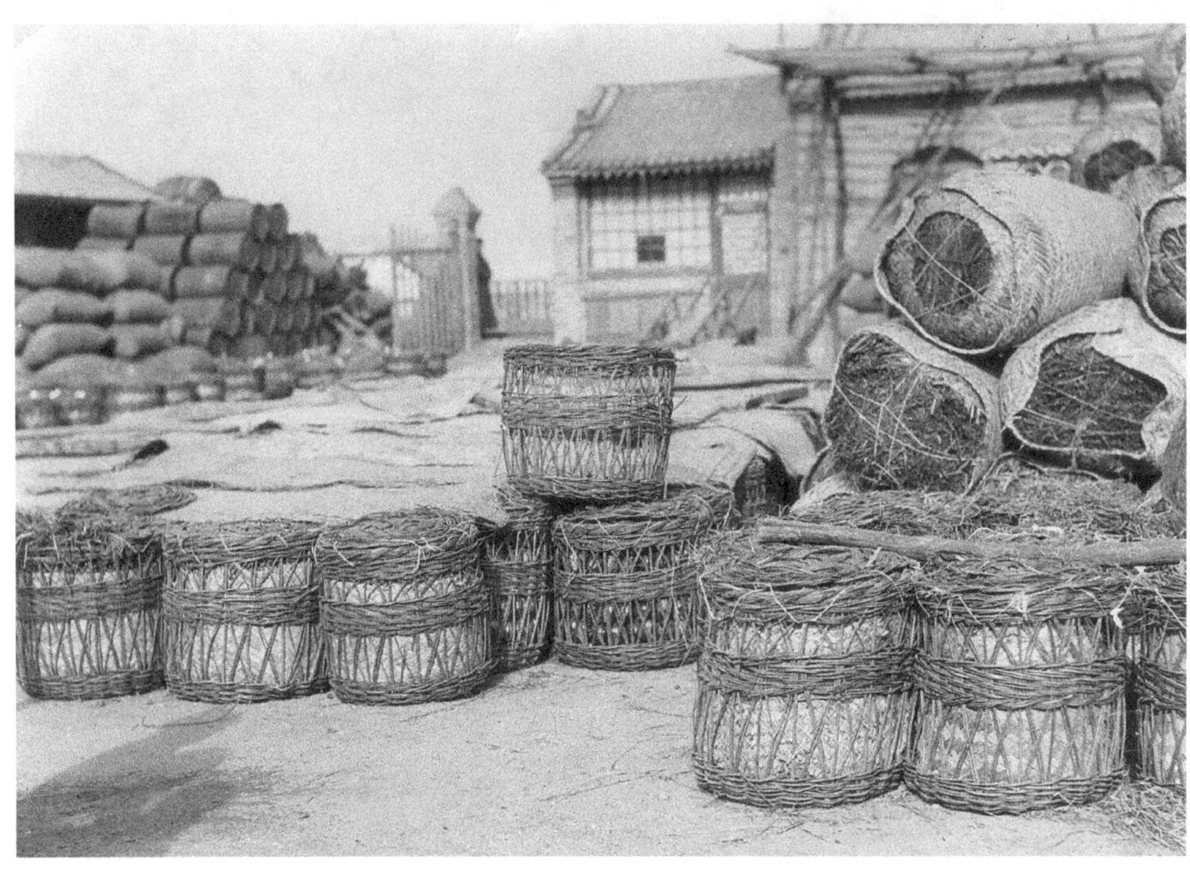

Req. 438. *Donkey panniers filled with fruit ready for transport to the city.*

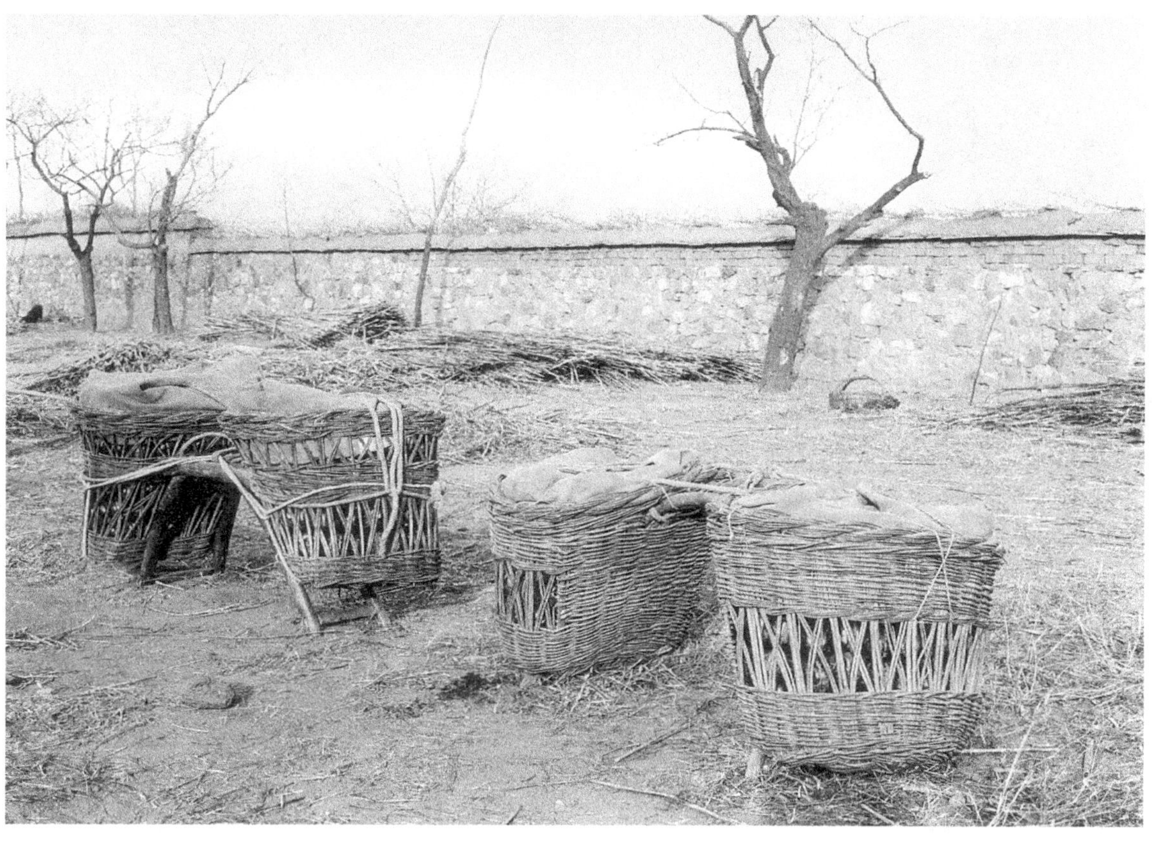

38043. *Nov. 28, 1924. Tai Ling Yuan. A close-up picture of mule and donkey packs filled with persimmons and ready to be loaded on the animals' backs. A mule's load is 500 fruits, a donkey's 300, and a camel's 1000.*

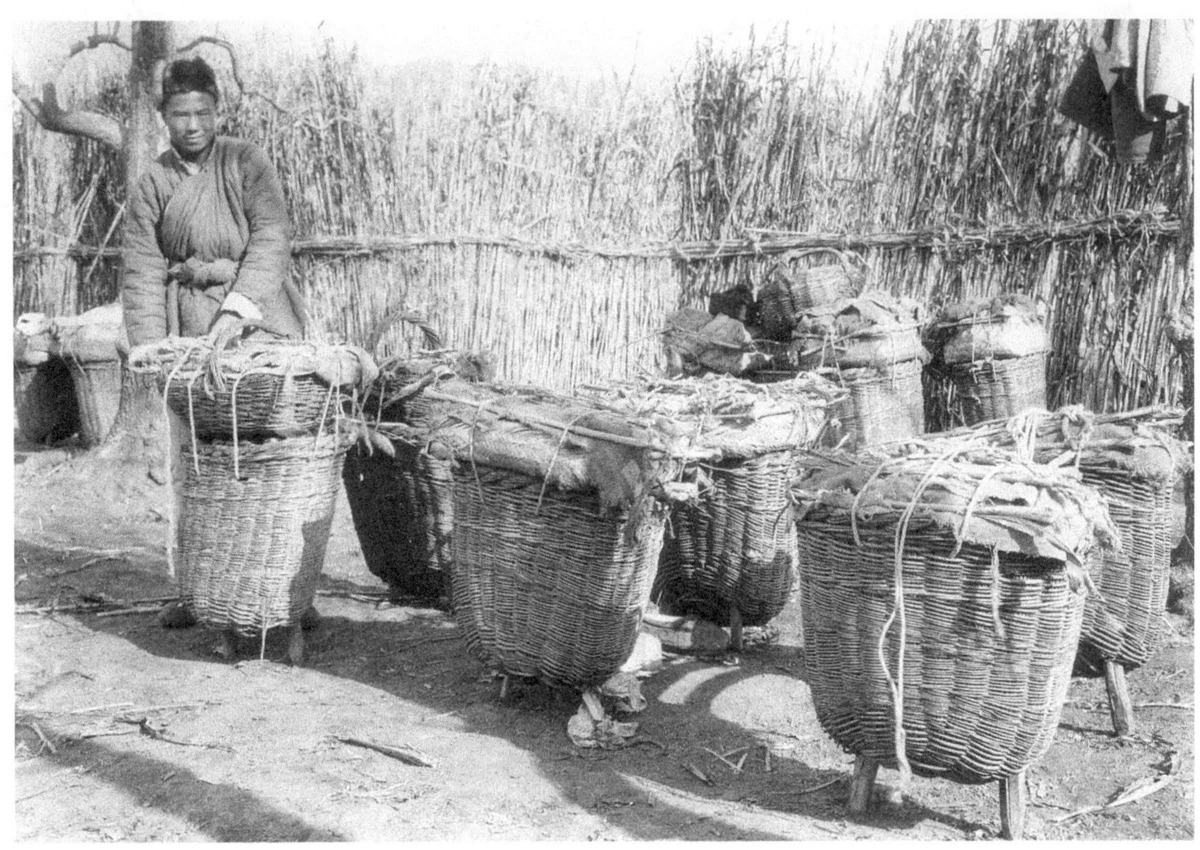

46224. *Hsiang Tang village. Donkey baskets ("Lung tuos") of persimmons tied up ready for loading on donkeys.*

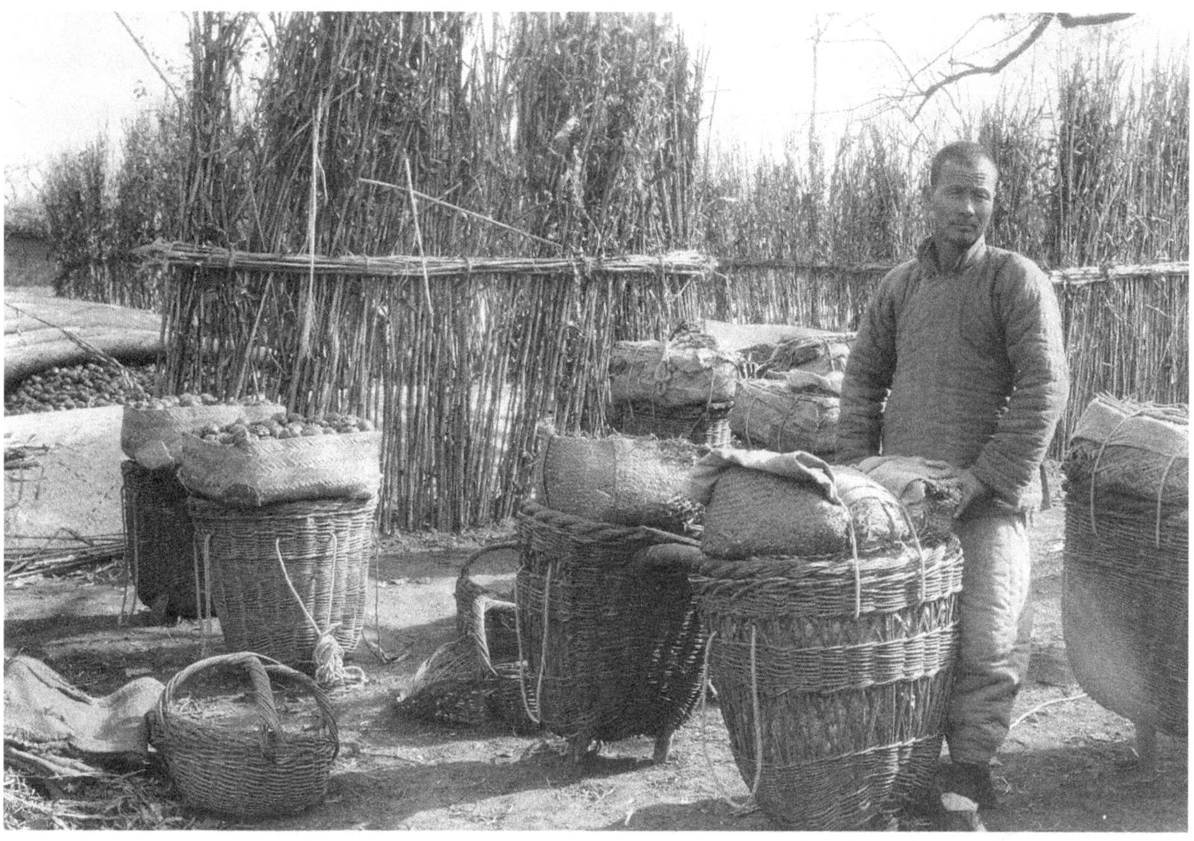

46222. *Nov. 14, 1930. Hsiang Tang. A nearby view in the storage yard of Mr. Chu Li Chi in the above village, where from Nov. 7 to Feb. 27 we secured temperature records of the air and persimmons in open storage beds. In the foreground there are several "Lung tuos" or donkey panniers filled with persimmons. It will be noted that each of the baskets has been augmented with another smaller basket of about 100 fruit each. At the right, a donkey man has just finished covering and lashing one of the small additional baskets to one of the panniers. To the left, and a little further back, sitting on top of donkey panniers are auxiliary baskets yet to be covered and roped in place. Still further back are partly uncovered beds of fruit.*

The temporarily constructed kaoliang (sorghum) fences along the south side of the beds are for the purpose of shading them and assisting in keeping the fruit cool in the early fall, and keeping the fruit frozen after it freezes.

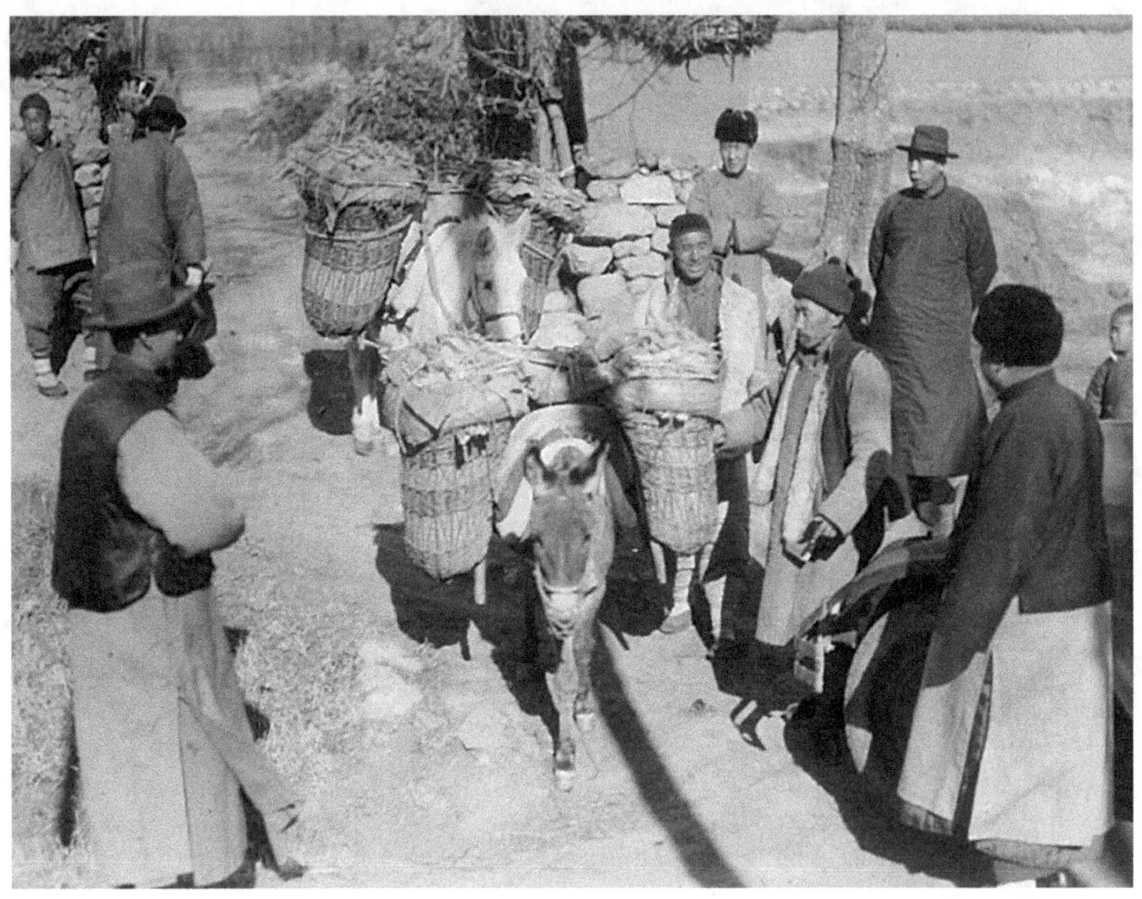

***46238.** Hsiang Tang village. Donkeys loaded with persimmons. These are part of a donkey train leaving the storage yard of Mr. Chi. The first man at the right is Mr. Peter Liu, our interpreter, and next to him is Mr. Chi.*

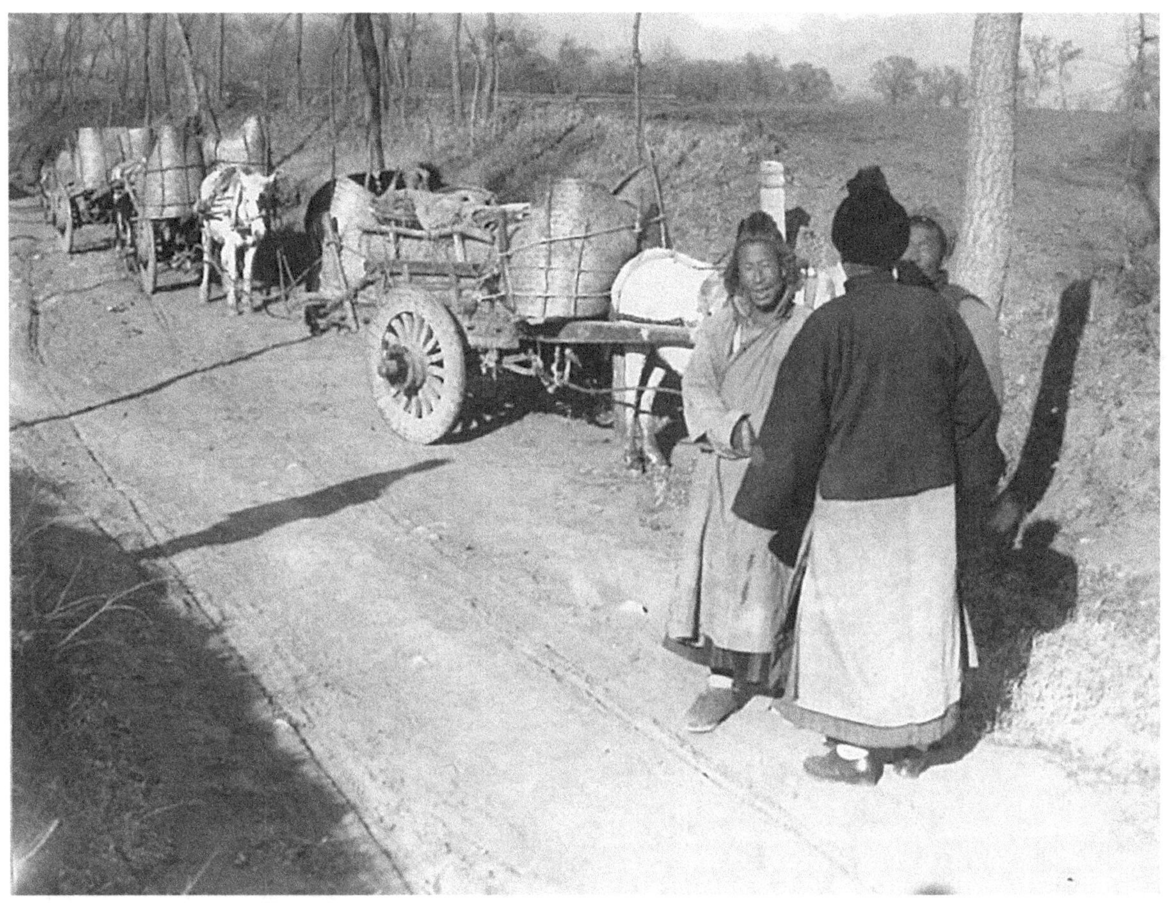

***46241.** Nov. 21, 1930. Three cartloads of persimmons along the road between Hsiang Tang and Tang Shan, en route to Peiping. Note in each the reed-grass matting body and the supporting sticks and ropes.*

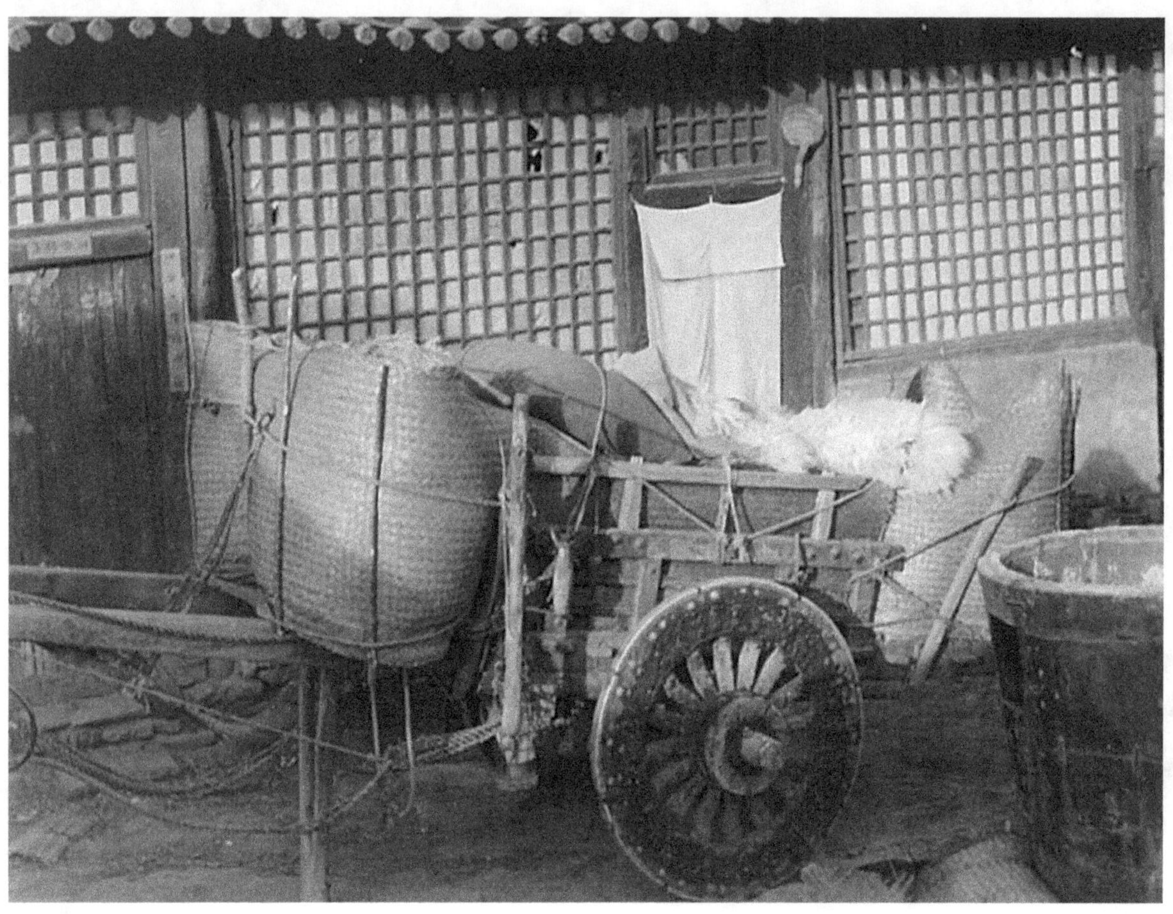

46204. *Nov. 11, 1930. Peiping. A fairly nearby view of a cartload of persimmons which pulled into the compound of the Wan Shun Tien Inn, where there was at the time two 6-container and one 8-container kilns in daily operation for the hot water treatment of persimmons to remove their astringency. A cartload of Tamopan persimmons is given as 6000 fruits, and of Lantern persimmons, 12,000.*

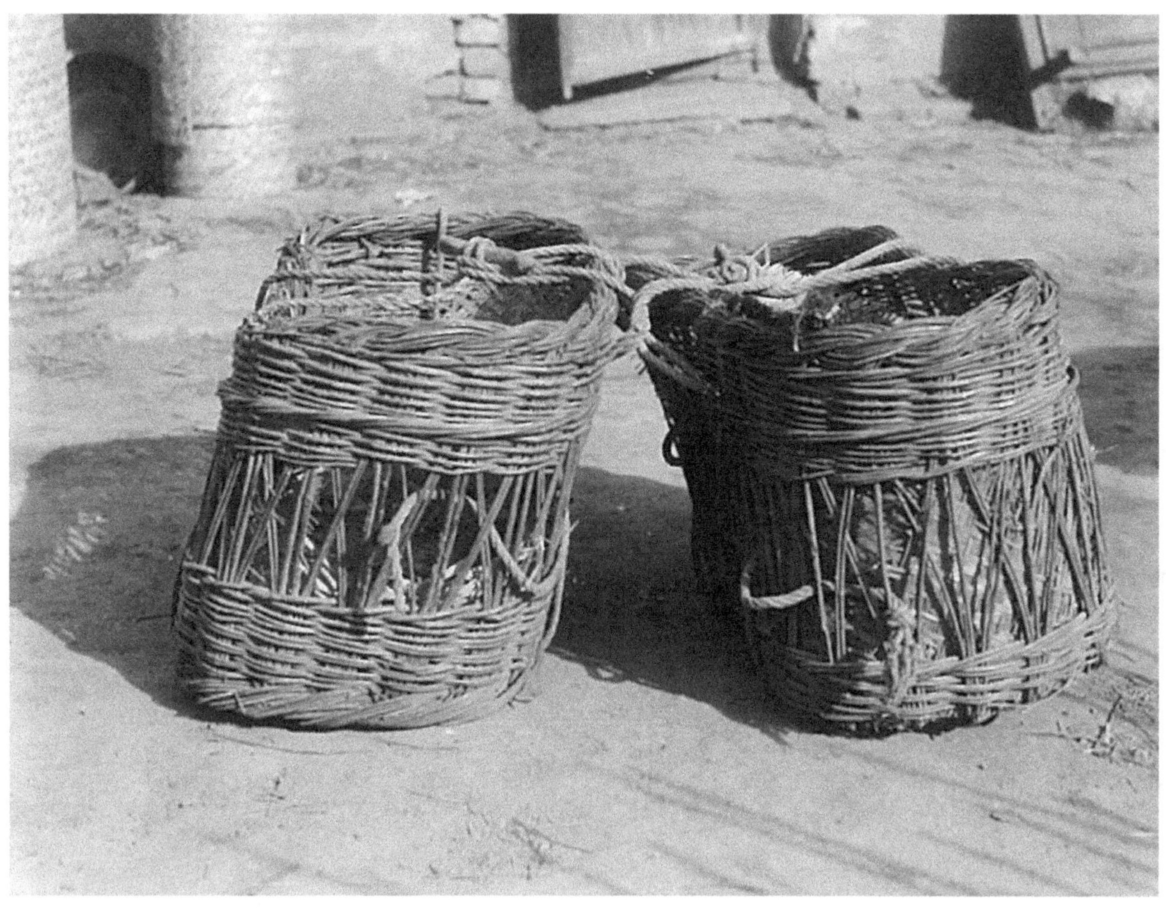

46202. *Nov. 11, 1930. Peiping. A nearby view of camel panniers. These baskets are sometimes made of small shoots of a species of* ***Lespedeza,*** *and also shoots of* ***Vitex.***

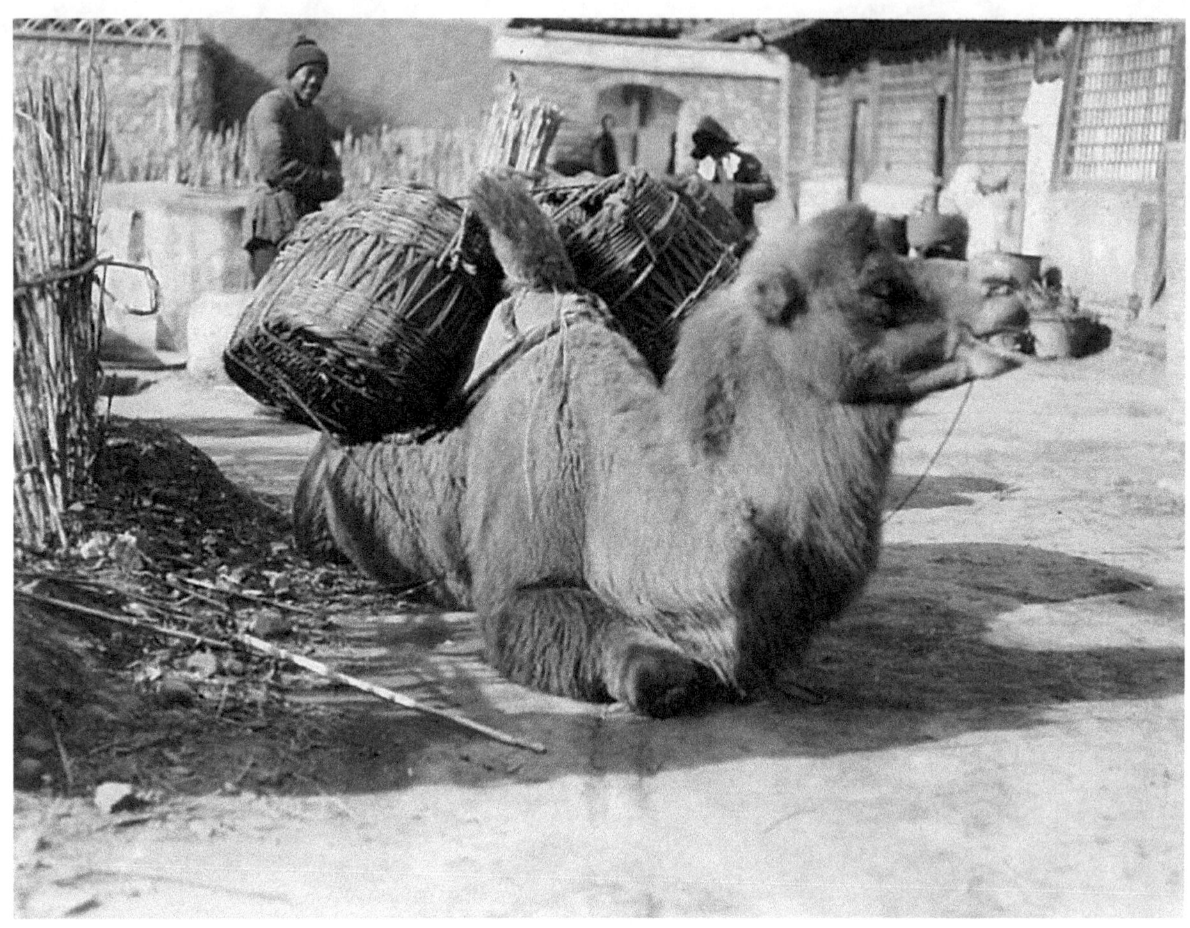

***46198A.** Nov. 11, 1930. Peiping. A nearby front view of a camel, showing its position and appearance at rest. This is also its position when being loaded or unloaded. The view also shows the position of the reed-grass (or sometimes felt) saddle pad, and the adjustment of the two empty "Tuo kuangs" or large panniers. Their adjustment is practically the same when filled.*

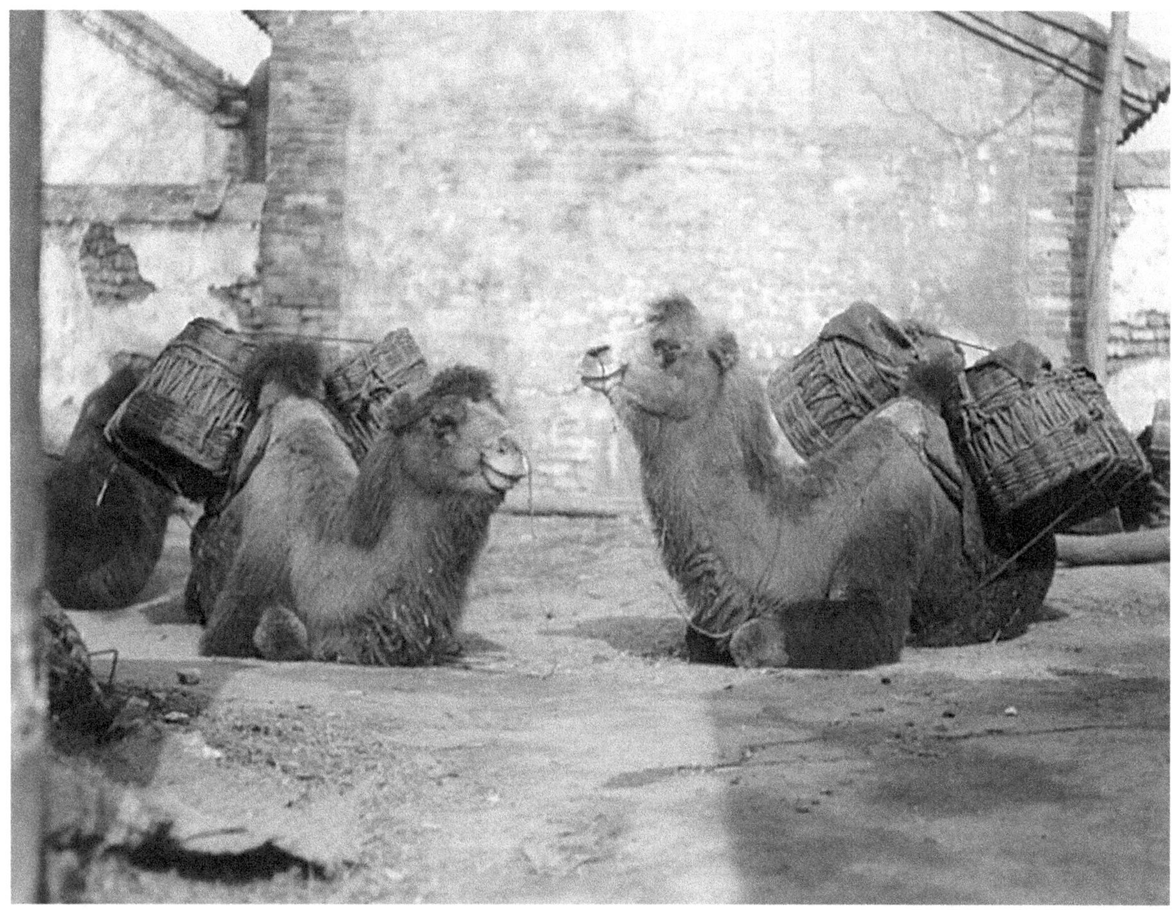

46200. *Nov. 11, 1930. Peiping. Camels in the Wan Shun Tien Inn compound where, between the middle of September and that of November, 1930, something like a million persimmons were depuckered by the hot water treatment. The "Tuo kuangs" meaning "camel baskets" or panniers are empty, and the camels are resting preparatory to their return trip of 1½ days into the persimmon growing district in the hills and valleys about Toli.*

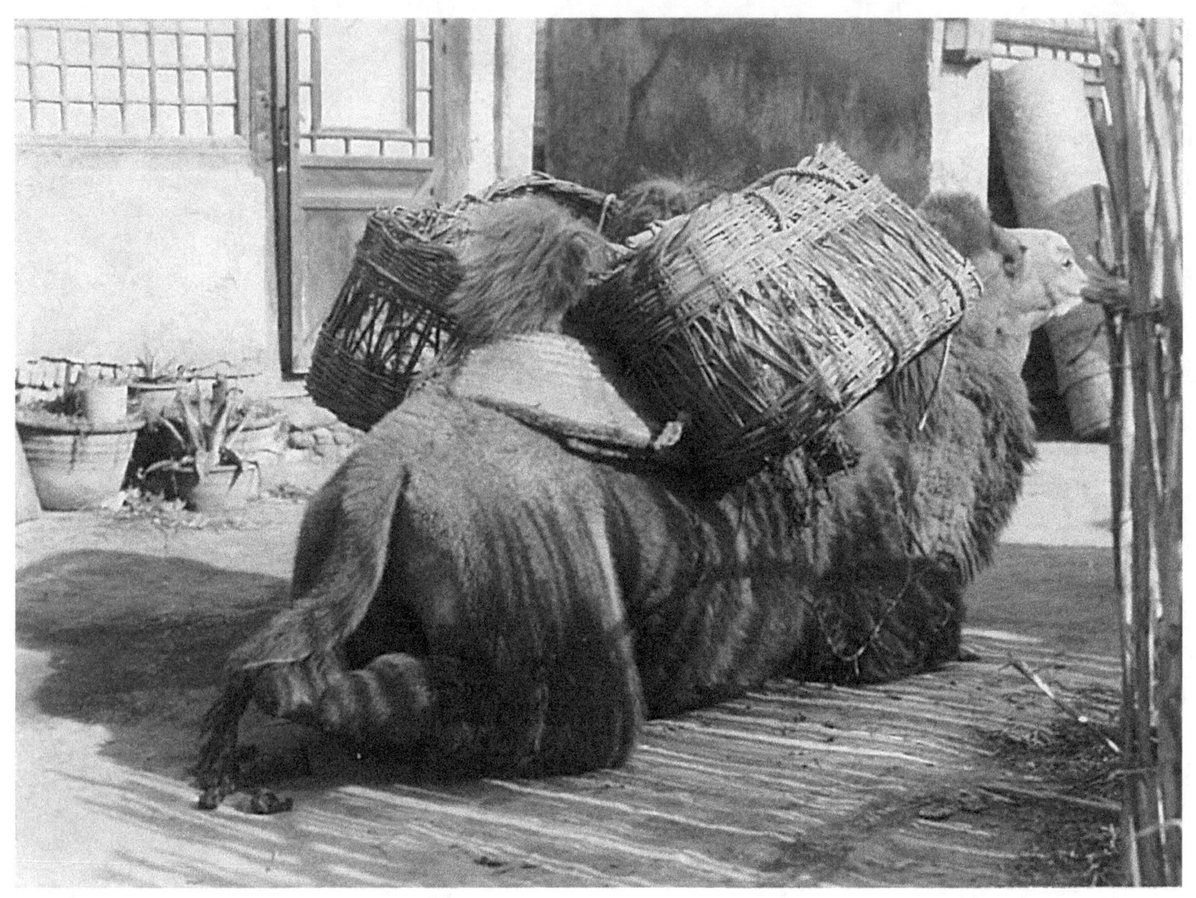

46198. *Nov. 11, 1930. Peiping. A nearby rear view of a camel and empty panniers.*

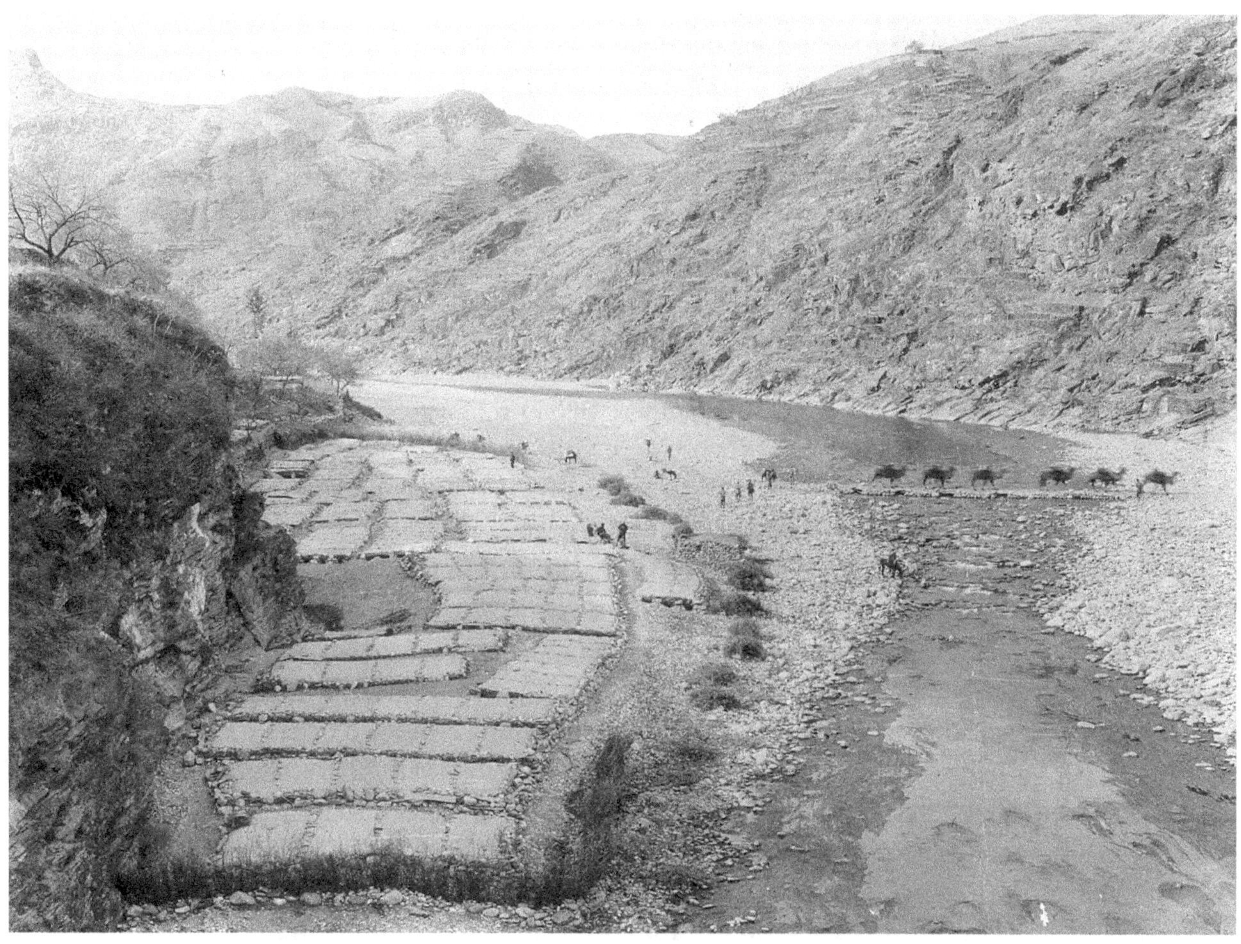

***29847.** Nov. 6, 1924. Fo Tzu Chuang. A persimmon storage ground on the sandy gravelly river bottomland next to the Clearwater River northwest of Peking. [Ed.: Note the camel train crossing the river in the distance.] The beds are covered with matting weighed in position with small stones. It is estimated that 1,000,000 persimmon fruits for the market in Peking are stored and transported from this yard.*

佛子庄柿子場

Fo Tzu Chuang shih Tzu Cháng
Persimmon storage at Fo Tzu Chuang

MARKETING

The harvested fruit is put into temporary piles and sold to visiting purchasers. It is also sent by donkey trains to nearby shipping points or direct to Peking or other markets. That which is not utilized in this way is stored in accessible storage grounds for winter use.

The marketing of persimmons begins in mid-September even before the fruit is fully mature, when artificial means (hot water processing) have to be employed to get rid of the astringency in order to make it edible, and continues until the open-air cold storage beds are exhausted, which in some seasons is as late as the last of March. The Chinese persimmon growers thus have a market season of nearly 6 months.

The numerous fruit stands in the Peking markets and on the streets are filled with this popular fruit which sells at reasonable prices, 3 to 5 coppers local currency per fruit, throughout the entire winter season. Americans and Europeans in China are generally fond of this fruit, and with these foreigners the persimmon as a breakfast fruit is as popular as the grapefruit is in the United States.

One of the men interested in the persimmon game appeared to us to be a pretty bright fellow, and apparently was not only very familiar with the persimmon-growing districts in the vicinity of Peiping, but was also quite well posted as to the quantity of persimmons produced in each district. From him we not only got the names of the villages included in each district and their average annual production, but also the estimated percent of the persimmons produced in each district which are marketed in Peiping, including, of course, both the inner and outer cities. This detailed information follows:

Estimated Number of Persimmons Produced Annually in the Different Growing Regions Near Peiping, Chihli, China

(1) The region from Toli to Ch'ang T'ao, a distance of almost 19 miles, produces about 20,000,000 fruits. Half of these persimmons come to Peiping, and half of them are shipped away from Liu Li Ho station of the Peiping-Hankow railway.

(2) The region starting from Mentoukou and extending southeast to Shang Wan, Hsiao Ying, Hou Hua Ying, Wang Ling, Shih Pau Ying and Ta Yu, a distance of about 10 miles, produces about 20,000,000 fruits, and about 70% come to Peiping.

(3) Starting from San Chia Tien to the northwest, and extending to Nan An Ho, Pei An Ho, Tai Tou, Ch'ien Sha Chien, and Shih Jen Tou, a distance of about 14 miles, about 5,000,000 are produced, all for the Peiping market.

(4) Starting from Nankou and westward, Tao Yii Wa, Hua Ta, K'u Chiang, Pai Yii K'ou, Mal Feng Suan, Ch'i Yuan Tsun, Nan Liu Tsun, and Pei Liu Tsun, a distance of about 14 miles, about 15,000,000 fruits are produced. About half go to Peiping and the other half go to Kalgan.

(5) From Nankow toward the Ming Tomb valley, the names of the villages are Tai Ping Chuang, Hsiao Kung Men, Tai Ling Yuan, Ting Ling, Chao Ling, Chang Ling, and Lao Chun Tang, a distance of about 10 miles. This region produces about 15,000,000 persimmons, and half come to Peiping and half go to Kalgan.

(6) From the villages from Kuan Yao to Tung Shan Kou, about 7,000,000 persimmons are produced. From Pa Chien to Peng Shan, about 5,000,000 are produced. From Tsui Tsun, Ma Yii, and Hsiang Tang, about 14,000,000 are produced. And Ch'in Ch'eng and Tao Lin produce about 5,000,000. Persimmons from these four different regions are about 70% large persimmons and 30% Lantern (small) persimmons. Approximately 80% of these fruits come to Peiping, while 20 % are either sold locally or are transported and sold somewhere else.

(7) Therefore, total estimated production from all regions near Peiping = 106,000,000 persimmon fruits.

Mr. Chi of Hsiang Tang village stated that selling prices of persimmons direct from storage beds are as follows:

1st grade Tamopan (large persimmon)	$7.50 Mex. per 1000.
2nd grade Tamopan (large persimmon)	$6.50 Mex. per 1000.
3rd grade Tamopan (large persimmon)	$5.00 Mex. per 1000.

First and second grades of Lantern variety are put together and sell for $4.00 Mex. per 1000. The third grade Lanterns are not sent to market but are sold in the village at about a copper each.

Mr. Chi, in response to our questions, said that quite frequently persimmon growers bed down their own fruit and also buy fruit on others' trees and pick it themselves or hire it picked to increase their quantity of stored fruit. Occasionally a man who does not own or control an orchard buys fruit from orchardists who do not have enough fruit to store or cannot afford to store, and stores it for the winter market.

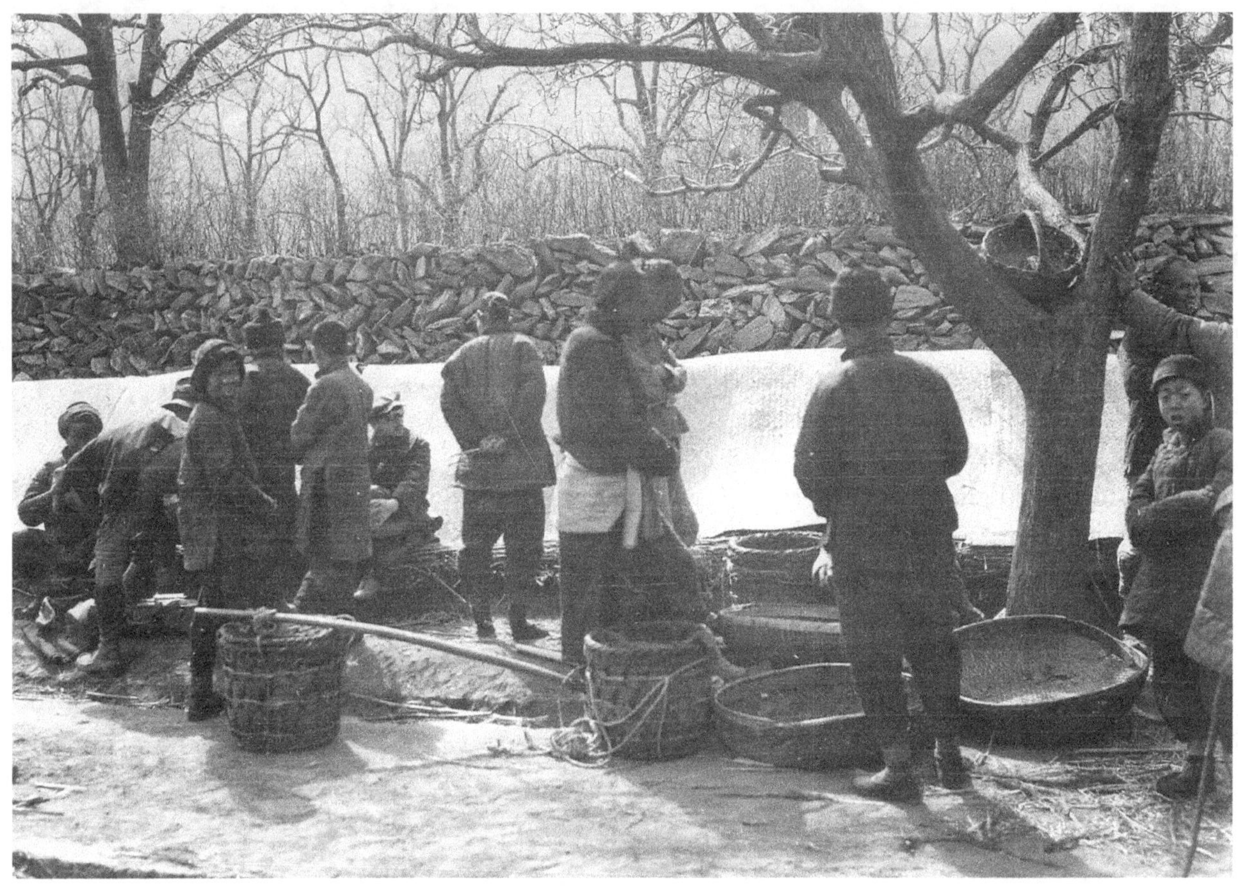

38498. *Mar. 8, 1925. Pan Pi Tien. A close-up picture of a number of persimmon purchasers who are dickering with Mr. Li. When we went to get some pictures of the storage bed in the background, it was about empty.*

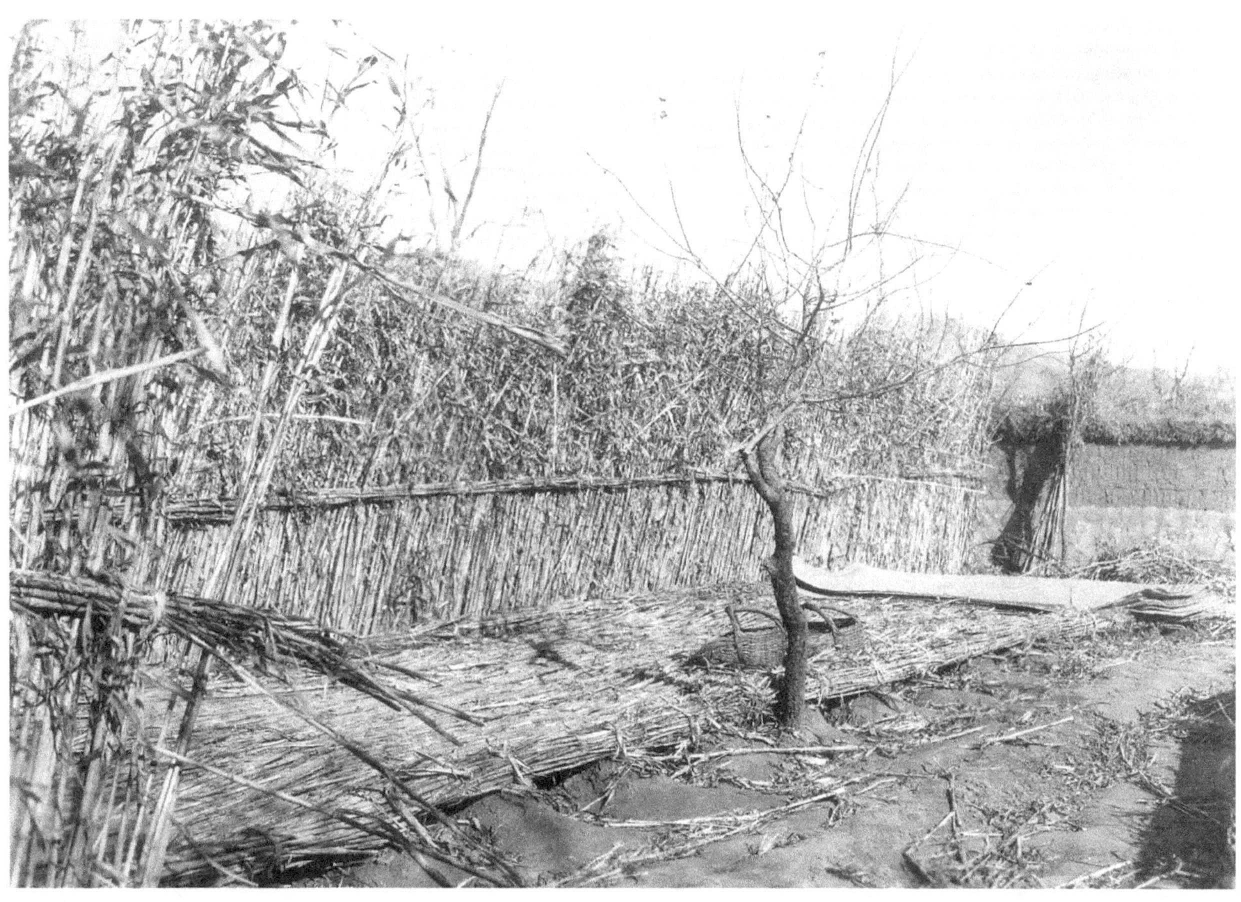

46236. *Hsiang Tang village. Empty persimmon storage bed; a week ago, this bed was filled with many thousands of beautiful 4-inch seedless persimmons. The reed-grass mats used to cover the fruit at night and on bad days are now in a pile at the further end.*

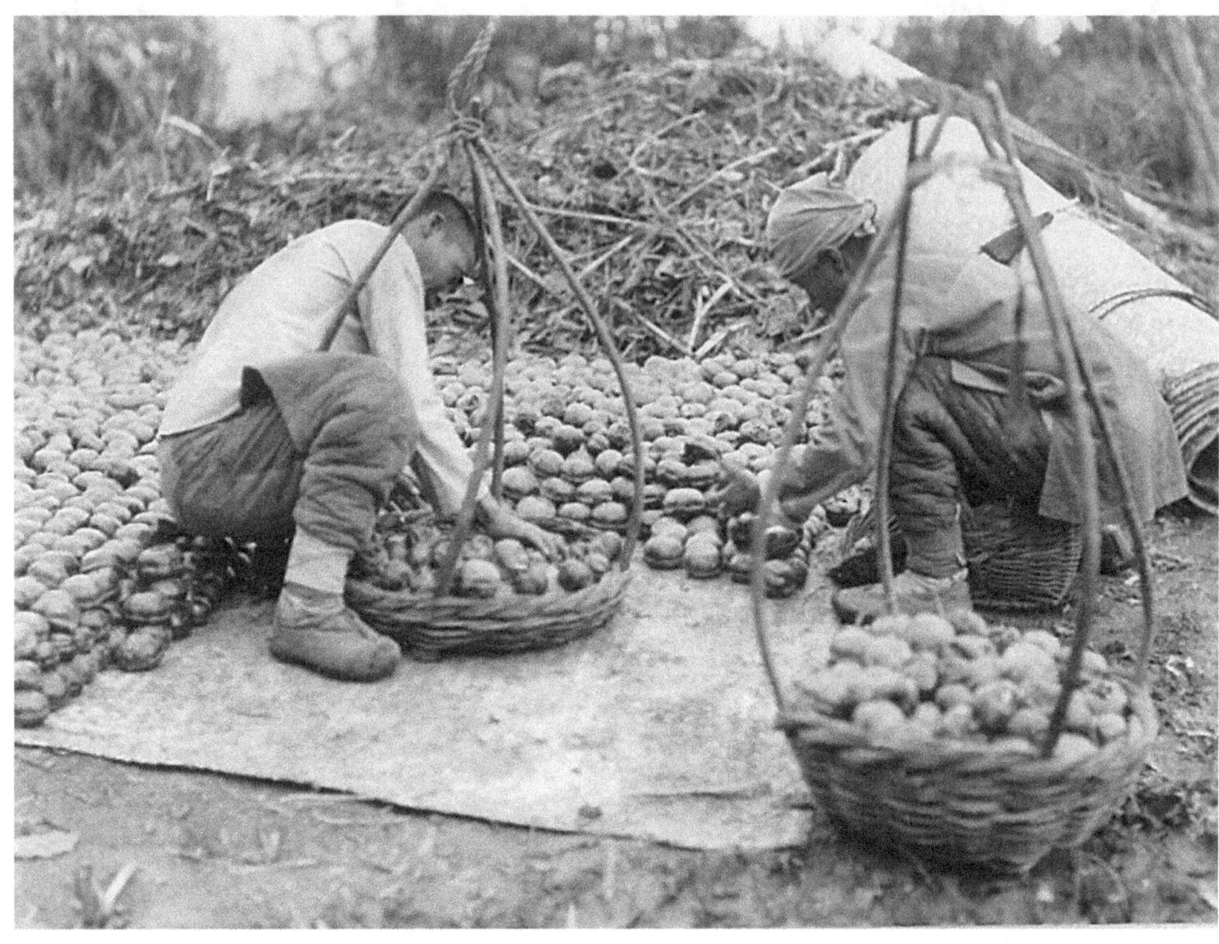

46170. *Nov. 11, 1930. Peiping. One of the common types of baskets used by the Chinese in carrying persimmons and other fruits, also flowers, vegetables, and other commodities. This type of carrying basket is mostly used within the city and at the storage yards when bedding down persimmons, as shown here. When well filled, these baskets each hold from 75 to 100 or even more good-sized fruits.*

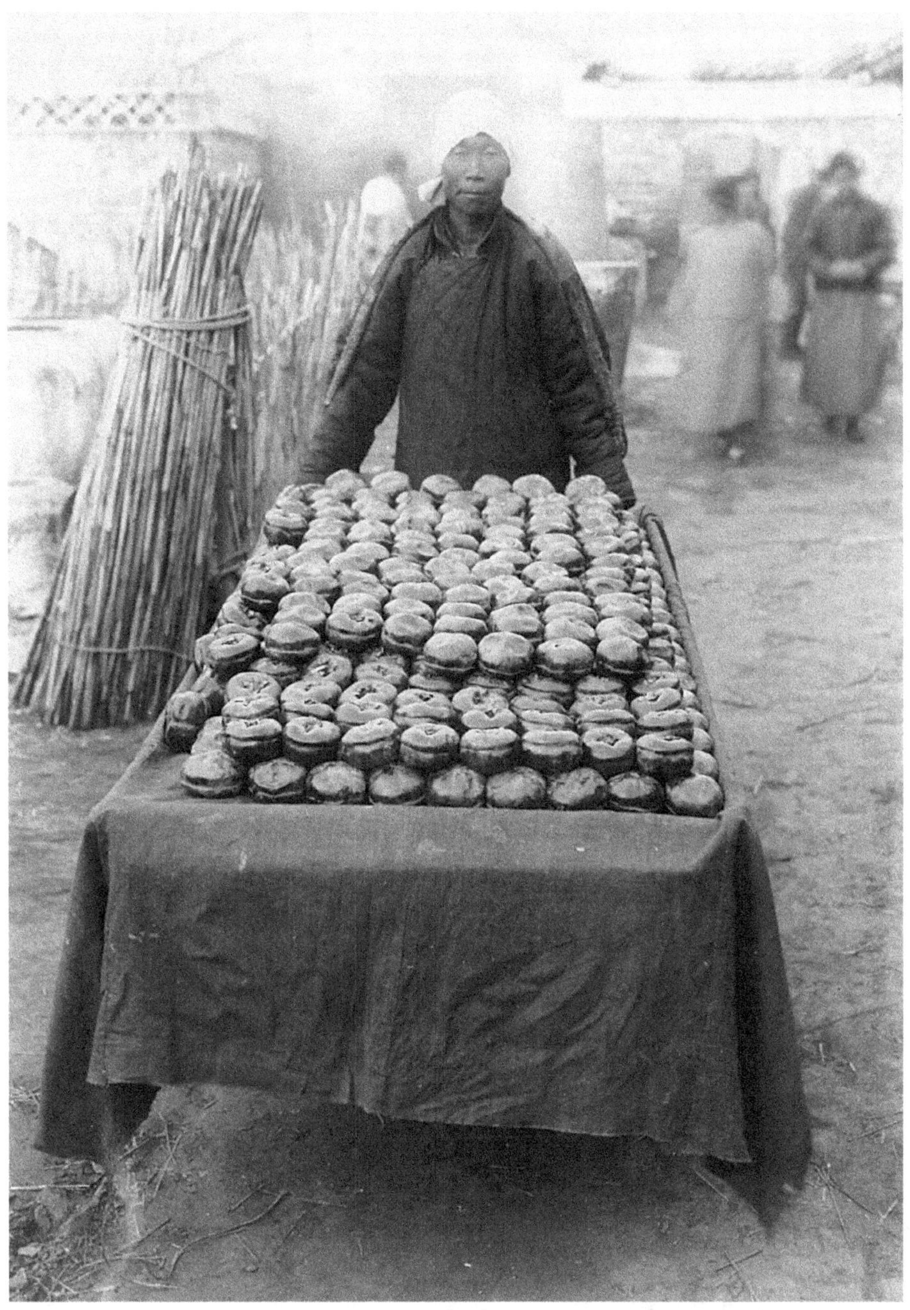

46217. *Nov. 12, 1930. Peiping. A large-wheeled wheelbarrow loaded with something like 500 large (Tamopan) persimmons fresh from a kiln in the compound of the Wan Shun Tien Inn, where on the previous night they were depuckered by the Chinese method of hot water treatment. These large-wheeled wheelbarrows are very commonly seen in the city and also on the highways heavily laden with produce, fuel, and other transportable products. A load for a man with one of these wheelbarrows for short and long hauls up to fifteen or twenty miles, is frequently equal to or even in excess of that of one mule cart.*

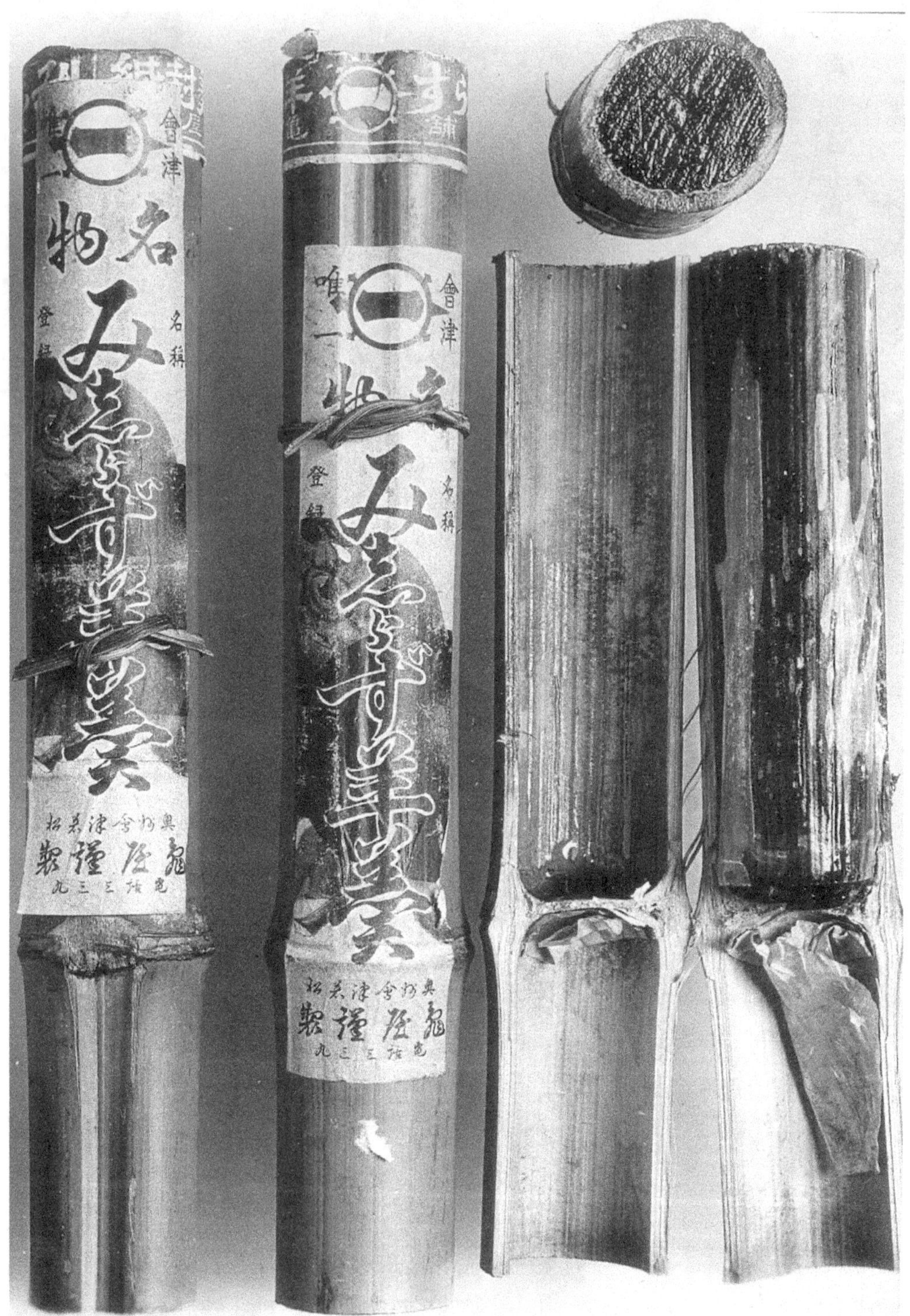

45335. *Dried persimmons sold commercially, stuffed into hollow bamboo stems.*

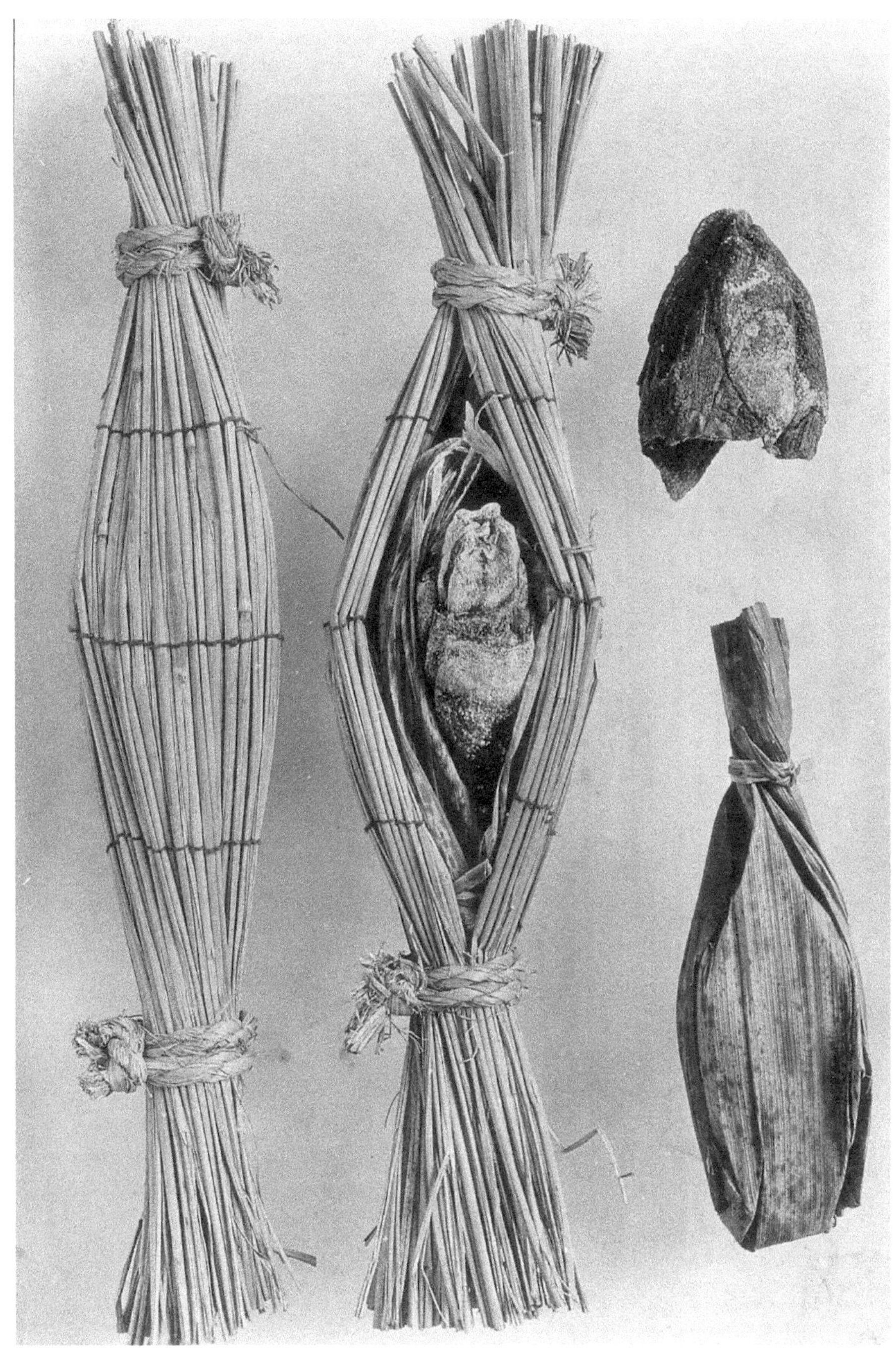

44754. *Dried persimmons sold in tied grass packages.*

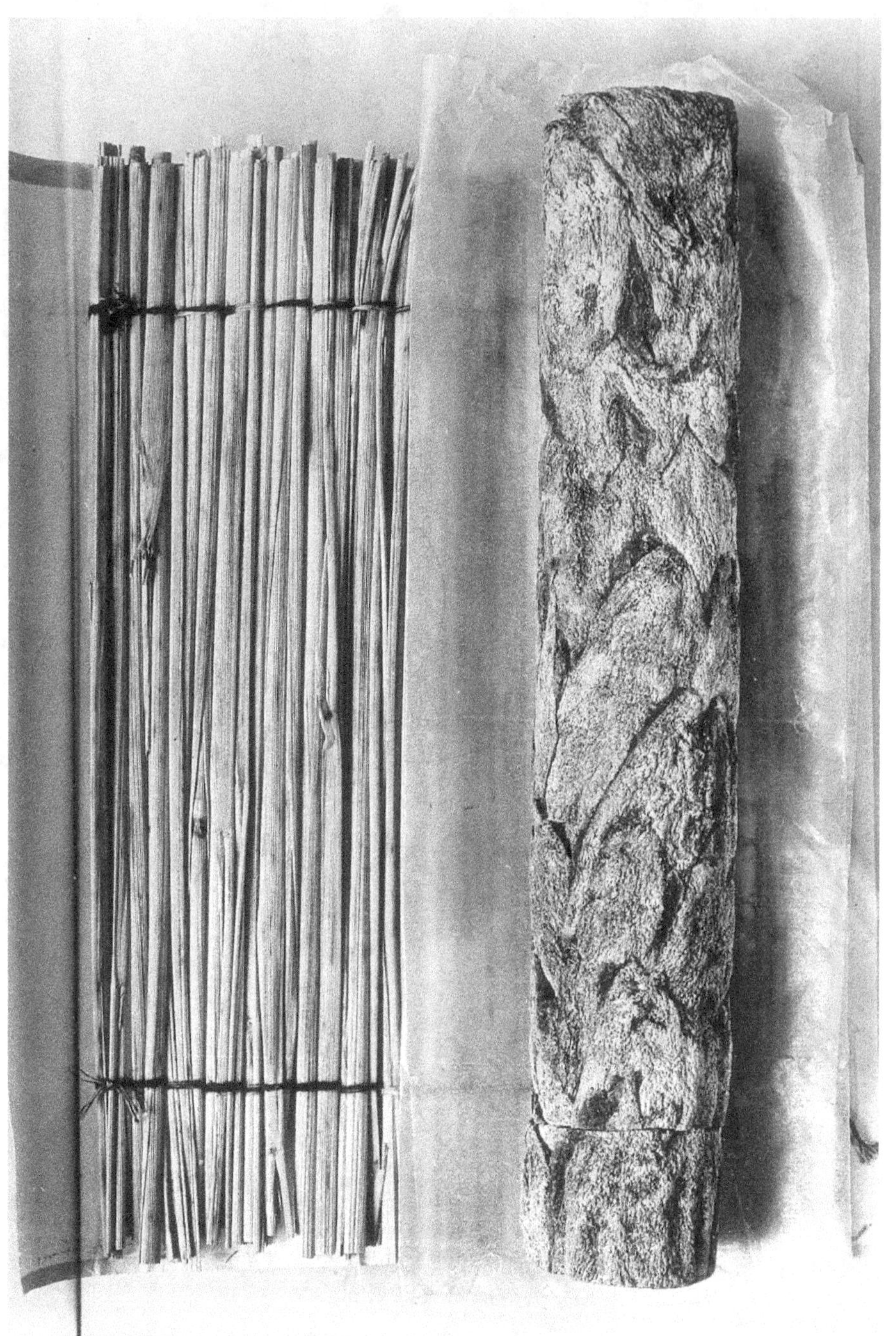

43397. *Dried persimmons sold in Japan in long pressed columns and protected by grass packaging, with outer commercial label removed.*

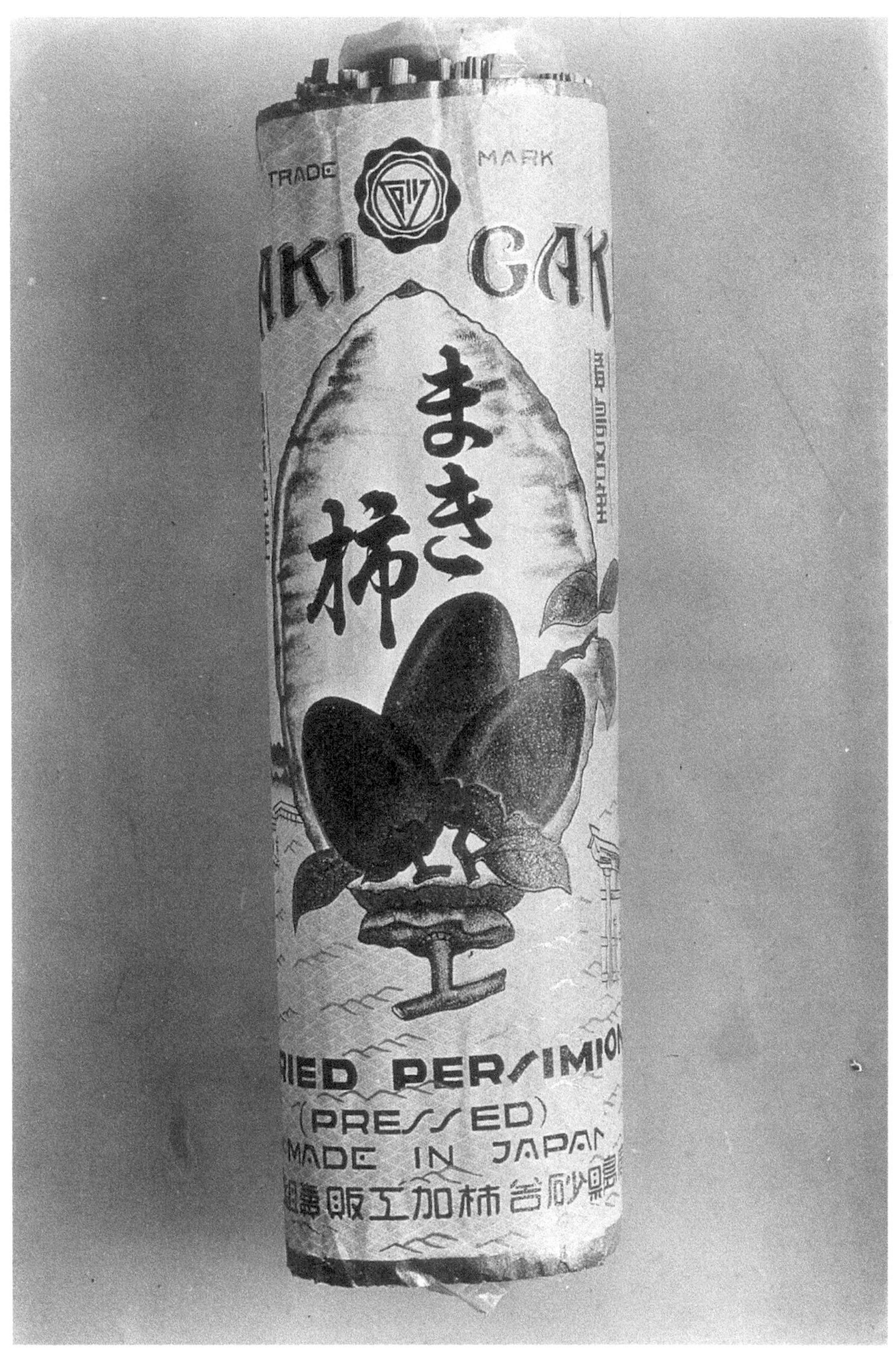

43396. *[Ed.: Commercial package of dried persimmons as sold in Japan. Purchased and photographed by Dorsett.]*

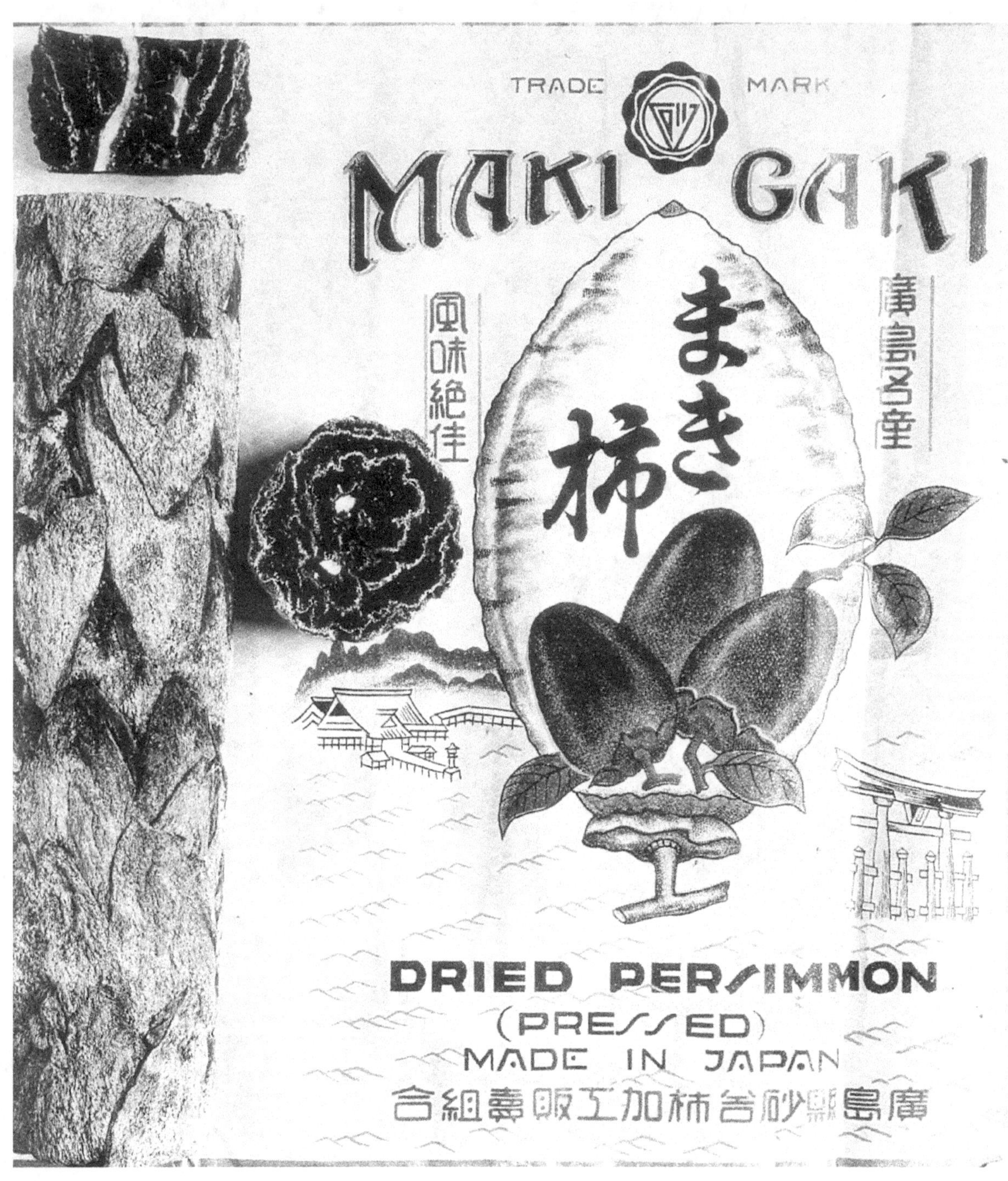

43398. *Commercial label removed from a package of dried persimmons.*

LABOR

[Ed.: A topic not addressed directly by the Dorsetts was labor. While there seemed to be little effort by the orchardists to prune trees or control insects, as noted by the writers, there obviously was a great deal of labor required for most other tasks associated with harvesting, processing, storing, and transporting persimmon fruits.

Presumably many of the residents of each village near each orchard had to be employed to pick the fruits. *Diospyros kaki* does not release its fruits readily, and most bearing trees appeared to be large and tall. Likely many pairs of workers (one in the tree, the other on the ground to catch the fruits) were needed for harvest.

More people were needed to transport the fruits from the orchard to the storage beds, and still more were needed to arrange the fruits in the beds according to set patterns (5 layers of fruits face down, top layer face up). The beds had to be prepared in advance, with trenches dug or redug, and layers of sorghum stalks prepared and placed over the trenches. After the fruits were placed in the beds, coverings of reed mats were rolled over them, and (later) dried grass mulching was put on top of the mats.

Workers grew the sorghum, harvested it, prepared the stalks for support mats, and used them also for windbreak fencing. The reed mats also had to be prepared (or purchased), another labor task. Some of these tasks likely were carried out well before persimmon harvest time.

More labor was required to construct transport baskets, bags, and rolls, and more labor required to fill them for transport from the orchard to the storage beds and from the beds to the market. People, donkeys, mules, and camels were used for transporting fruit to urban markets or to railroad depots. More work was required to care for the animals and to load the fruit onto the animals. Men had to accompany the laden animals to their destinations.

Some fruits were processed in hot water kilns to remove astringency. Some of the resulting non-astringent fruits were peeled and strung into caltics of 10 fruits each to be dried, wrapped, and in some cases, labeled. These tasks required a great deal of labor.

Fortunately China had a large population of rural laborers in the early part of the 20th century. These workers had to be willing, able, competent, and very sturdy to accomplish all of the required tasks of the persimmon fruit industry, and they obviously met all of these standards in good measure.]

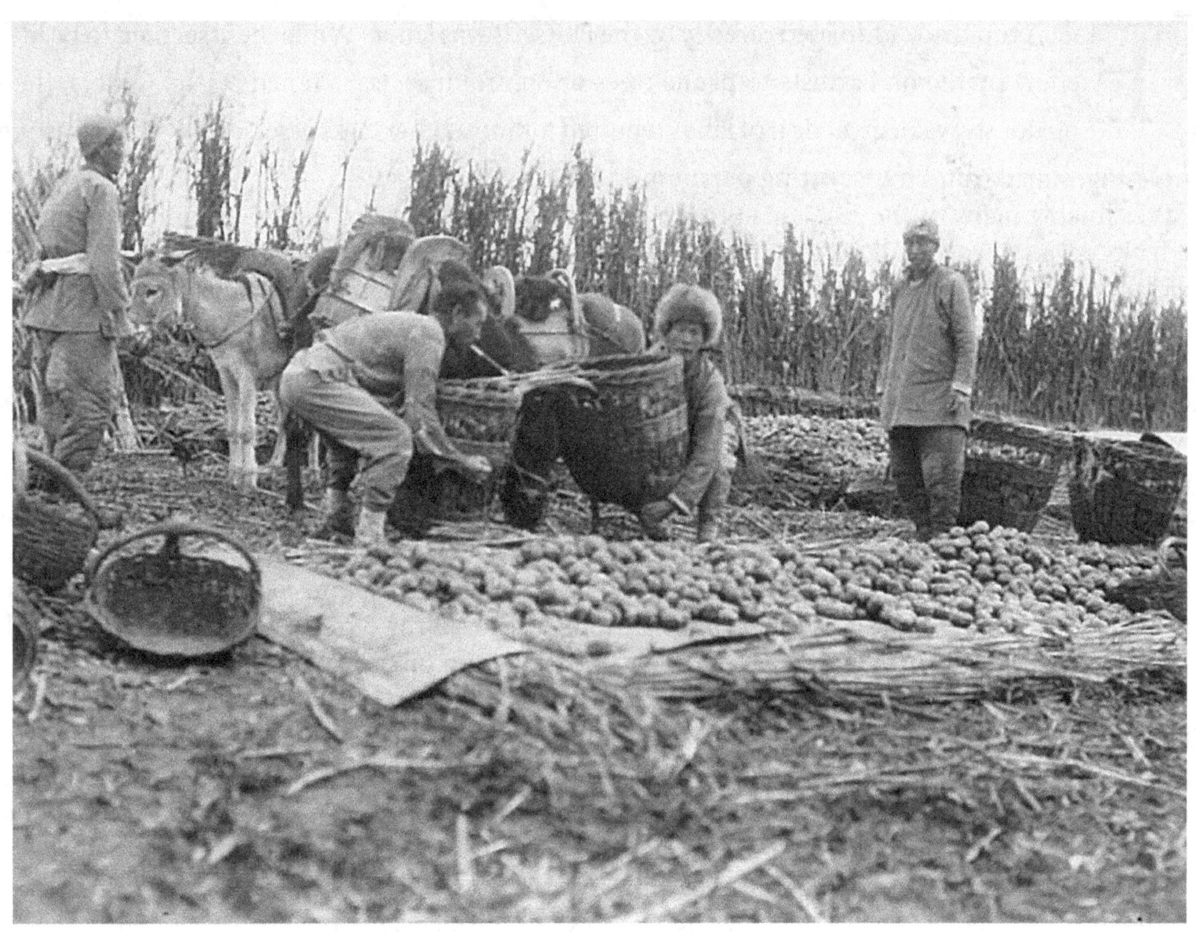

***46172.** Hsiang Tang. Unloading persimmons from donkeys and donkey baskets in an open-air winter storage yard in the outskirts of the above village.*

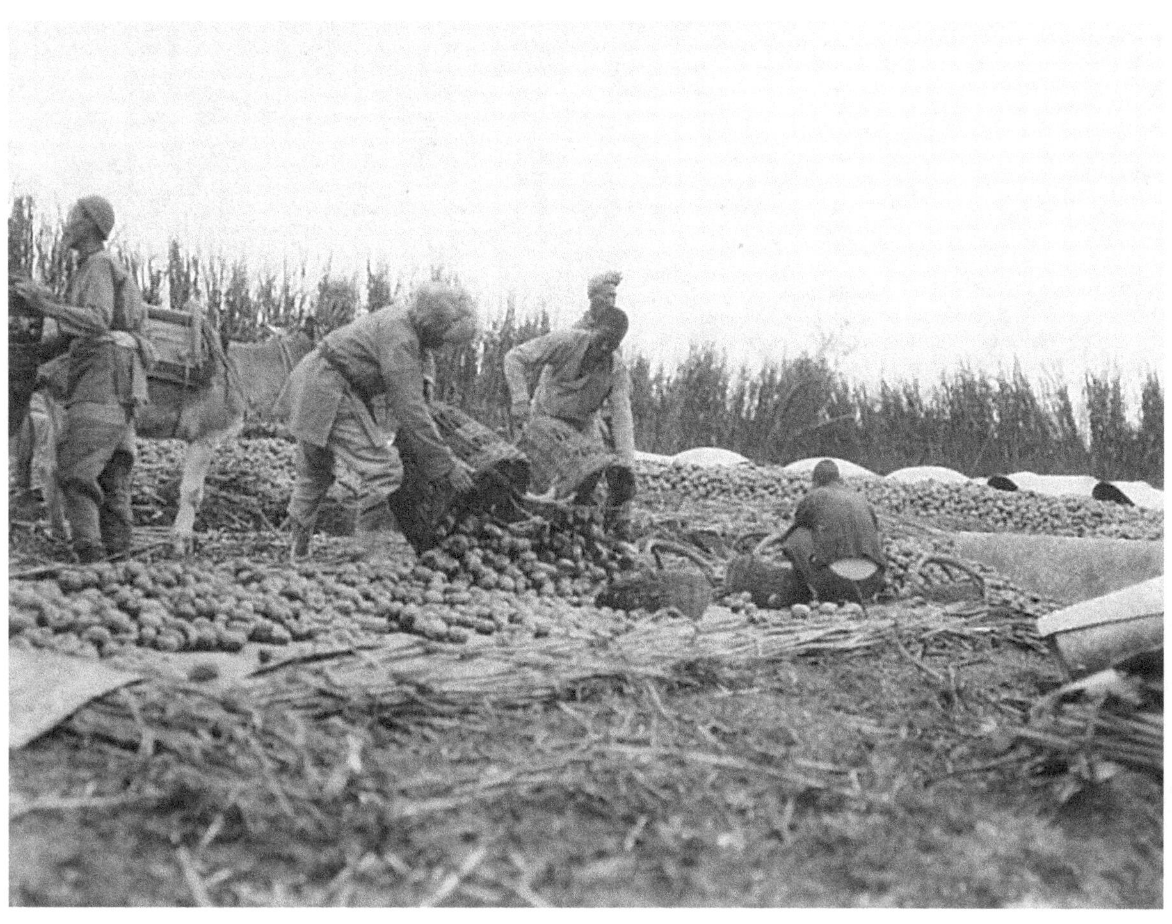

46171. *Hsiang Tang village. Showing the dumping of persimmons onto beds from donkey-carrying baskets.*

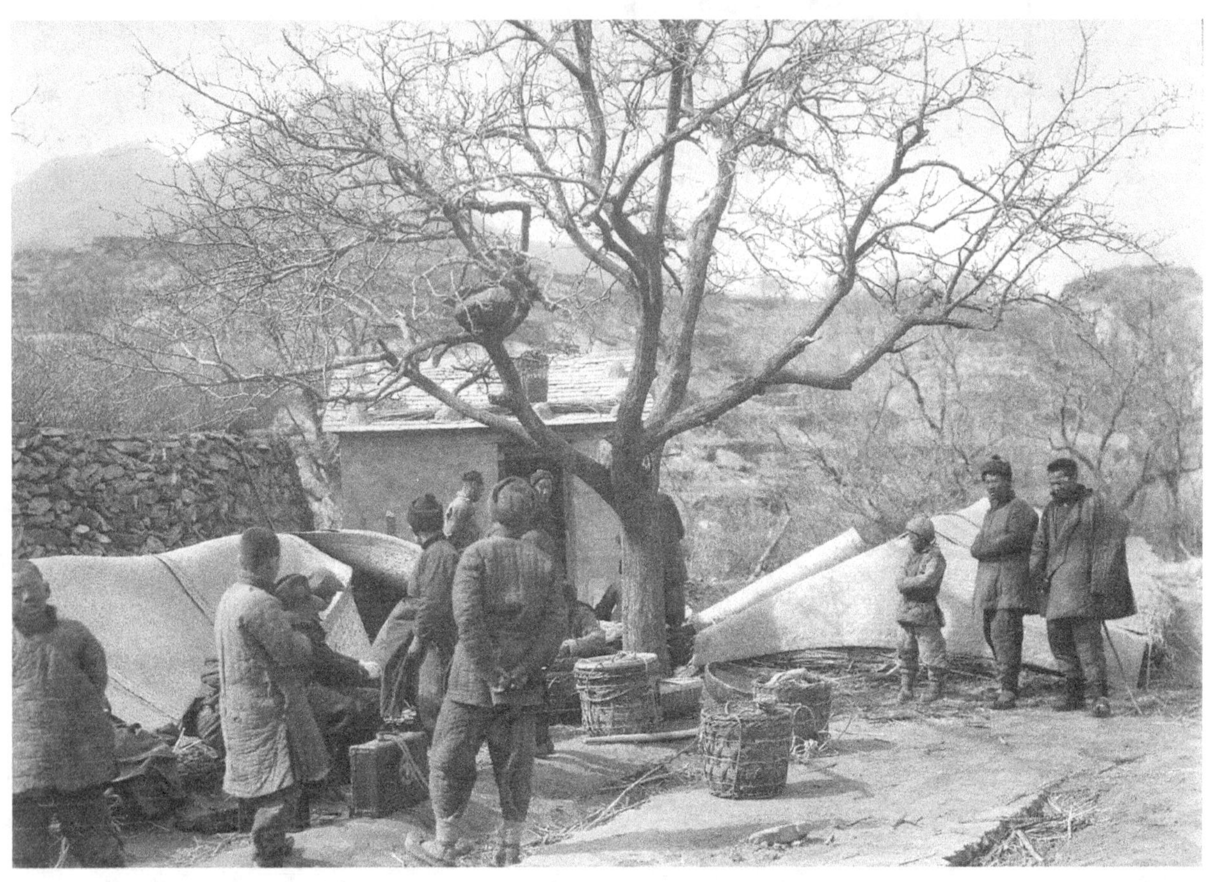

38496A. *Mar. 8, 1925. Pan Pi Tien village. View of young and adult workers gathering around the home and persimmon storage ground of Mr. Li Yung Shen near the village.*

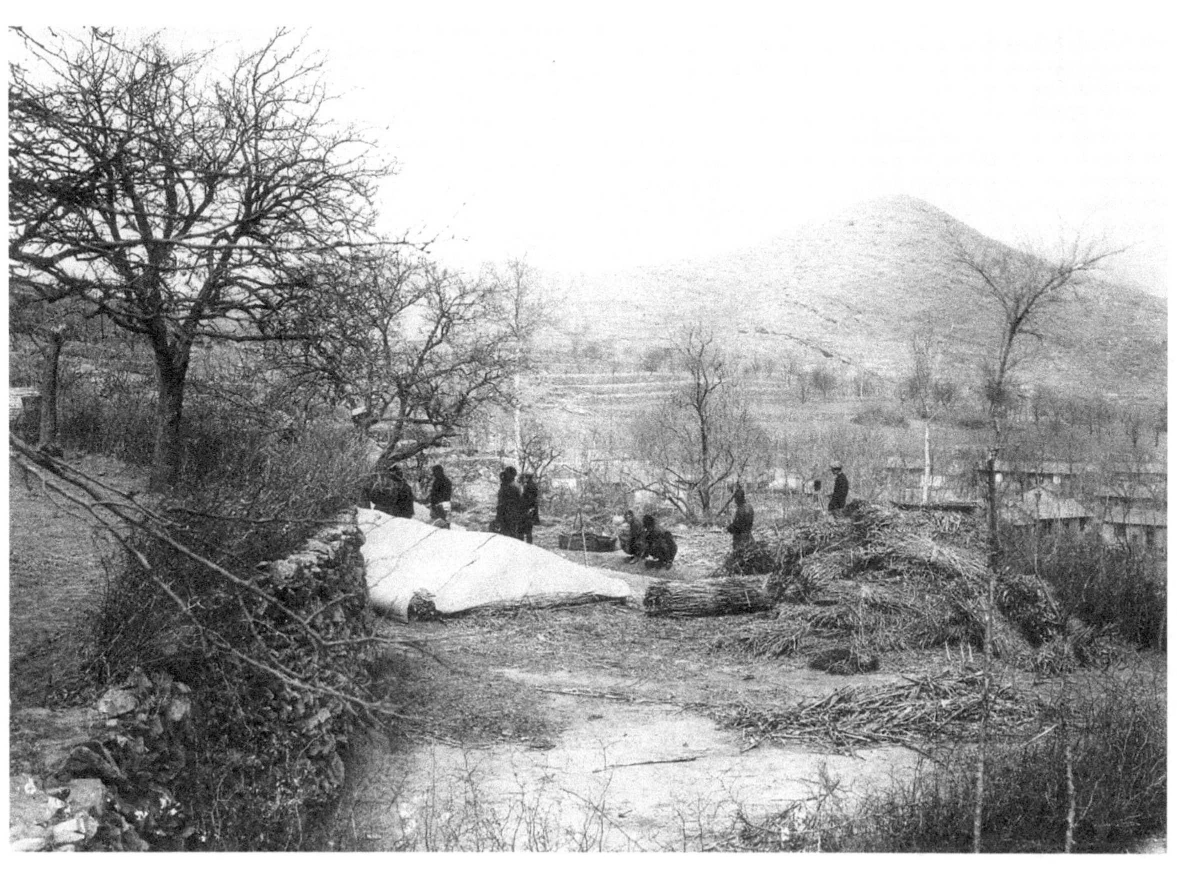

38497. *Mar. 8, 1925. Pan Pi Tien village. Workers preparing a persimmon storage ground of Mr. Li's near the village.*

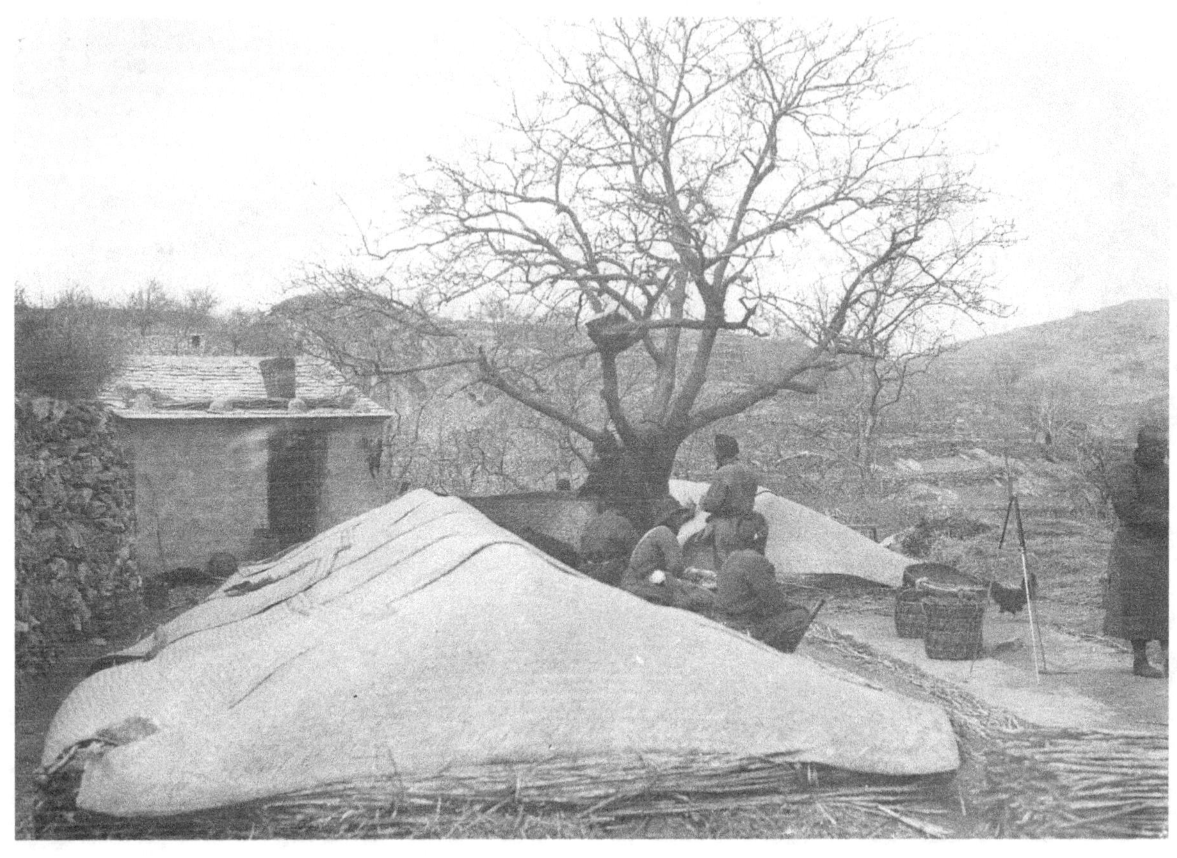

38496. *Mar. 8, 1925. Near Pan Pi Tien village. Workers resting following preparation of a storage bed at Mr. Li's; his house is in the background.*

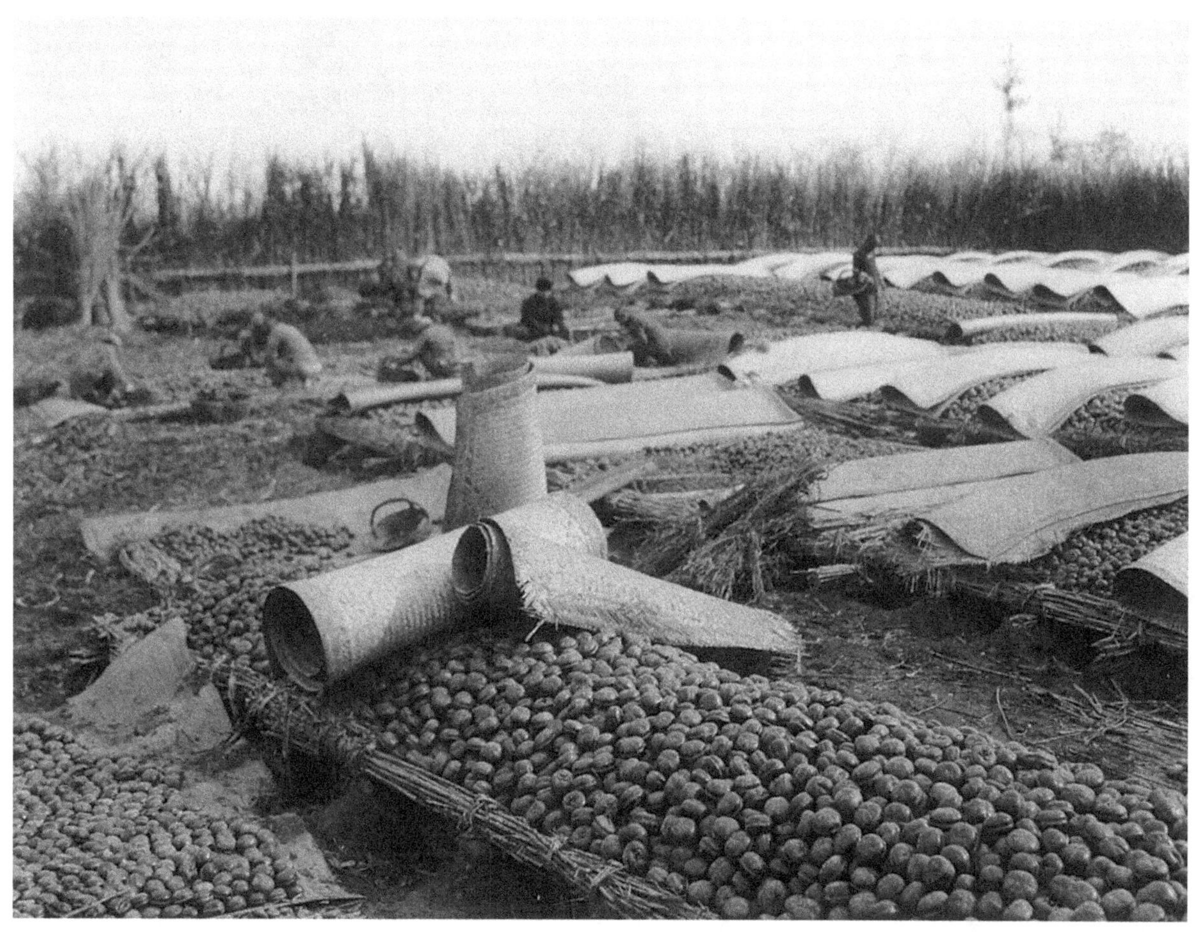

46174. *Hsiang Tang village. View of workers in a persimmon storage yard, where 800,000 to 1,000,000 persimmons are piled in storage beds on kaoliang (sorghum) stalk mats on the ground.*

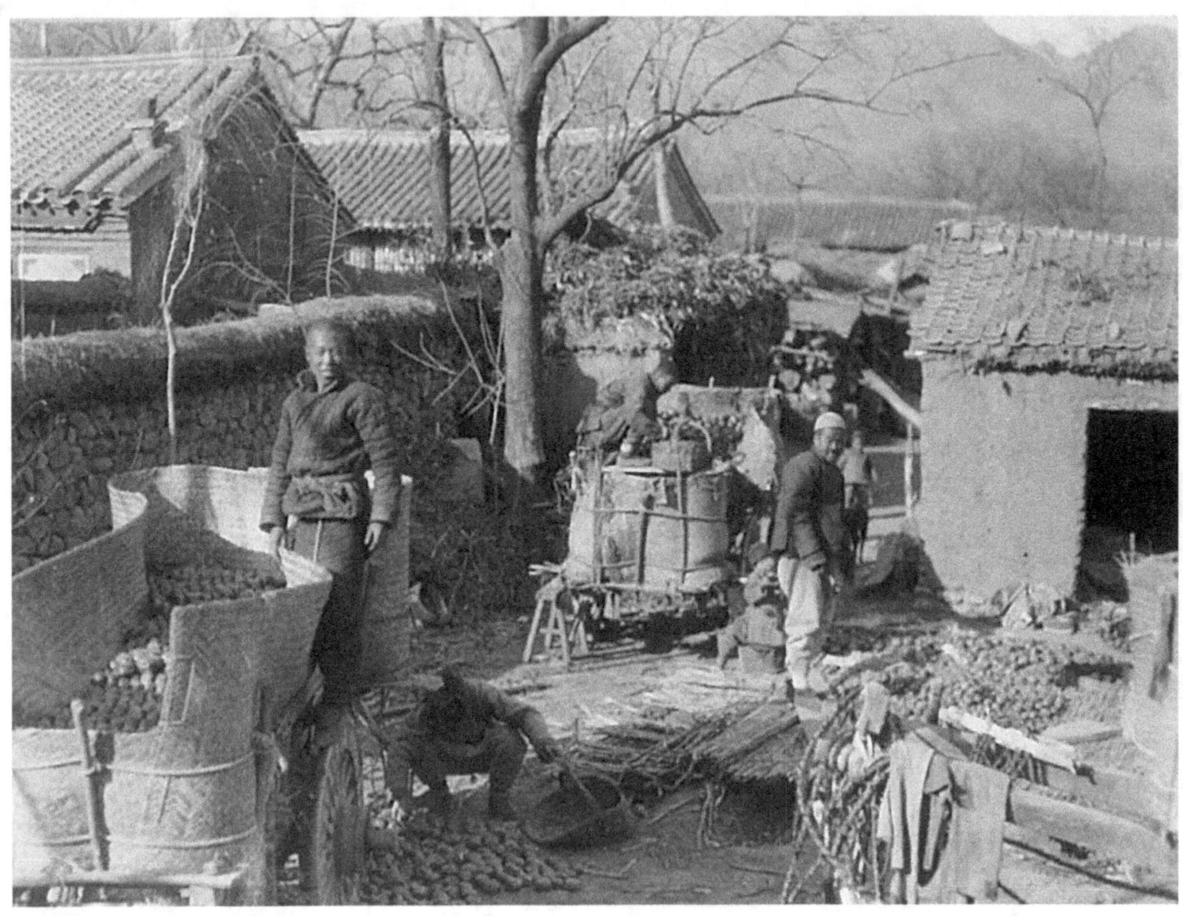

46371. *Dec. 5, 1930. Hsiang Tang. Loading persimmons from winter storage beds onto carts. The fruit is counted into an open-sided basket, such as the man at the right of the cart is using, and when full, is passed to the man standing on the cart wheel, who empties the persimmons into the cart.*

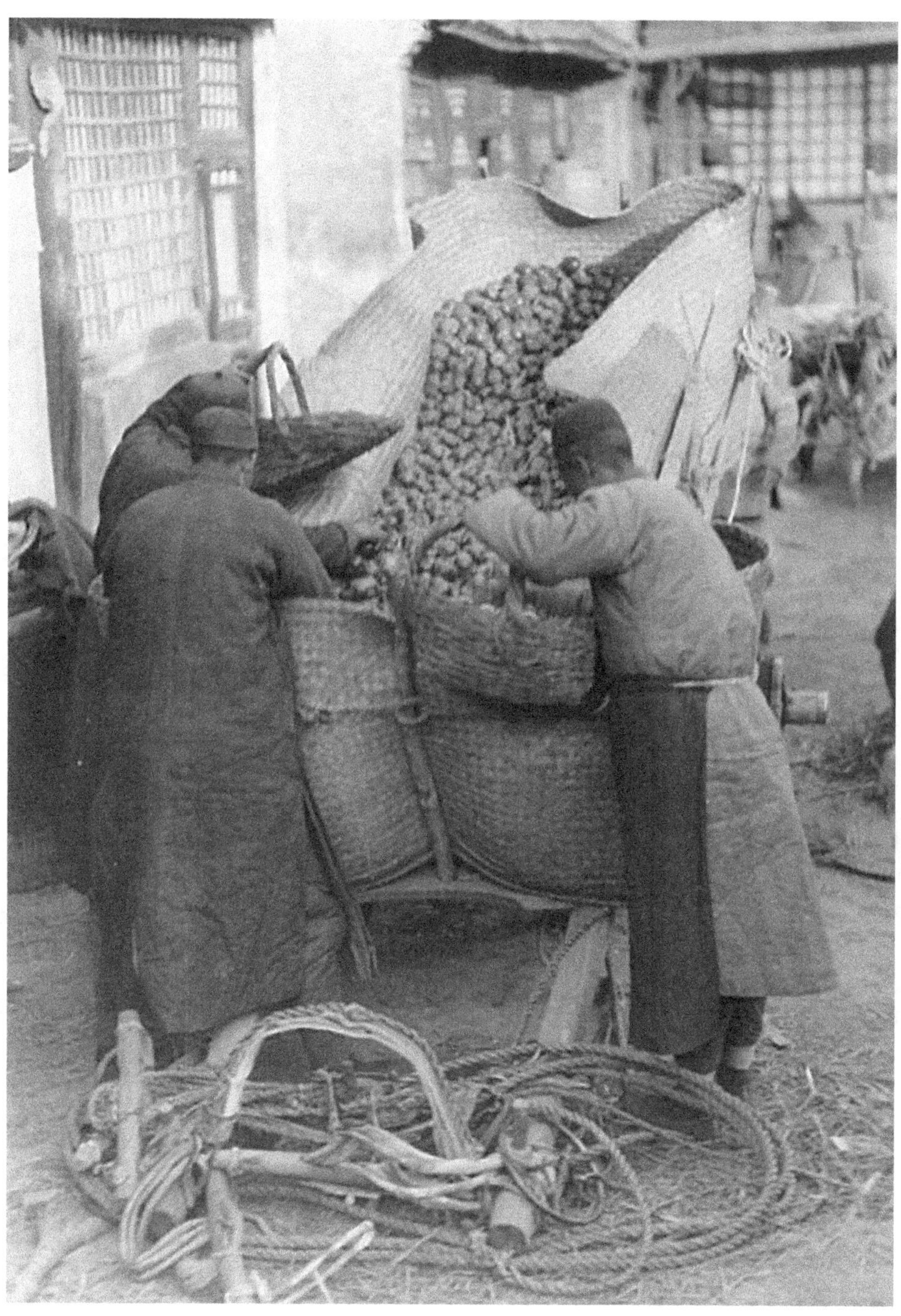

46203. *Nov. 11, 1930. Peiping. A nearby view of a cartload of persimmons being unloaded in the Wan Shun Tien Inn compound where this fruit is hot water treated for some eighteen hours to remove its astringency.*

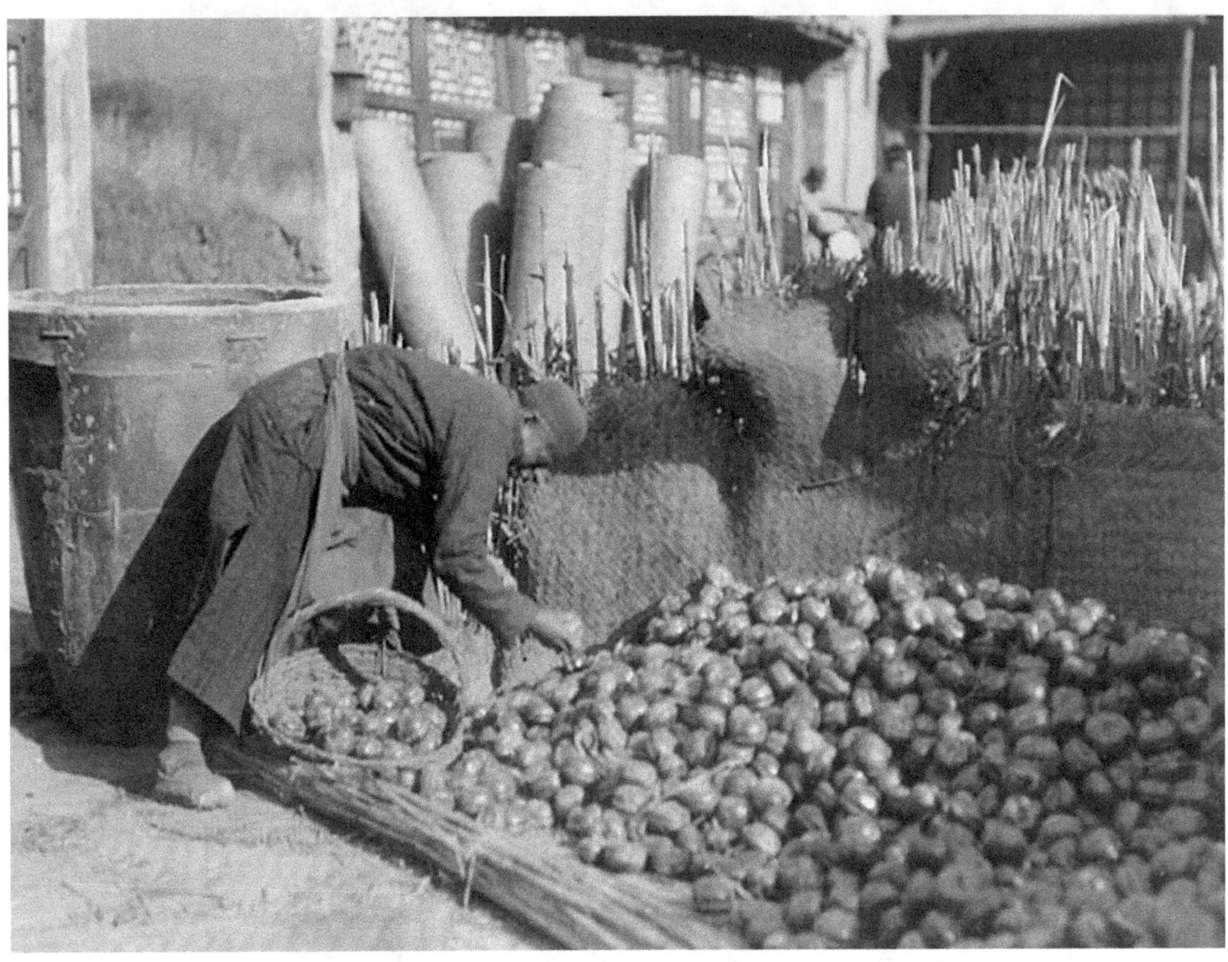

46207. *Wan Shun Tien Inn, Peiping. Sorting persimmons for the hot water treatment to transform the tannin in the fruit to a non-puckering substance.*

FUTURE USE IN THE U.S.

A careful survey of the persimmon industry in the Orient appears to warrant the statement that this fruit deserves a more prominent place in American horticulture.

There are a number of species and many varieties of persimmons distributed throughout the world, especially in Japan and in the great domain of China, and efforts should be made to introduce as many of these as possible for use in extending this industry in the United States. This goal can be attained only by determining the varieties and stocks best adapted to different regions and the commercial sorts best suited for cold storage and freezing. This is an important work which should be carried forward as promptly as possible.

The winter outdoor cold storage of persimmons as practiced by the Chinese in the vicinity of Peking justifies the belief that through American methods of cold storage (freezing) of American-grown oriental persimmons, their market season could be materially prolonged, and they could be marketed around the world. In other words, the markets of the world would be opened to American-grown oriental persimmons.

[Ed.: Now, seventy five years later than when the Dorsetts wrote the above conclusions, we can observe that the oriental persimmon has not become significantly more popular in the U.S. One reason is the successful production and marketing of beautiful and delicious apples, pears, and citrus during the fall and winter. Another reason is the problem of astringency in the most delicious and commonly marketed variety of oriental persimmon in the U.S., Hachiya, edible only when soft. A third reason is that many U.S. residents are familiar with the small seedy native persimmon fruit of *D. virginiana* that is very astringent until it is soft, shriveled, and unattractive. This latter circumstance will disappear as the U.S. population becomes more urban and never encounters the native fruits.

Dorsett noted that the most commonly grown large persimmon in North China was the Tamopan variety. This variety has been grown in the U.S. and found to be hardy as far north as Maryland. However, the flavor of the Tamopan fruits grown in the U.S. is relatively bland, compared to that of Hachiya, and so Tamopan has not been widely grown or accepted. The Lantern variety is also hardy as far north as Maryland and has a somewhat better flavor than Tamopan, but is not widely grown.

Today's oriental persimmon growers in the U.S. are now beginning to market more fruits of the non-astringent types, such as the Fuyu variety. These are nearly as delicious as Hachiya, and can be eaten while still firm, and can be stored, transported, and marketed over several months while the fruit is still firm. Also, there are now increasing numbers of people who are familiar with the oriental persimmon fruit, and others who are willing to try new flavors. Thus the groundwork set by plant explorers F. N. Meyer and P. H. Dorsett will more likely come to fruition in this 21st century.]

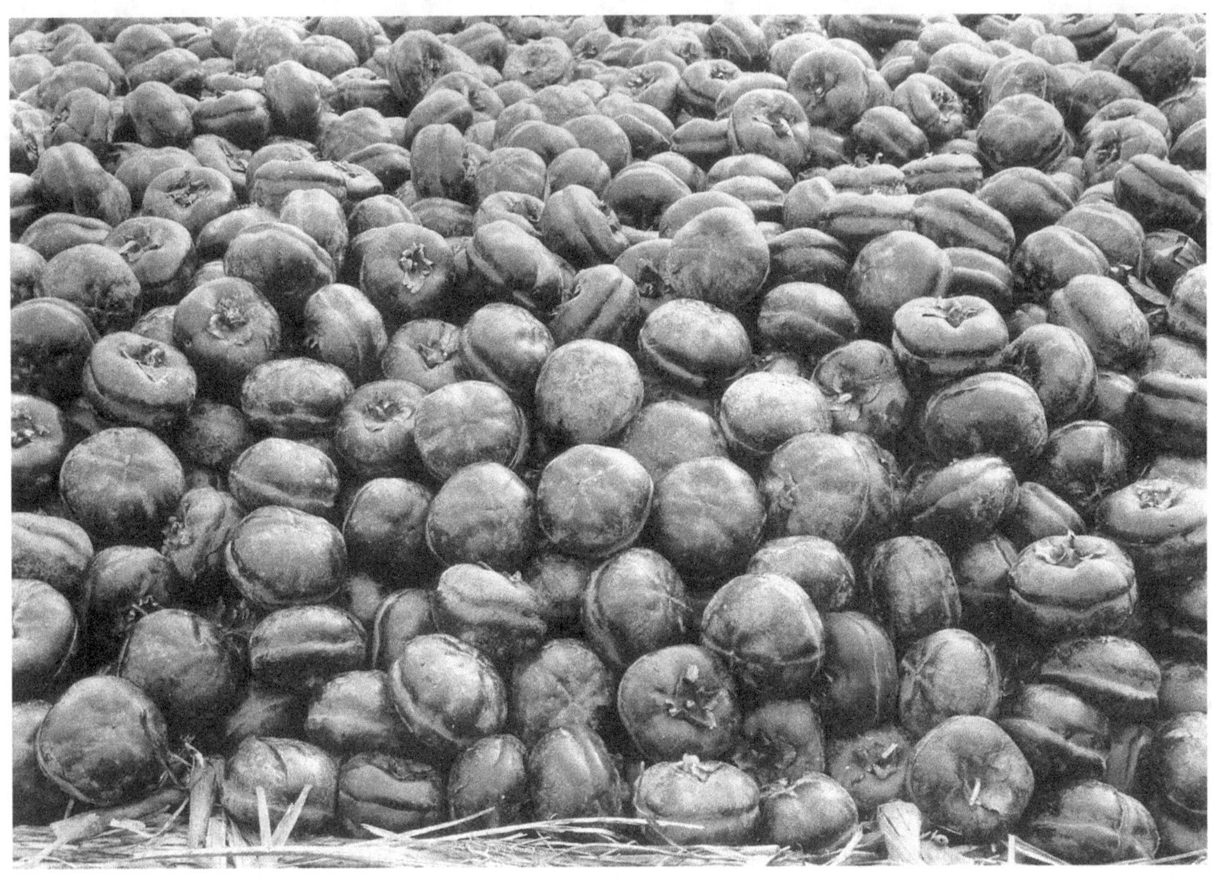

46181. *A close-up view of large (Tamopan) persimmons in a storage bed, awaiting transfer to Peiping for processing mid-September to mid-November or for direct sale from mid-November to late March.*

AUTHOR'S NOTES

In developing the contents of this book, I have strived to use P.H. Dorsett's own language and descriptions. However, I have, in some cases, rearranged photo legends for uniformity and completeness throughout the book (e.g., photo negative number, followed by date, then location, preceding the descriptive text). Also, in many legends, I eliminated certain repetitive wording such as "China" and "Diospyros" which were in most of the original legends. I occasionally chose different wording for clarity, but P.H. Dorsett generally used the English language quite well.

In a few instances, where more information regarding the topics under discussion was appropriate, I have added my own comments, using my experience in growing, studying, and evaluating oriental persimmons over the past 50 years. These additions are clearly marked. Otherwise, the language and content are strictly Dorsett's.

The narrative text for each section was derived principally from the USDA Circular No. 49, Nov. 1928, which Dorsett and his son James published. Additionally, I used excerpts from Dorsett's notes and informal records, which were available at the National Agricultural Library (NAL) in Beltsville, MD. This latter source of information provided many of the more descriptive legends for pictures taken in the 1930-31 expedition, and for details on temperature measurements undertaken by Dorsett.

Photographs used in this book that were not in my own collection were obtained from NAL. The following list of Dorsett's photo negative numbers represents the photographs that were supplied by NAL:

- 46162
- 46163
- 46166-46174
- 46179
- 46186-46188
- 46195
- 46196
- 46197A
- 46198
- 46198A
- 46200

- 46202-46204
- 46206-46208
- 46210-46212
- 46214-46219
- 46221
- 46223
- 46233-46235
- 46237-46241
- 46371
- 46384
- 46454
- 46455

RELATED LITERATURE

Cunningham, Isabel Shipley. 1984. Frank N. Meyer, *Plant Hunter in Asia.* Iowa State University Press. 137 pp.

Dorsett, P. H., and J. H. Dorsett. 1928. *Culture and Outdoor Winter Storage of Persimmons in the Vicinity of Peking, China.* U. S. Dept. of Agriculture Circular No. 49. 12 pp.

McClure, F. A. 1925. *Some Preliminary Notes on Persimmons in Kwangtung.* Lingnaam Agricultural Review: 91-98 + 16 figures.

Preston, William H. 2006. *Exploring for Hardy Oriental Persimmons.* Pomona 39(2):38-43.

Preston, William H. 1966. *Current Status of the Oriental Persimmon in Temperate Eastern United States.* 57th Annual Report of the Northern Nut Growers Assoc., Inc.:112-123.

Preston, William H., and Michael J. Newell. 2006. *Status of Oriental Persimmon Planting at Eastern Shore of Maryland.* Pomona 39(2):43-49.

Ryerson, Knowles. 1927. *Culture of the Oriental Persimmon in California.* Univ. of Calif. Coll. of Agric. Bull. 416: 63 pp.

Shanks, James B., Michael J. Newell, and William H. Preston. 1998. *Persimmons for Maryland—An Alternative Crop or Home Fruit.* Hort. Res. Bul. No. 1. 8 pp. Dept. Nat. Res. Sci. & Landsc. Arch., Univ. of MD.

Smith, J. Russell. 1929. *Tree Crops—A Permanent Agriculture.* Chapter XI. *The Persimmon: A Pasture Tree for the Beasts and a Kingly Fruit for Man.* Pp. 94-100. Harcourt Brace & Co.

U. S. Dept. Agriculture, National Agricultural Library. Special Collections: *Dorsett-Morse Oriental Agricultural Exploration Expedition.* 1928-1932.

U. S. Dept. Agriculture. *Seed and Plant Introductions.* 1899-1930. Eight bound volumes covering over 80,000 accessions.

OTHER PHOTOGRAPHIC TOURS TAKEN BY DORSETT
In the Orient

Photographic album entitled *"Bamboo", 1929-1930.* USDA Special Collection Box 19

Photographic album entitled *"Farm Views", 1929-1930.* USDA Special Collection Box 20

Photographic album entitled *"Landscapes", 1929-1930.* USDA Special Collection Box 21

Photographic album entitled *"Miscellaneous", 1929-1930.* USDA Special Collection Box 22

Photographic album entitled *"Ornamentals", 1929-1930.* USDA Special Collection Box 23

Photographic album entitled *"Parks and Gardens"*, USDA Special Collection Box 24

Photographic album entitled *"Temples and Shrines"*, USDA Special Collection Box 25

IMPORTATION OF ORIENTAL PERSIMMONS INTO U.S. 1900-1930

Ed.: Using the USDA's Seed and Plant Introductions inventories from 1900-1930, I have assembled the following information regarding the importation of *Diospyros kaki*, the Oriental persimmon, into the United States:

(1) Scionwood accessions for grafting obtained from various sites in China numbered 180 types or varieties, from Japan 301, and 1 to 3 each from Korea, India, New Zealand, Algeria, and Bermuda. Some of these accessions were duplicative.
(2) Seeds from 17 selections of *D. kaki* varieties or types came from China, and 1 to 3 from Japan, the Philippines, and France.
(3) Scionwood collections of non-astringent varieties or types totaled 69 accessions, and there were probably more than these.
(4) Scionwood and/or seeds from staminate (male-flowering) trees were sent from at least 3 sources, and there were probably more.
(5) At least 47 persons were directly involved in the collection and shipment of *D. kaki* accessions to the U.S. during this period. The most prolific collectors were Frank N. Meyer (who confined his collections to China), F. A. McClure (also China), and W. T. Swingle (Japan). All were employed by USDA to collect plant material in these countries. Also, substantial submissions were made by the Yokahama Nursery Company of Japan, and by Professors T. Tanikawa, T. Onda, and Ishiwaea of the Government Horticultural Experiment Station in Okitsu, Japan.

It should be understood that scionwood sent from such long distances at that time did not always arrive in the U.S. in good enough condition to permit successful propagation by grafting. We can assume that most of the scionwood was sent to Plant Introduction stations at Chico, CA and Savannah, GA. A few may have been sent to the station at Glenn Dale, MD. Grafting was undertaken using native *D. virginiana* seedlings as understock, as well as *D. lotus* and *D. kaki* seedlings.

Imported seeds of *D. kaki* may have fared better in transit than scionwood, but generally required stratification after arrival and had the problem of not coming true to type or variety.

Many varieties and types from China came in with descriptions but no name; they were, however, assigned a P.I.(Plant Introduction) number. A review of surviving *D. kaki* in the U. S. reveals that very few of these unnamed accessions survived.

At least 17 (and probably more) *D. kaki* varieties were alive at the Chico station in 1960, but the station was closed soon after and the orchard has probably been demolished. The Savannah station was closed earlier than 1960 but there are about 10 varieties alive in the surrounding communities. Also, more are likely still alive in North Florida, such as at Glen St. Mary, where a nursery there had many varieties established. The station at Glenn Dale, MD had none or very few varieties established there, and none were present by 1948. But the station very likely supplied some scionwood to J. Russell Smith's Sunny Ridge Nursery in Round Hill, VA during the 1920's and '30's. Dr. Smith claimed he had 29 varieties fruiting in the 1930's. His orchard no longer exists, but scionwood was collected from the surviving trees in 1958-64 and was distributed to a few interested nurseries such as at Glen St. Mary, FL.

A persimmon variety orchard was established by Dr. James B. Shanks at the Univ. of MD Wye Research & Education Center at Wye, MD in 1966-84. This orchard contained up to 84 varieties, some of which came from the Smith orchard. Thirty varieties still survive. One variety, PI 15832 Tsurushigaki, obtained from the Smith collection and originally collected in 1923 in Japan, still survives. (The collector stated this variety was good for drying.) A number of commercial varieties such as Hachiya, Fuyu, and Tanenashi probably are derived from the early collections.

The following *D. kaki* varieties imported during 1900-1930 were known to be established in the U.S. for a period of time. Some varieties were imported several to many times during 1900-1930 and also later on.

- Aizu Michirazu
- Akadansu
- Benigaki
- Delicious
- Fuji
- Fuyu
- Fuyugaki
- Giboshi
- Gosho
- Hachiya
- Hanagosho
- Hira Tanenashi
- Honan Red
- Hyakume
- Jiro
- Kawabata
- Lantern
- Kubo
- Manerh
- Midzushima
- O'gosho
- Okame
- Saijo
- Shaumopan
- Sheng
- Tamopan
- Tanenashi
- Triumph
- Tsurushigaki
- 20th Century
- Yamagaki
- Yemon
- Yokono
- Yotsumizu
- Zengi
- Zengi Maru

ABOUT THE EDITOR

William Preston began his interest in the Oriental persimmon in 1958 when he worked for USDA's New Crops Research Branch. A horticulturist with three degrees from the University of Maryland, he has traveled to many sites in the Eastern U. S. to locate and view Oriental persimmon trees.

He has written many articles about this crop, and the subjects include fruit ripening, ornamental value of trees, exploring for varieties, taste panel tests, variety comparisons, marketing, orcharding, history, and culture. To keep abreast of horticultural topics, he maintains membership in the American Society for Horticultural Science, the American Horticultural Society, and the North American Fruit Explorers. He maintains a two-acre commercial orchard of Oriental persimmons in Calvert County, Md. He resides in Glenn Dale, Md. with his wife Corinne.

www.ingramcontent.com/pod-product-compliance
Lightning Source LLC
LaVergne TN
LVHW061243100826
845148LV00008B/1014
* 9 7 8 0 9 8 0 2 3 8 0 6 8 *